mproving Money Stock Control

Economic Policy Conference Series

Cosponsored by
The Center for the Study of American Business at Washington University, St. Louis, Missouri
and
The Federal Reserve Bank of St. Louis

Previously published books in the series:

Meyer, Laurence H., *The Supply-Side Effects of Economic Policy*

Improving Money Stock Control

Problems, Solutions, and Consequences

edited by
Laurence H. Meyer
Washington University

Springer Science+Business Media, LLC

Chapter 3 is reprinted with the permission of the Bank of England.

Library of Congress Cataloging in Publication Data
Main entry under title:
Improving money stock control.

(Economic policy conference series)
Contains the papers and comments delivered at the 6th annual conference cosponsored by the Center for the Study of American Business and the Federal Reserve Bank of St. Louis, held Oct. 20–31, 1981.

1. Monetary policy — Congresses. 2. Money supply — Congresses. 3. Monetary policy — United States — Congresses. 4. Money supply — United States — Congresses. I. Meyer, Laurence H. II. Washington University (Saint Louis, Mo.). Center for the Study of American Business. III. Federal Reserve Bank of St. Louis. IV. Series.
HG230.3.I45 1983 332.4′973 82-13011

ISBN 978-94-017-1847-9 ISBN 978-94-017-1845-5 (eBook)
DOI 10.1007/978-94-017-1845-5

Originally published by Kluwer Nijhoff Publishing in 1983
Softcover reprint of the hardcover 1st edition 1983

Contents

Preface

On October 30–31, 1981, the Center for the Study of American Business and the Federal Reserve Bank of St. Louis cosponsored their sixth annual conference, "Improving Money Stock Control: Problems, Solutions, and Consequences." This book contains the papers and comments delivered at that conference.

The Federal Reserve System has moved, over the last decade, toward setting policy in terms of explicit and publicly announced monetary aggregate targets — specifically, growth ranges for alternative measures of the money supply. This conference, as the title suggests, was wide ranging in its discussions of monetary control. But rather than dealing with the merits of monetary aggregate targeting, its focus was instead on solving the problems associated with, and evaluating the consequences of, improved monetary control.

The initial paper outlines the current operating procedures followed by the Federal Reserve and suggests reforms to improve monetary control. The following three discussion papers in Part I critically examine the Fed's operating procedures. The two papers in Part II discuss the experience of other countries with monetary aggregate targeting — the United Kingdom and Switzerland, respectively — and Part III examines the consequences of improved monetary control.

In "Nonborrowed Reserves Targeting and Monetary Control," David E. Lindsey, assistant director of the Division of Research and Statistics at the Board of Governors of the Federal Reserve System, outlines the principles underlying the current operating procedures, discusses the choices available among both alternative monetary aggregate targets and alternative reserve aggregate operating targets, and presents a program of reforms to enhance the precision of monetary control. Lindsey's presentation carefully develops the current procedures. The Fed's operations begin with the setting of annual growth ranges for multiple monetary aggregate targets, but they also involve setting shorter-term (or interim) ranges and a wide band for the federal funds rate at Federal Reserve Open Market Committee meetings, and end with target paths for nonborrowed and total reserves. Lindsey goes on to discuss the relative merits of narrow versus broader money supply measures (*M1* and *M2*) as targets, and he notes how recent experience suggests the usefulness of the current practice of multiple targets. He also defends the Fed's choice of nonborrowed reserves as the operating target and argues against moving to a broader operating target, such as the monetary base or total reserves. Lindsey ends his paper with a thorough discussion of reforms that might improve the precision of monetary control under reserve aggregate operating targets.

Lindsey's paper is followed by comments by R. Alton Gilbert, William Poole, and W. Lee Hoskins. Gilbert, a senior economist at the Federal Reserve Bank of St. Louis, takes issue with Lindsey's defense of nonborrowed reserves as an operating target and presents the case for a broader target, either the monetary base or total reserves. This disagreement between Gilbert and Lindsey illustrates the difficulty of empirically demonstrating the effects of policies that have not been implemented. Gilbert also cautions against an optimistic assessment of the gains to monetary control that are likely to be associated with the reforms suggested by Lindsey. Gilbert views the current imprecision in monetary control as a reflection of the Fed's failure to exploit the potential of existing institutional arrangements due, first, to indecision concerning which of the monetary aggregates to emphasize and, second, to continuing concern with objectives other than monetary control that interfere with the Fed's pursuit of monetary growth targets.

William Poole, Professor of Economics at Brown University, agrees with Lindsey that reforms are badly needed to improve monetary control, but he criticizes the Fed for failing to present to Congress the case for such reform "regularly and consistently." Poole carefully considers Lindsey's proposal for a graduated marginal discount rate and concludes that it does not offer a clear advantage over competing proposals for staggered reserve accounting and penalty carry-overs.

W. Lee Hoskins, senior vice-president and chief economist at the Pittsburgh National Bank, presents the first-hand perspective of a participant in money and credit markets. Hoskins suggests that the October 1979 change in operating procedures did little more than widen the federal funds band. Market participants continue to believe that the Fed is operating with an interest rate constraint. He documents occasions on which the Fed seemed more concerned with maintaining or smoothing interest rates than in maintaining a pattern of reserves growth consistent with its monetary growth targets.

The papers in Part II describe the experience of central banks in the United Kingdom and in Switzerland with monetary control. In "Targeting the Monetary Base: The Swiss Case," Kurt Schiltknecht, director, Economic Division, Swiss National Bank, discusses the Swiss experience with monetary aggregate targeting. In 1975, the Swiss National Bank (SNB) began to conduct its monetary policy in terms of a money stock target. From the outset, the SNB chose to implement this policy by operating on the monetary base, unlike many central banks, such as those in the United States and the United Kingdom, where monetary control was initially pursued via control over interest rates.

The Swiss monetary aggregate targets were also viewed from the beginning as medium- or long-term targets. In particular, the Swiss National Bank avoided a policy of activism or fine tuning, that is, it did not make short-run adjustments in its monetary aggregate targets for purposes of domestic stabilization. However, the SNB was prepared to depart from its monetary aggregate targets to dampen excessive fluctuations in foreign exchange rates.

The use of monetary aggregate targets was temporarily abandoned between the fall of 1978 and spring of 1979, during which time the Swiss National Bank's major efforts were directed at intervention in the foreign exchange markets. Thereafter, the SNB returned to targeting monetary aggregates but chose to target the monetary base directly rather than to use the monetary base to achieve explicit money supply targets.

John Wenninger, manager of the Monetary Research Department, Federal Reserve Bank of New York, commenting on the Schiltknecht paper, questions whether or not the SNB procedures are, as often alleged, an example of a monetarist approach to monetary aggregate targeting — an approach that can be defined in terms of adhering to a long-run target and avoiding a response to short-run economic developments. He notes that, in contrast to this view of monetary aggregate targeting, the practice of the SNB consistently involves changes in base growth in response both to changes in economic conditions and to exchange rates. Wenninger concludes that the SNB policy is in fact "highly discretionary" and suggests this may account for its poor record in achieving its monetary growth targets. Wenninger also points to some aspects of the Swiss experience that have made the central bank's task somewhat easier. First, the Swiss government does not generally run large deficits that the central bank would be under pressure to monetize. Second, the policy trade-offs in Switzerland are very different because recessions tend to result in the reduced use of foreign workers rather than increases in unemployment.

In "Recent Developments in Monetary Control in the United Kingdom," William Allen, assistant advisor on monetary policy, Bank of England, describes the evolution of the practice of monetary aggregate targeting since the Bank of England began to announce target ranges for monetary growth in mid-1976. Allen begins by reviewing research on the stability of money demand equations and on the precision of the relation between monetary aggregates and nominal income and inflation. The evidence does not yield a definite answer concerning which aggregate — *M1, M3,* or sterling *M3* — to target. The decision was reached, however, to target a broad aggregate, sterling *M3*. Allen discusses the reasons underlying this choice.

At first, monetary control operated through interest rates — with the Bank of England setting its discount rate (the minimum lending rate, *MLR*) to be consistent with the monetary growth targets. However, because the effect of interest rates on sterling *M3* was "slow and uncertain," and because the announcement of changes in the *MLR* tended to have disruptive effects, the Bank of England abandoned this operating procedure and moved in 1980 to exercise control over monetary aggregates via control of the monetary base. Thus, open market operations rather than changes in the discount rate have become the main instrument of monetary policy. The Bank of England, however, continues to be concerned about interest rate volatility, and interest rates remain an official objective of policy through the setting of wide bands for short-term rates. In addition, there is some movement away from a focus on *M1* and *M3* and toward a new aggregate, to be known as *M2,* the sum of retail deposits and currency, a measure of retail transactions balances.

In commenting on the Allen paper, Michael Parkin, Professor of Economics at University of Western Ontario, criticizes the logic underlying the Bank of England's choice of a monetary aggregate target. He notes the importance of considering the interest elasticity of the aggregate as well as the stability of its relation to income and the stability of its demand function. He suggests the criteria of finding the aggregate with a strong Granger-causal relationship to the price level but a weak Granger-causal relationship with real variables. Parkin also notes that the new techniques employed by the Bank of England are *not* monetary base control, and the Bank of England has not committed itself to move to monetary base control. Although the Bank of England has ceased to announce official interest rate targets, official targets continue to be set and this information continues to be available to the public. He concludes that the new techniques introduced by the Bank of England are, in fact, almost identical to the previous technique of operating through the setting of the discount rate. In Parkin's view, this approach to monetary control lacks theoretical and empirical support and leaves Britain in desperate need of a monetary standard.

The papers in Part III discuss the consequences of central bank policy for interest rate and price level variability and for the real effects associated with changes in the monetary growth targets set by the central bank. In "Monetary Stabilization and the Variability of Prices and Interest Rates," Jeremy Siegel, Associate Professor of Finance, Wharton School, University of Pennsylvania, discusses the effects of central bank policy on interest rate and price level variability. Siegel defines central bank policy in terms of the central bank's movement of high-powered money in response to changes in market interest rates. Siegel demonstrates that the appropriate direction of response in high-powered money to an increase in the market interest rate depends on the source of the disturbance moving the interest rate. This leaves the difficult problem of identifying the source of the disturbance moving the interest rates. Siegel develops a simple criterion, involving the correlation between unanticipated changes in the price level and interest rates, to determine what disturbances are dominant and, therefore, what should be the appropriate direction of response of high-powered money to changes in market rates. Siegel goes on to discuss the targeting of aggregates broader than high-powered money and to examine the trade-off between variability in interest rates and the price level. He concludes that central banks should give more weight to price level variability because of the greater opportunity to hedge interest rate fluctuations.

Phillip Cagan, Professor of Economics at Columbia University, commenting on the Siegel paper, accepts the author's basic theme that the appropriate central bank response to interest rate changes depends on the source of the disturbance generating the movement in the interest rates. Cagan suggests, however, that the traditional practice of central banks can be seen as an attempt to neutralize short-run money market disturbances by stabilizing interest rates over short periods and to offset the more persistent aggregate demand disturbances by stabilizing monetary growth over the longer run. Cagan therefore suggests an extension of Siegel's framework to allow for different frequencies in money market and aggregate demand disturbances. In addition, Cagan notes other limitations in Siegel's model: its failure to take account of uncertainty about model parameters or to allow for lags, especially in the response of the price level to disturbances. As a consequence of limitations in Siegel's analytical framework, Cagan is reluctant to accept Siegel's simple criterion for determining the appropriate direction of policy response to changes in market interest rates.

In their paper, "On the Real Effects of Imprecise Monetary Control," Laurence H. Meyer and Charles Webster, Jr., Professor and Assistant Professor of Economics, respectively, at Washington University, discuss the effects that improved control over the money supply can have on the speed with which expectations of monetary growth converge with the rate set by the Federal Reserve. This speed of convergence is shown to be directly related to the effectiveness of the Fed in meeting its monetary growth targets. Slow convergence in expectations, in turn, results in long periods of unanticipated monetary change and, hence, large real effects when the Fed alters its monetary growth targets. The precision of monetary control, therefore, directly affects the real costs involved with reducing inflation via a policy of reducing the rate of monetary growth. Meyer and Webster present simulations with the Barro rational expectations model to develop an estimate of the size of the real effects associated with changes in the precision of monetary control.

Robert Rasche, Professor of Economics at Michigan State University, in his comments on the Meyer and Webster paper, raises questions about the specification of the initial conditions at the time a monetary target is announced. He argues that there are two reasonable alternatives, both different from the initial conditions assumed by Meyer and Webster: complete credibility or complete absence of an information base from which private economic units can make judgments about future Fed policy. Rasche also suggests that the variance of the money supply should not be taken as a technical parameter, but rather as something subject to change by the policy authorities. It is, therefore, something for which the public must develop an estimate by observing the behavior of the money supply.

Finally, Rasche suggests that Meyer and Webster should have replaced the Barro expected monetary growth equation with their Bayesian learning specification and then jointly reestimated the entire model before running their simulations.

In his luncheon talk, Albert M. Wojnilower, managing director for First Boston Corporation, develops a "historical and institutional approach" to analyzing financial markets. Wojnilower develops three basic themes. The first is that "essentially all the recessions of the last 30 years were triggered by credit crunches." High interest rates alone — without an accompanying credit crunch — may slow the economy, but will not induce a recession. His second theme is that high interest rates cause inflation, rather than (or at least more than) high inflation causes high interest rates. Finally, Wojnilower traces how the response of the financial system to restrictive monetary policy and regulatory constraints has made it more difficult to implement anti-inflationary monetary policy and has increased the importance of the Federal Reserve's role as lender of last resort.

Acknowledgments

Many people associated with the Center for the Study of American Business and the Federal Reserve Bank of St. Louis have contributed to the planning of this conference and to the production of this proceedings volume. I would particularly like to thank Marcia B. Wallace, of the Center for the Study of American Business, who supervised the arrangements for the conference and helped edit the manuscripts and prepare them for publication.

I THE UNITED STATES EXPERIENCE

1 NONBORROWED RESERVE TARGETING AND MONETARY CONTROL

David E. Lindsey

Two years have passed since the Federal Reserve revised its operating procedures to emphasize control over reserve aggregates, using nonborrowed reserves for day-to-day policy operations. On the first anniversary of this change in policy implementation, the Federal Reserve System staff undertook what Milton Friedman has characterized as an "excruciatingly detailed analysis of the experience since October 6, 1979."[1] A year later I would like to review the entire period from a broader perspective. This paper aims at consolidating the results of previous basic research on monetary control, rather than contributing to that research per se. However, some controversial interpretations are advanced which I hope will stimulate further testing of the underlying theories. Because some of my comments are deliberately intended to be provocative, and even argumentative, I would like to dissociate them at the outset from the views either of the Board of Governors or of other members of the Board staff, who may not necessarily agree with all the personal judgments contained in this paper.

The first section of the paper briefly discusses the principles underlying the Federal Reserve's procedures for controlling money. The second section then reviews the reserve oriented operating procedures in practice, focusing on how the basic mechanisms are revealed in the data, rather than on technical minutiae. The third section briefly interprets recent movements in various monetary aggregates, and assesses their relative reliability as intermediate targets; the next section then analyzes recent movements in various reserve aggregates and their multipliers, and draws conclusions regarding their relative reliability as potential operating targets. A final section proposes certain reforms to the regulatory environment that, in my opinion, would assist the conduct of monetary policy.

The Operating Procedures in Principle

The principles underlying the operating procedures for controlling money are reasonably straightforward.[2] Having established annual ranges for the monetary aggregates, the Federal Open Market Committee (FOMC) selects at each meeting interim money growth targets over the next several months typically designed to return money to the longer-run objective over time. For the upcoming intermeeting period, FOMC also specifies a relatively wide federal funds rate band that serves as a trigger for consultations, and may also choose an initial discount borrowing assumption used for constructing the nonborrowed reserves path. The Board staff then derives intermeeting-period target paths for nonborrowed and total reserves that are consistent with the Committee's decisions.

During intermeeting periods, the trading desk at the Federal Reserve Bank of New York engages in open market operations designed to attain the nonborrowed reserve target, as adjusted for incoming information. These technical adjustments to the nonborrowed (and total) reserve targets are made when new data indicate that certain variables are diverging from path levels in a way that disturbs the multiplier relationship between total reserves and money. Simply put, these technical adjustments are designed in principle so that a divergence of the money stock from its intermeeting target gives rise, essentially atuomatically, to proportional dollar changes in the gap between total reserves demanded and nonborrowed reserves supplied; however, other unexpected shocks altering the multiplier relationship between total reserves and money do not affect this gap. Specifically, over the intermeeting period, the induced movement of borrowings away from their initially assumed level equals the assumed average required reserve ratio in transactions deposits at member banks times the divergence of the money stock from its intermeeting target path (but with the deposit components lagged two weeks in reflection of lagged reserve requirements).

Thus, in principle, these operating procedures involving nonborrowed reserve targeting automatically permit deviations of money from intermeeting targets to produce proportional movements of discount window borrowings. An overshoot of money, for example, will cause borrowings to rise. Given the discount window rate structure and administrative procedures, the rise in borrowings will tend to be associated with an increase in the federal funds rate spread over the discount rate. This increase occurs because institutions must be induced to overcome their heightened reluctance to borrow in response to the stronger administrative pressure accompanying enlarged adjustment borrowings. The higher federal funds rate, in turn, sets in motion balance sheet adjustments on the part of depository institutions and the public that will tend both to raise other short-term interest rates and to reverse over time the initial overshoot in money from the interim target.

If the money stock deviation from the intermeeting target stems from a "permanent" movement in the money demand schedule, perhaps owing to a strengthening of aggregate spending, then these automatic forces would not be sufficient to reverse fully the emerging overshoot in money. This would certainly be true within the same intermeeting period, given the distributed lag of the effects of interest rates on the quantity of money demanded. (Even over the long run, money would not fully return to path in this case if, hypothetically speaking, the nonborrowed reserve target were left unchanged, because the implied money supply schedule is not vertical with respect to short-term interest rates, but has a positive slope owing primarily to the interest elasticity of borrowings.)

Thus, to reduce the extent of the deviations of money from target, both in the current intermeeting period and prospectively, additional options are available between FOMC meetings under the operating procedures. A discretionary policy adjustment to the nonborrowed reserve path relative to the total reserve path — as opposed to the technical adjustments described earlier — can be made in the direction opposite to the money stock overshoot. Or the discount rate can be raised. Exercising the first option would raise discount borrowings for a given discount rate and tend to raise the federal funds rate above where it would be otherwise. Exercising the second option also would tend to raise the federal funds rate above its level otherwise, given the target for nonborrowed reserves. Either policy action would tend to speed up the process of returning money to target. In gauging whether such actions are warranted, the size of the gap between estimated total reserve demands and the adjusted target for total reserves is monitored. Prior to discretionary adjustments to the nonborrowed reserve path, this gap also equals, by construction, the induced movement in borrowings implied by the updated nonborrowed reserve target away from the initially assumed borrowings level. (See the Appendix for a simple theoretical model of this process.)

The Operating Procedures in Practice

The principles underlying the Federal Reserve's monetary control procedures are illustrated in figures 1–1 and 1–2, which provide a bird's-eye view of monetary policy since October 1979 that is far enough removed from the trees to bring the forest into focus.[3] The behavior of *M1* and *M2* levels relative to their annual ranges are shown by monthly data in the top two panels. Old definitions of *M1* and *M2* are shown relative to their ranges for 1979, while redefined *M1B* and *M2* are shown for 1980 and 1981. *M1B* in 1981 is adjusted to remove inflows to NOW accounts estimated to have come from sources other than demand deposits.

Levels of selected reserve aggregates are shown in the bottom panel. Except for a temporary variation in precautionary holdings of excess reserves around the implementation of the Monetary Control Act, total reserves track required reserves fairly closely. The shaded area between total reserves and nonborrowed reserves represents adjustment (and seasonal) borrowings at the discount window.

M1B and *M2* strengthened together relative to their longer-run ranges in four episodes — the fall of 1979, late winter of 1980, the fall of 1980, and the spring of 1981. In each case, adjustment borrowings increased in the month *M1B* rose the most relative to its upper bound and in three cases widened in the subsequent month as well. *M1B* and *M2* both weakened relative to their longer-run ranges in early winter 1979, markedly so in the spring of 1980, and again in late winter of 1981. In each case, adjustment borrowings fell in the month of the greatest weakness of *M1B* relative to the lower bound of its longer-run range, as well as in the subsequent month.

Since May of 1981, *M1B* has run below its lower bound while *M2* has been near or above its upper bound. Adjustment borrowings have been gradually trending downward over this period. For a time this summer the FOMC, concerned about the strength of *M2*, specified a directive to the Desk that permitted partial accommodation of the nonborrowed reserves

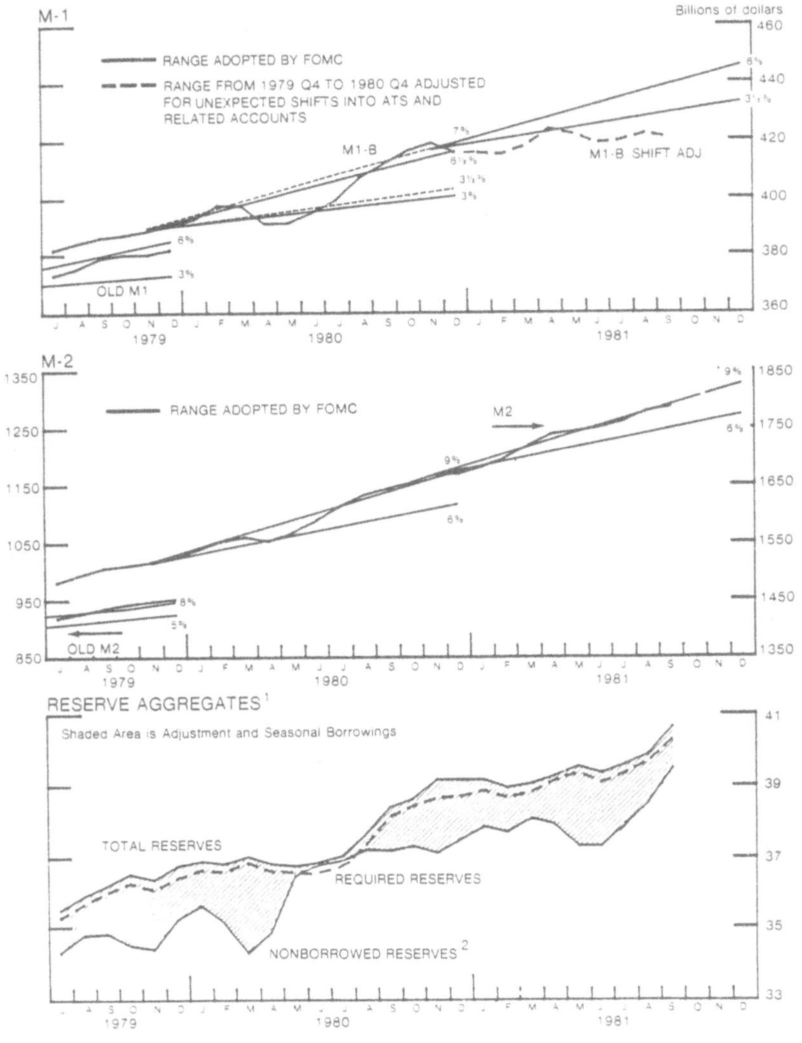

[1]The reserve aggregates series have been adjusted to remove discontinuities associated with changes in reserve requirement ratios and the distorting effects of weekend reserve avoidance activities in 1979 and 1980.

[2]Includes extended credit.

Figure 1–1 Monetary and Reserve Aggregates

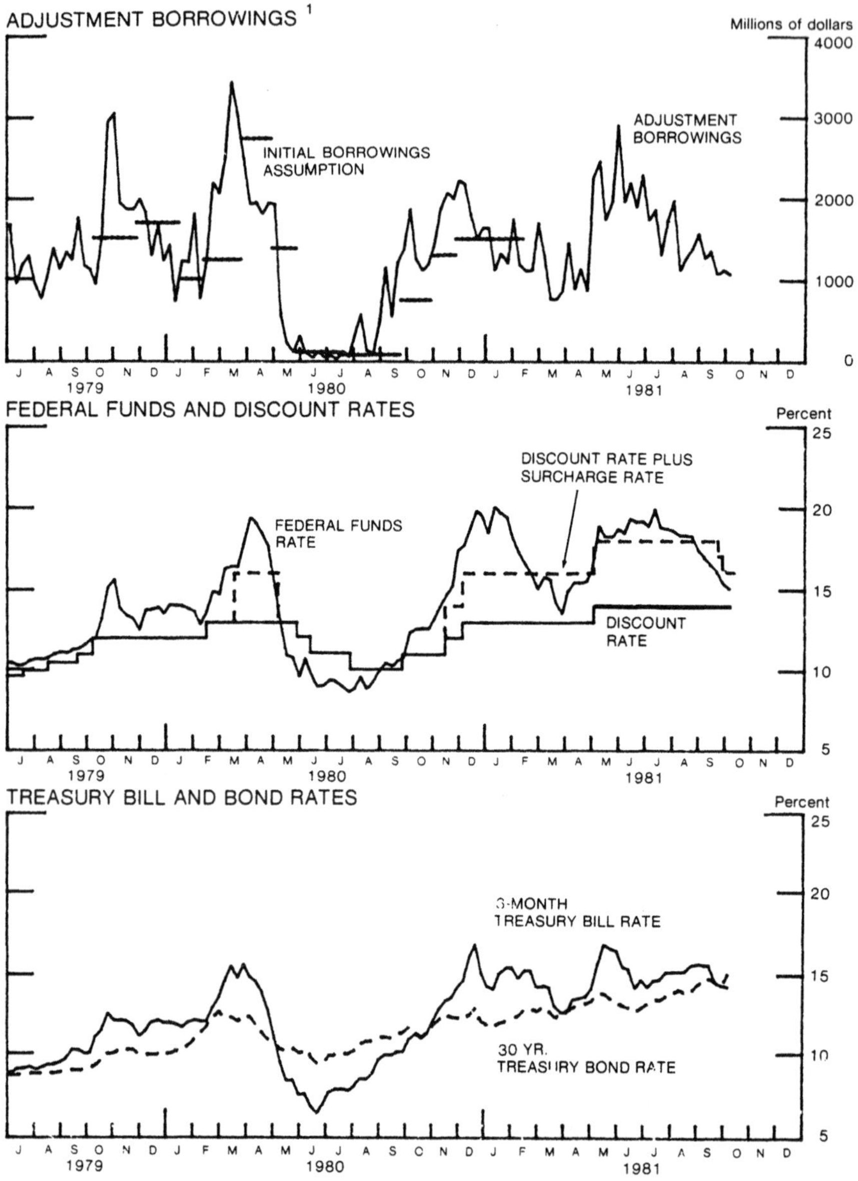

[1]Includes seasonal borrowings.

Figure 1–2 Adjustment Borrowings and Interest Rates

path to the weakening of *M1B*, which muted the automatic decline of borrowings.

The relationship between the amount of adjustment borrowings and the spread of the funds rate over the discount rate is indicated by weekly data in the top two panels of figure 1–2; the spread clearly tends to vary directly with adjustment borrowing.[4]

The horizontal lines in the top panel represent those levels of the initial borrowings assumption that are publicly available at present.[5] The figure clearly shows that induced movements or discretionary actions have occasionally caused borrowings to differ significantly from the level assumed in constructing the initial reserve paths. Substantial movements in the initial borrowing assumption itself from one intermeeting period to the next also have occurred upon occasion.

The relationship — such as it is — between the federal funds rate and both the three-month treasury bill rate and the thirty-year Treasury bond rate may be seen by comparing the middle and bottom panels of figure 1–2. Through 1980, both short-term and long-term government securities rates tracked the federal funds rate reasonably closely, with variations in longer-term rates, of course, displaying less amplitude.[6] In 1981, however, this relationship appears to have weakened, particularly on the long end. For example, the federal funds rate has been trending downward since early July, but bond yields continued their upward march through late September and Treasury bill rates rose through late August. Regarding bond yields, adverse expectations about the federal government's prospective demands on credit markets apparently were engendered by the congressional passage of the tax cut package, and perhaps inflationary expectations were adversely affected as well.

The last financial relationship relevant to monetary control is the money demand function. It is the final one to be examined in the context of figures 1–1 and 1–2. The nexus going from interest rates to money demand is captured in the bottom panel of figure 1–2 set against the top two panels of figure 1–1. Any indirect connection going from interest rates to real income and prices and then back to money through its demand function is, of course, only implicit in the figures, and the independent effects of the real sector, prices, and other factors on money demand are ignored altogether.

Unfortunately, at this stage the eyeball technique runs into trouble. Although turning points in money are generally preceded or accompanied by movements in interest rates in the opposite direction, as upswings in money typically reverse downswings (and vice versa), no clearcut money demand relationship between interest rates and money leaps out from the figures. What impresses me in this comparison is another relationship. Money and short-term interest rates have tended to move in the same direction, with turning points in money leading turning points in interest rates typically by a month or so.

What is the proper interpretation to be placed on the empirical regularity of movements in short-term interest rates tending to follow movements in money with only a brief delay over this period? The answer should be obvious from our previous discussion, and yet is is rarely even noted by academic economists making pronouncements about such relationships. The data are essentially tracing out an upward sloping money supply function over intervals of a month or more created by the nonborrowed reserves target operating procedure. For example, a nontargeted rightward movement in the money demand schedule raises total reserves demanded relative to the nonborrowed target, which, in turn, automatically increases adjustment borrowings and tends to push up the federal funds rate. Expectations of future federal funds rates then are adjusted upward, also partly in response to the publication of the unexpectedly stronger money statistics and their perceived implications for future reserve demands and supplies; this causes other short-term rates to come under upward pressure. On occasion, the Federal Reserve also takes discretionary action to lower the nonborrowed reserves target relative to the total reserves target or to raise the discount rate, thus further boosting the interest rate impact of the initial surge in money demand.

Notice that, in explaining this *positive* association between money and short-term rates, no recourse need be made to adjustments of inflationary expectations in response to faster observed money growth or to feedbacks from the real sector to money and credit demands. Besides, it strains one's credulity to think that three-month bill rates tend to jump up immediately when the Federal Reserve publishes a large weekly increase in *M1B* because expectations of inflation *over the next three months* have been altered. It is also difficult to imagine that changes in money can significantly affect real spending or credit demands in some direct fashion independent of interest rate channels and, hence, feedback to interest rates over an interval of only three months. This is not to deny the increasing role of influences such as inflationary expectations or credit demands on interest rates as their maturities lengthen beyond three months. Nor do I mean to deny that both inflation and real economic activity affect the position of the money demand schedule and, hence, have a powerful indirect effect on short-term interest rates. Indeed, recognizing this influence only reinforces the previous explanation.

Moreover, recourse to the so-called short-run liquidity effect — in which an increase in the money stock reduces interest rates as the public moves along its money demand function — does not seem needed to explain the tendency for turning points in money to be associated briefly with continued movements in Treasury bill rates in the opposite direction. Besides, if this tendency for money and bill rates to move in opposite directions for a short time arose from a liquidity effect associated with money supply-side disturbances, one would not expect it to be reversed so quickly, in light of what we know about the timing of the transmission mechanism of monetary impulses to economic activity and prices — the theory of macro rational expectations notwithstanding.[7] This temporary leading relationship between money and bill rates is explained largely, I believe, by a combination of factors that are generally ignored by academic analysts. The factors include: (1) the two-week lag in required reserve accounting that delays the impact of changes in deposits on required reserves;[8] (2) the carryover privilege, which permits depository institutions to delay at least some of the reserve position adjustments implied by deposit swings for an additional week beyond the time their required reserves are affected; (3) the unavoidable delay in data collection and hence publication of the monetary aggregates, which prevents market participants from knowing immediately of money stock developments and simultaneously incorporating this information into market interest rates.

The positive association, aside from this brief delay, between money and interest rates traced out by the data implies that the downward sloping money demand schedule (in the interest-rate-money space) has varied over a much wider range than the upward sloping money supply schedule. Thus, there is a prima facie case that the explanation for the observed variation in interest rates and the money stock over this two-year period should be sought primarily in an examination of the instability of the money demand schedule. This analysis suggests that the observed variation in short-term interest rates during the last two years primarily represented Federal Reserve resistance through nonborrowed targeting to shifts in the position of the money demand schedule. Because the money supply function has a positive slope, instability in the observed stock of money, though muted, will accompany instability in the position of the money demand schedule.

In this connection, the greatest instability in observed money during the years under consideration occurred in the last three quarters of 1980. It seems irrefutable, at least in retrospect, that the imposition and subsequent removal of the special credit restraint program in the spring and summer strongly affected the public's money demand. First, the imposition of the program initially led to a reduction in spending and the real income scale variable; real GNP fell by 9.9 percent at an annual rate in the second quarter of 1980. In addition, the accompanying repayment of bank loans apparently gave rise to large negative errors in standard money demand functions in the same quarter. These effects worked in reverse in the two quarters following removal of the program.[9] These special influences were external to the new monetary control procedures; they do not so much raise questions about the fundamental efficacy of the procedures as they do about the wisdom of attempting to stabilize money growth in the face of such temporary shocks to money demand, at least of the second type.

The other major episode in which *M1B* strayed from its annual range was in 1981, when it has generally been below its lower bound. However, *M2* has been near or above its upper bound in every month since February. Is one to conclude that the FOMC should have expanded nonborrowed reserves more rapidly over this period in an attempt to attain the lower bound for *M1B* sooner, but in so doing drive *M2* above its upper bound? Or should growth of nonborrowed reserves have been more restrained so as to bring *M2* well within its range, but in the process forcing *M1B* further below its lower bound?

Movements in the Various Monetary Aggregates and Their Reliability as Intermediate Targets

The previous questions point out the importance of determining which monetary aggregate is the most reliable intermediate target. Cross currents in 1981 certainly raise this familiar question anew. In light of its importance, this issue will be addressed in some detail in this section. Suffice it to say in summary that an unexpectedly large downward shift in the demand for transactions balances — which apparently was induced by historically high interest rates this year — has made shift-adjusted *M1B* overstate the degree of monetary restraint, while an unpredictably large increase in the share of the nontransactions component of *M2* bearing market-related yields has made *M2* understate the degree of restraint. It is by no means clear that monetary policy on balance so far this year has been either too easy or too tight. This experience also lends credence to the Federal Reserve's practice of announcing ranges for more than one monetary aggregate.

The introduction of nationwide NOW accounts in 1981 has added uncertainty to the interpretation of movements in the narrow monetary aggregates. For example, the other checkable deposit component of *M1B* has surged from \$28 billion in December of 1980 to \$72 billion in September of 1981. Some portion of these inflows originated from sources other than demand deposits and has boosted the growth of *M1B* above what it would have been otherwise. The observed growth of *M1B* tends to overstate the expansiveness of monetary policy, other things equal, owing to this effect.[10]

In order to abstract from the impact of shifts into NOWs from savings instruments, the Federal Reserve has published and targeted an *M1B* measure adjusted for such shifts, based on evidence from sample surveys and econometric modeling concerning the proportion of inflows to NOWs coming from nondemand deposit sources in 1981.[11] While potentially subject to error, the adjustment procedure has, I believe, captured this impact reasonably well, making the chances of an upward bias and a downward bias about equal. I say this, even though shift-adjusted *M1B* typically has been running well below the lower bound of its annual range so far this year, which might lead one to believe that the adjustment has been too large. I think the explanation lies elsewhere, specifically, in an unexpectedly large downward drift of the true demand function for transactions balances in which transactions balances are accurately captured by *shift-adjusted M1B*.[12]

Table 1–1 provides evidence in support of this view. Column 3 shows prediction errors of annual growth rates of adjusted *M1B* from the rather conventional money demand function embedded in the Board's quarterly econometric model. After the last episode of substantial downward shift in the mid-1970s, this equation's annual growth rate errors were below 1 percentage point for four consecutive years. But, so far in 1981, a substantial annual drift of 6 percentage points has appeared. Compare this result with that obtained using an equation estimated by Richard Porter and Thomas Simpson of the Board staff.[13] This equation includes a complicated five-year bond rate ratchet variable with an increasing elasticity as the current rate rises above its moving average of past levels. This variable is designed to proxy incentives for innovation in cash management, thus internalizing such sources of downward demand shifts. As in recent years, Porter and Simpson's equation has predicted growth of adjusted *M1B* quite accurately on balance so far this year, with the error (shown in the last column) amounting to only −0.2 of one percentage point. This result suggests to me that the shift-adjustment procedure has been fairly reliable in measuring the underlying growth in transactions balances; however, money holders have responded to historically high intermediate-term interest rates much as the equation would have predicted by engaging in unusual efforts to economize on transactions balances.[14]

It is worth examining the monetary policy implications of this equation, as an aid to our interpretation of recent *M1B* growth. Figure 1–3 indicates the shape of the money demand curve for shift-adjusted *M1B*

Table 1–1. Actual and Predicted Growth of Adjusted *M1B* (annualized percent change from previous year's fourth quarter base; based on seasonally adjusted data)

		Board Quarterly Model Equation		*Porter-Simpson Equation*	
	*Actual Adjusted M1B**	*Predicted Adjusted M1B*	*Error (actual minus predicted)*	*Predicted Adjusted M1B*	*Error (actual minus predicted)*
1975:4	5.1	9.0	−3.9	8.2	−3.1
1976:4	6.8	9.3	−2.5	7.9	−1.1
1977:4	8.2	9.1	−0.9	8.9	−0.7
1978:4	7.9	8.4	−0.5	8.5	−0.6
1979:4	6.6	7.1	−0.5	6.0	0.6
1980:4	6.5	7.3	−0.7	6.0	0.5
1981:3	1.2	7.1	−5.9	1.4	−0.2

* Actual growth of adjusted *M1B* in 1981 corresponds to the growth of the published adjusted *M1B* series (except for rounding error). In earlier years, additional adjustments are based on the assumption that the introduction of ATS accounts nationwide, and NOW accounts in the Northeast had an expansionary effect and savings accounts for businesses and state and local governments had a depressing effect on *M1B* growth. The adjusted *M1B* series for these years is constructed as an estimate of what *M1B* would have been if these new deposit categories had not been created. The adjustments essentially consisted of subtracting one-third of other checkable deposits and adding one-fourth of business savings deposits and one-fifth of state and local government savings deposits. Since the latter two series tend to fluctuate with interest rates, the actual adjustment is made by assuming that these series grow at half the rate of increase of nominal income after the initial introductory phase for each.

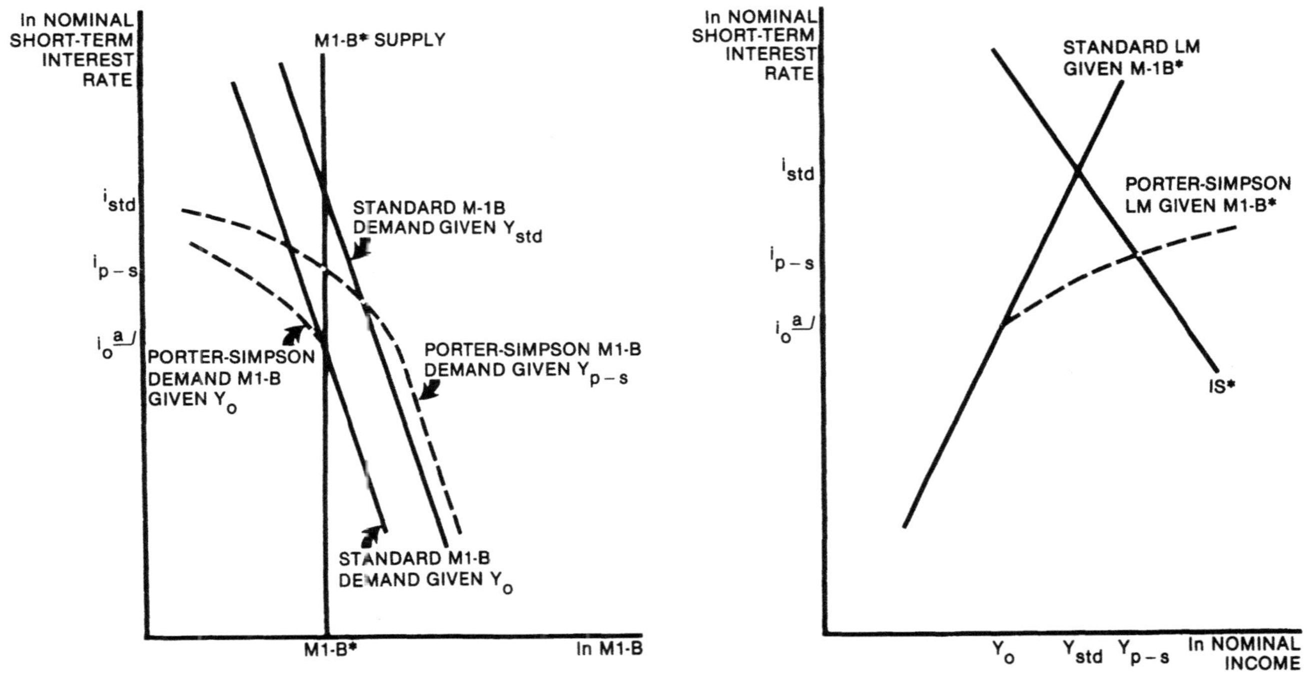

[a] i_0 is the short-term interest rate associated with a five-year bond rate equal to a moving average of past five-year bond rates; std is the standard demand function; and p-s is the Porter-Simpson demand function.

Figure 1–3 Money Demand and Monetary Policy Implications of the Porter-Simpson Money Demand Function for *M1B* implied by this equation, as well as the shape of the associated *LM* curve drawn for a given level of *M1B*.

Notice that the *classical* and *Keynesian* regions occasionally found in money and banking textbooks are effectively reversed by the Porter-Simpson equation. The upper reaches of the money demand and *LM* curves, associated with high interest rates, become quite interest elastic, while the lower ranges of both curves, associated with low interest rates, appear relatively inelastic. The implication of this characterization is clear. The stronger the advance of autonomous nominal aggregate demand, the less additional resistance will be provided by the monetary sector, since further upward shifts in the *IS* curve induce smaller interest rate increases. This result implies that downward adjustments to the targets for narrow money in the face of strong aggregate nominal demands for goods and services would be more appropriate in a world characterized by the Porter-Simpson money demand function than in a world with a more standard demand function. Turning back to the real world, the preceding analysis suggests that, in light of the consequences for money demand of historically high interest rates this year, the unexpected weakness of shift-adjusted *M1B* relative to the lower bound of its longer-run range need not, in itself, raise concerns about an overly restrictive monetary policy.

Ironically, a comparable analysis for *M2* leads to essentially the opposite conclusion about this broader aggregate; the interest-elasticity of demand for *M2* has probably continued to fall this year, rather than rising appreciably as did that of *M1B*. The primary reason is that the proportion of the nontransactions component of *M2* bearing market-related yields, shown in figure 1–4, has been growing rapidly in recent years, including 1981.[15] The chart indicates that such assets were relatively insignificant as late as mid-1978, prior to the introduction of the money market certificate in June. However, by year-end 1980, assets in *M2* bearing yields related to market interest rates had ballooned to nearly 45 percent of the nontransactions component of this aggregate, and only eight months later this fraction had reached 56 percent.

From December 1980 through September of 1981, shares in money market mutual funds have expanded by $81 billion, an unexpectedly whopping growth, six-month money market certificates (MMCs) have advanced by $54 billion, and 2½-year small saver certificates (SSCs) by $19 billion — with the advance of these latter accounts accelerating since the cap on SSCs, which was instituted in February, was removed in early August. At the same time, overnight RPs and Eurodollar deposits have added another $4 billion. (Retail RPs, not presently included in *M2*, have

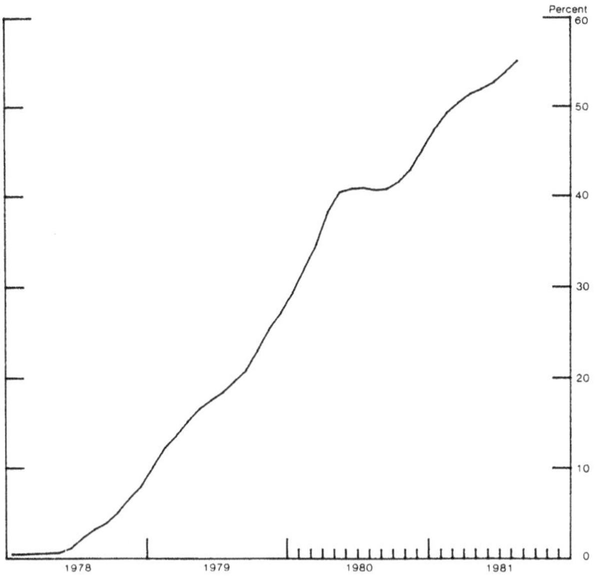

Figure 1–4 Share of Nontransactions *M2* Bearing Market-Related Yields

grown by $11 billion this year, mainly in recent months, depressing somewhat the measured growth of *M2*. By year-end, however, many retail RPs will have switched into the all saver certificates (ASCs), offered October 1, and the residual downward distortion to *M2* will be small. However, some new upward distortion may be introduced into *M2* by ASCs themselves, which will acquire some funds previously held in other market instruments outside of *M2*.) By contrast, deposits subject to fixed rate ceilings continued to run off, as savings deposits declined by $59 billion and small time deposits other than MMCs and SSCs fell by $8 billion — with these funds lodging primarily in *M2* assets bearing market-related yields. Similarly, the large preponderance of funds shifted out of *M1B* as money holders economized on transactions balances also surely found their way into these components of *M2*, making this aggregate virtually immune from the sizable downward shift of *M1B*.

These brute facts have implications for the demand function for *M2*. As indicated by figure 1–5, the increasingly market-sensitive average own rate of return on *M2* balances has successively lowered the elasticity of demand of *M2* with respect to market interest rates and shifted the *M2* demand schedule toward the right, given the observed income and market

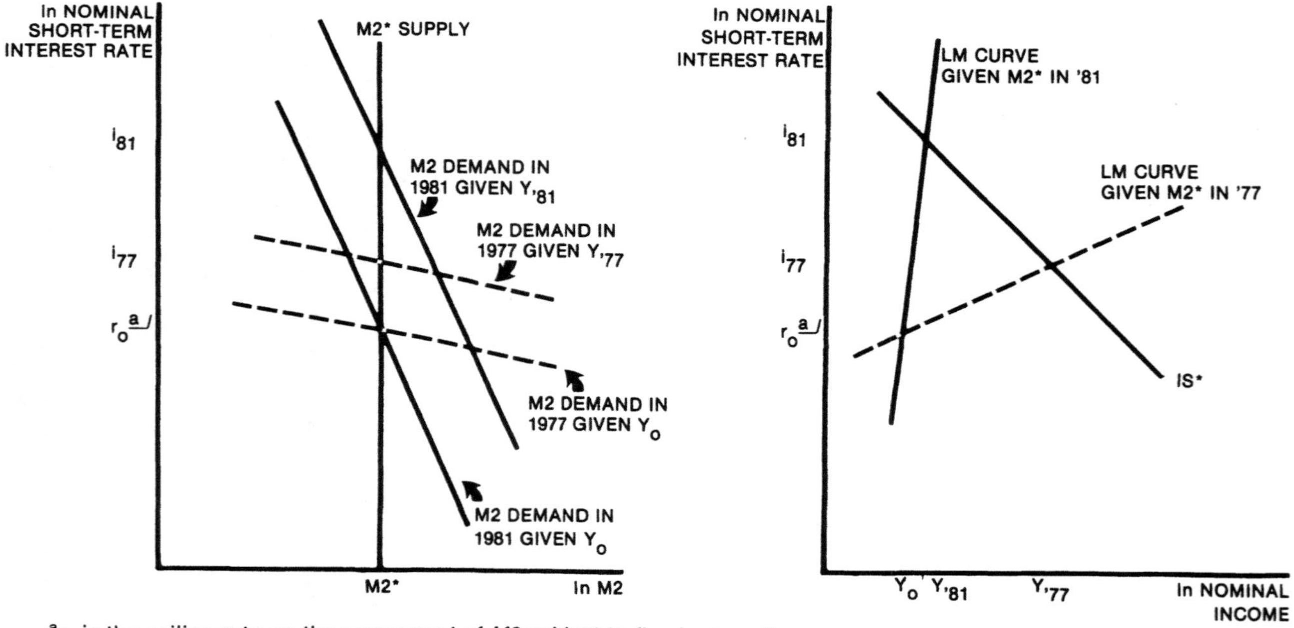

[a] r_o is the ceiling rate on the component of *M2* subject to fixed rate ceilings.

Figure 1–5 Money Demand and Monetary Policy Implications of the Increasing Fraction of *M2* Bearing Market-Related Yields interest rates in each of the past four years. These effects have steepened the slope of the *LM* curve drawn for a given level of *M2*.[16] This means, of course, that a strengthening of nominal demand for goods and services and the accompanying upward shift in the *IS* curve will meet with more resistance from the monetary sector for a given *M2* than would have been the case in earlier years. Thus, a given growth rate range for *M2* presently implies much more restraint on nominal economic activity than was the case as recently as 1977; moveover, the degree of restraint has increased with each passing year since then. This analysis suggests that the strength of *M2* relative to the upper bound of its long-run range in 1981 need not, in itself, imply undue monetary ease, since even as high a growth rate of *M2* as 9 percent could be associated with considerable restraint on nominal economic activity, given the interest rate implications of holding *M2* growth to this rate.

In closing this section, let me admit to a predilection toward thinking that the narrow money stock, in principle, provides a more meaningful indication of monetary impulses than do the broader aggregates. It seems to me that holdings of important components of *M2*, particularly money market mutual fund shares, are so dominated by investment motives and are such close substitutes for market instruments as to render the interpretation of movements in *M2* quite difficult and the variance of both *M2*'s demand function and the *LM* curve drawn for *M2* rather large. Moreover, according to my intuition, a change in the stock of money transmits its impacts to interest rates, real income, and prices through its interaction with the transactions demand function for the medium of exchange. Nevertheless, while I think that there exists such a "true" demand function at each point in time, predicting its location and setting targets for *M1B* over time on this basis has become a rather chancy business. For a year now, I have had some confidence that the Porter-Simpson equation could aid in this effort — indeed, more confidence than do Porter and Simpson themselves. But because this approach must rely so heavily on forecasts of intermediate-term interest rates, it too is subject to pitfalls. Besides, such an approach really represents only a band-aid cure for a serious malady. The basic problem lies with the incentive structure built into the regulatory framework that, in an inflationary environment, virtually guarantees the kind of innovations in cash management techniques and in transactions-type instruments that have made targeting on narrow money so problematical since the mid-1970s. In my view, radical surgery to the regulatory structure to remove the artificial impediments to a market-related return on all transactions balances offers the only reliable hope over the long run; I shall return to this issue in the last section of the paper.

Movements in the Various Reserve Aggregates and Their Reliability as Operating Targets

Our review of operating procedures over the last two years raises the issue of how observed growth in the reserve aggregates, particularly over short periods, should be interpreted. Let me indicate the kind of misleading analysis one commonly hears in this connection. It is often alleged that total reserves or the monetary base provide the stuff out of which money is created and thus that acceleration in the growth of these measures presages faster monetary expansion. After all, it might be argued, the total reserves multiplier for shift-adjusted *M1B* varied only between 10.9 and 10.6 from October 1979 to August 1981; such trivial variation ensures that movements in narrow money will follow movements in total reserves with only little delay. Concerns along these lines recently have been expressed by some market participants who fear that the annualized growth of total reserves in August and September of 8¼ and 23 percent, respectively — and even faster expansion of nonborrowed reserves — indicate a loss of resolve on the part of the Federal Reserve in conducting a policy of monetary restraint.

In addressing this general point, let us first analyze reserve movements in these two months, and then put the issue in somewhat broader perspective. Table 1–2 decomposes the growth in total reserves in these months by source.[17] Of this growth, 7½ percentage points in August and 6¼ percentage points in September may be attributed to the accommodation of a rapid expansion in large time deposits at member banks. Another 4 percentage points in August and 3¼ percentage points in September supported growth in member bank savings and small time deposits. Thus, "total reserves available to support *M1B* deposits" fell by about 3½ percent in August and rose by about 14½ percent in September, for an average of about 5½ percent over the two months.[18] To be sure, somewhat more ease is suggested by the average growth of about 13½ percent in "nonborrowed reserves available to support *M1B* deposits" during the two months. Actually, however, shift-adjusted *M1B* rose at an average annual rate of 1¼ percent over the two months, while *M2* expanded at a 9 percent average clip.

Stated somewhat differently, some of the variation in growth of reserve aggregates represents movements that offset the effects of multiplier variability on the money stock. In addition, some sources of multiplier variation, particularly those stemming from variations in money demand, cannot be offset fully by opposite movements in reserves over short periods, and, hence, are associated with observed variation in the money

Table 1–2. Sources of Growth in Total Reserves by Component in August and September 1981 (seasonally adjusted)

	Contribution to Growth in Total Reserves			
	Millions of Dollars[a]		Annual Growth Rates[a]	
	August (p)	*September (p)*	*August (p)*	*September (p)*
Required Reserves Held Against				
1. Member commercial bank deposits (sum of 2, 3, and 4)	295	603	8.9	18.1
2. Transaction deposits (OCD, demand deposits, U.S. government, net interbank, telephone transfers)	−85	284	−2.6	8.5
3. Savings and small time deposits	136	111	4.1	3.3
4. Large time deposits	244	208	7.4	6.3
5. Nonmember commercial banks and others	28	5	0.8	0.2
Reserve Aggregates				
6. Total required reserves	323	608	9.8	18.3
7. Excess reserves	−48	157	−1.5	4.7
8. Total reserves (sum of 6 and 7)	274	765	8.3	23.0
9. Adjustment borrowings[b]	−337	−184	−10.2	−5.5
10. Nonborrowed reserves[c] (8 less 9)	611	949	18.5	28.6

[a]p = preliminary.
[b]Includes seasonal borrowings.
[c]Includes extended credit.

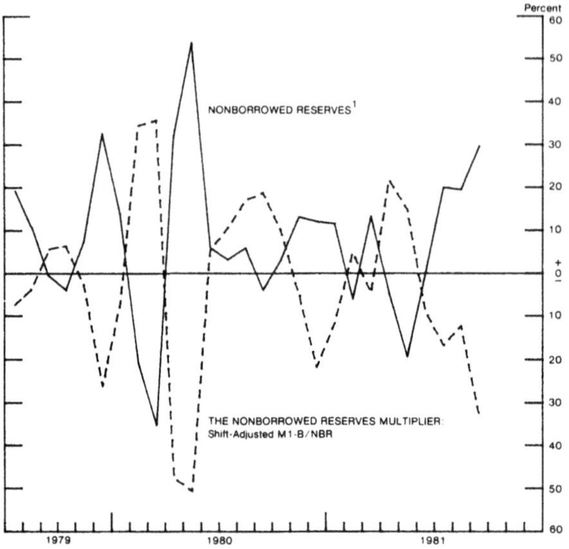

[1]*NBR* includes extended credit.

Figure 1–6 Nonborrowed Reserves and Its Multiplier (annualized growth rates)

stock. Indeed, adjustments of nonborrowed reserve targets opposite to money demand movements may offset some of the effects of the demand-side disturbance on the observed money stock; at the same time, however, they will increase the variation of the multiplier itself.[19] Finally, it turns out that the variation in reserve multipliers is not so trivial after all.

This last observation is confirmed by figures 1–6, 1–7, and 1–8, which show month-to-month percent changes at an annual rate in the multipliers for nonborrowed reserves, total reserves, and the monetary base, respectively, together with the growth rates of these reserve aggregates themselves. These charts are presented mainly to indicate the range of month-to-month variations in the reserve multipliers and to suggest that variations in growth of the narrow reserve aggregates and in growth of their multipliers tend to be offsetting (negatively correlated). One lesson is simply that short-run money growth cannot be inferred merely by examining growth of reserves or the base over similar periods.

Perhaps another example will drive the point home. The change in total reserves accelerated from a negative 6½ percent at an annual rate in February 1980 to positive rates of 1½ and 2½ percent in March and April, respectively. Even so, *M1B* collapsed at around a 17 percent annual rate

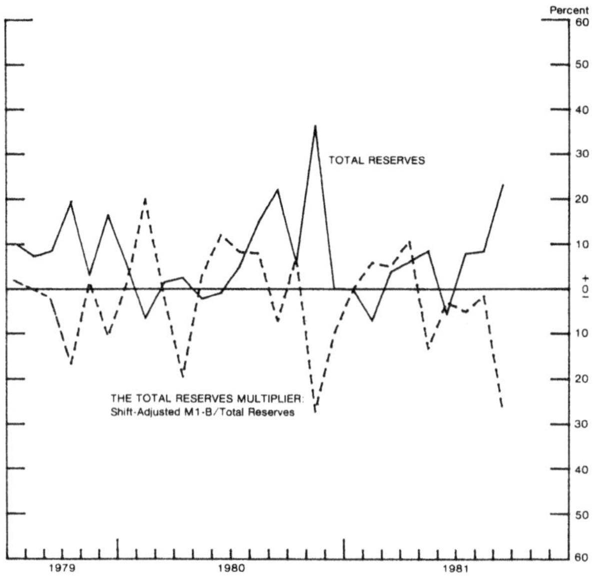

Figure 1–7 Total Reserves and Its Multiplier (annualized growth rates)

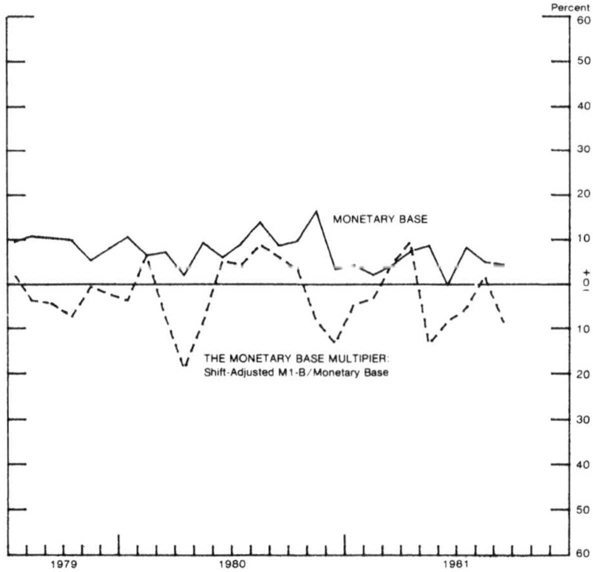

Figure 1–8 Monetary Base and Its Multiplier (annualized growth rates)

in April as its multiplier fell by 19½ percent. The monetary base (Board definition) was a somewhat better indicator of money growth over this period, owing to the sharp deceleration of currency growth in April. Over the February-to-April period, the base grew at 6½ percent, 7 percent, and 2 percent rates; nevertheless, in April its *M1B* multiplier dropped at about a 19 percent annual rate as *M1B* declined.

Despite this episode, the month-to-month percent changes of the monetary base multiplier in figure 1–8 may be seen to be more stable on average than the changes of the reserve multipliers shown in the two preceding figures. Such behavior of the base multiplier has persuaded Anatol Balbach, of the Federal Reserve Bank of St. Louis, that *M1B* could have been fairly closely controlled, at least over 1980 as a whole, if the monetary base had simply been set on a constant growth path month by month. His oft-quoted study also indicated that even better control would have occurred if the base had been set each month on the assumption that the multiplier in the current month would be equal to last month's value.[20] In another study, by James Johannes and Robert Rasche, which was publicized by the Shadow Open Market Committee, the monetary base multiplier was found not only to be more stable month-to-month than narrower reserve multipliers, but to be more predictable as well.[21] Johannes and Rasche concluded, as did Balbach, that the Federal Reserve should switch its operating target to the monetary base, even under the existing regulatory structure.

I would respectfully contest this conclusion, on the basis of evidence contained in the Federal Reserve staff study of February 1981, confirming once again that appearances can be deceiving and that correlation does not imply causality.[22] We found that the base multiplier was only as stable and predictable as it was during 1980 because the base was not tightly controlled over this period. With nonborrowed reserves as the operating target, unanticipated shifts in the demands for currency, transactions deposits, and member bank borrowings caused observed movements in the same direction in *both M1B and the monetary base*. Surges in currency demand raised the base directly, while unexpected jumps in transactions deposits and borrowing demands raised the base via the associated increases in total reserves as borrowings rose. With such disturbances affecting both the numerator and denominator of the multiplier in the same direction, variation in the multiplier was muted, compared to what would have occurred if the monetary base in the denominator had been held at a predetermined level. In this latter case, an increase in currency demand, for example, would not have been allowed to change the level of the monetary base, but would have caused a reserve drain of equal magnitude and a multiple contraction of deposits and money. This outcome would have been associated with a comparatively large decline in the base multiplier.

Although it is not theoretically certain that the monetary base multiplier is more predictable when the base is not exogenously controlled, we found that such a result held empirically when the Board money market model was simulated with the actual errors that disturbed each equation in the first year of the new procedures. In the case corresponding to actual experience, in which disturbances to money were permitted to induce endogenous movements in the base, the model's monthly predictions of the base multiplier had an annualized root mean squared error of only 5 percentage points. By contrast, in the hypothetical case in which the base was determined exogenously — such as targeted on a constant growth path and attained come hell or high interest rates — the comparable monthly error of the model's multiplier prediction jumped to 9.9 or 10.4 percentage points, depending upon the exact procedure employed. The latter results compare unfavorably to the misforecasts of the nonborrowed reserves multiplier, which averaged 6.5 or 8.2 percentage points when this measure instead was assumed to be selected as the exogenously determined operating target.[23] Money errors with nonborrowed reserves exogenous were lower than those with the base exogenous because disturbances to currency demand were less damaging and because the discount window was allowed to act as a cushion against disturbances on the money supply side.

These results indicate that, under the current regulatory structure, short-run targets for the monetary aggregates would be attained more closely by using nonborrowed reserves rather than the monetary base as a predetermined short-run operating target. The empirical work suggests even more strongly that a predetermined target for total reserves would yield less monetary control precision than one for nonborrowed reserves. Considering the possibility of judgmentally adjusting reserve targets during intermeeting periods to offset recognized disturbances — as is, of course, present practice — would make these conclusions less certain. Nevertheless, I believe the burden of proof has now been passed to the proponents of the base or total reserves.

An Immodest Proposal for Reform

Having come this far, I cannot resist the urge to add in conclusion my own "program for monetary stability."[24] Others wiser than I have offered their proposals in the past and new sages, perhaps learning just this semester that demand curves slope downwards, will surely do so in the future. I cannot claim much originality for my package; most of these proposals have been around for some time and the implementation of several of them is already underway. Indeed, what is most original are a few glaring *omissions* from the list; my reasons for rejecting these probably will stir up more controversy today than my justifications for the items I am pushing. In any event, here is the list of regulatory changes that I would like to see instituted:

1. Repeal of the prohibition of interest payments on demand deposits
2. Phase-out of interest rate ceilings on all deposits
3. Payment of interest on required reserve balances at the Federal Reserve at a rate equal to the return on the Federal Reserve's security portfolio in the preceding calendar quarter
4. Continued phase-in of reserve requirements under the Monetary Control Act
5. Extension of reserve requirement coverage to all transactions-type balances, regardless of issuer
6. Return to essentially contemporaneous required reserve accounting on transactions deposits, combined with a limited liberalization of the carryover privilege

Another possible reform deserves further study:

7. Establishment of a graduated marginal discount rate that depends on adjustment borrowing as a percent of the institution's lagged required reserve balance plus required clearing balance at the Federal Reserve, with elimination of administrative pressure and arbitrage restrictions but with the basic discount rate and the gradient set at the Board's discretion

The first three items, while offering gains in economic efficiency and resource allocation, are primarily designed to reduce the present artificial incentives to demanders and suppliers of money for adopting sophisticated cash management techniques and inventing new transactions or near-transactions instruments.[25] Market-determined interest rates on all transactions accounts would minimize the opportunity cost of holding them, while interest payments on required reserve balances would eliminate the tax on reservable liabilities that is now passed on to depositors in the form of lower implicit or explicit returns. In terms of priorities, I consider the need for the first three reforms just as pressing as for the others, even though they have not received the attention in public discussions that they deserve.

The last four items are, of course, designed to improve short-run control over narrowly defined money through nonborrowed reserves targeting. Full phase-in of reserve requirements under the Monetary Control Act (MCA) will produce more nearly uniform and universal reserve requirements on transactions accounts and eliminate requirements on all other deposits except nonpersonal time deposits. The latter requirements could be reduced to zero at the Board's discretion. Continued phase-in of the MCA is included because the advantage of uniform and universal reserve requirements on the deposit component of the aggregate being controlled inexplicably has been overlooked in certain circles. Some monetarists opposed the extension of reserve requirements to nonmember institutions, apparently on the grounds that monetary control would be little improved. However, four empirical studies by Board staff, each quite distinct methodologically, have suggested the opposite.[26] The institution of universal reserve requirements evidently affords a noticeable improvement in the short-run predictability of the reserves multiplier, particularly to the degree that these reserve requirements are binding (that is, establish required reserves in excess of the levels of vault cash holdings that are desired for operating needs).[27]

A separate set of critics has argued, however, that binding but noninterest-bearing reserve requirements represent a tax on deposits which serves to spur innovations and hence impairs monetary control in the long run. Although this point is certainly well taken, these critics then go on to argue that reserve requirements should be eliminated and interest should be paid on reserve balances held at the Federal Reserve only on a *voluntary* basis.[28] This conclusion, however, is a non sequitur of the first order. To neutralize the tax effect, interest indeed should be paid on required reserve balances — much as it is implicitly paid at present on required clearing balances in the form of reduced service charges — but such interest payments would obviate the reason for eliminating reserve requirements. Paying interest exclusively on voluntary reserve balances simply compounds the multiplier slippage that would result otherwise from paying interest on excess reserves. Thus, such a proposal would end up greatly reducing the precision of monetary control. When throwing out the bath water, some attention should be paid to the baby.

Extension of reserve requirements to all transactions-type accounts regardless of issuing institution is a straightforward application of the principle of uniformity and universality of reserve requirements.[29] This condition is a prerequisite for close control through reserves of a narrow monetary aggregate, redefined to include any new transactions instruments as they come along.

I also support the switch from lagged reserve requirements (LRR) to contemporaneous reserve requirements (CRR), even though there is still some dispute about the size of the potential monetary control gains to be obtained by doing so, particularly under an operating procedure geared to nonborrowed reserves.[30] Even so, I believe that CRR offers advantages for monetary control and other objectives sufficient to outweigh its operational disadvantages.

Contemporaneous reserve accounting likely would imply less short-term interest rate volatility on settlement day and less rate volatility in response to money supply-side disturbances, since movements in required reserves over the reserve period would serve as an automatic stabilizing mechanism. Moreover, interest rate movements over periods of several months may well be muted by CRR. Because initial departures of money from target would be countered more effectively, smaller changes in short-term interest rates would be implied later in returning money to target by the end of any particular control horizon. One reason for this closer short-run monetary control under CRR is that the automatic response of aggregate reserve positions and short-term interest rates to movements in the money demand schedule would be speeded up.[31] In practice, other things equal, week-to-week volatility of interest rates would likely be enlarged by CRR, reflecting high frequency variations in money demand, some of which are transitory and self-reversing.[30]

The question arises as to whether the volatility of short-term interest rates arising from week-to-week variation in money demand should not be smoothed to some extent; I believe that some cushioning of the effects of transitory variations in reserve demands (and supplies) is appropriate. But the issue of the *size* of interest rate responses to money demand shocks can be separated from the issue of their *timing*; it is only the latter consideration that is fundamentally relevant to the choice between CRR and LRR. CRR affords an *immediate* — though not necessarily *large* — reaction of reserve positions and the federal funds rate to a short-run change in money demand; this seems appropriate to cover the possibility that the change is permanent and to get started the process of portfolio adaptations by banks and the public. This consideration is one reason why I favor CRR.

Regarding the issue of the size of the interest rate response, I believe that adherence to a total reserves target over short control periods would give rise to excessive volatility of reserve positions and of the federal funds rate in reaction to demand-side shocks. I say this recognizing that such rate variability is needed for more precise short-run monetary control and that, with CRR, monetary control probably would be closer with an operating target for total reserves, as opposed to nonborrowed reserves, at least once the MCA is phased in.[31] (The phase-in of more nearly uniform and universal reserve requirements will reduce the importance of money supply-side disturbances, which are more damaging with total reserves targeting.) Even then, however, I would prefer retaining nonborrowed reserves as the operating target to allow the discount window to cushion the response of money market conditions to temporary factors affecting reserve supplies and demands.

Various alternatives to the discount window for performing this function have been proposed, including considerably liberalized carryover, unlimited carryover with penalties, and staggered reserve periods.[32] In particular, a recent proposal for staggered accounting has gained adherents.[33] However, I find myself unable to support the adoption of any of these proposals.

A few observations are in order concerning staggering. Contrary to some assertions, staggering would not reduce the need for defensive open market operations as long as short-run reserve targets are retained. The same amount of operations to offset market factors affecting reserves would be needed to hit a reserve target over a given interval, whether reserve periods are staggered or coincident.

More importantly, staggering would impair monetary control by lessening the predictability of the reserves multiplier. It is precisely the fact that all depository institutions settle on the same day that now prevents the cumulation of reserve imbalances from week-to-week (apart from carryover, which is limited in both amount and duration) and keeps the total reserves multiplier dependent upon statutory required reserve ratios. Under staggering, however, the ability of settling institutions to borrow from or lend to nonsettling institutions in the federal funds market would permit reserve imbalances to be passed on from one week to the next.

If market participants inaccurately forecast the fundamental direction of interest rate pressures, the federal funds rate for a time could fail to respond to policy-induced changes in reserve availability or to changes in money demand. Consequently, institutions could delay basic balance sheet adjusments, which would lead to an accumulation of reserve imbalances over time. Once reserve managers recognized their error, an overreaction of balance sheet adjustments would be necessary in order to remove the enlarged reserve imbalance from the banking system. Sizable interest rate variation over the intermediate run would result from such a process, leading to an over- or undershooting of money from its sustainable equilibrium given reserves. This would be true even if, as often cited by its proponents, staggering normally reduced settlement day pressures.

These instabilities of interest rates and money presuppose that, for a time, reserve imbalances would be passed back and forth between classes of institutions through federal funds trading. Suppose instead, however, that in response to a reserve imbalance, settling institutions make the appropriate basic adjustments to their earning assets. Under certain plausible assumptions, a cycling of interest rates and deposits would still result.[34] It is the possibility that these dynamic instabilities may be inherent in staggered accounting per se that makes me wary of this system.

Would my alternative system work better than staggering? Admittedly, my preferred mechanism for the cushioning of temporary shocks — the discount window — is subject to certain drawbacks at present. The functional relationship between adjustment borrowings and the spread of the funds rate over the discount rate is subject to uncertainty, as noted above.[35] But this admission brings me to my last proposal, which I have courageously advanced as warranting further study.[36]

Under the proposal for a graduated discount rate system, administrative pressure and arbitrage restrictions would be eliminated. Institutions would have every incentive to equalize their marginal costs of various sources of funds, which would entail changing the level of adjustment borrowing until the marginal discount rate equaled the prevailing funds rate. Hence, all eligible institutions would incur the same amount of adjustment borrowings as a percentage of the sum of their lagged required reserve balance and their required clearing balance at the Federal Reserve, which is already set on a lagged basis.[37] Given these assumptions, the aggregate amount of borrowing for each federal funds rate would be perfectly predictable in advance. Thus, the error in the relation between adjustment borrowings and the federal funds rate would be eliminated, or, in practice, at least substantially reduced.

As a consequence, a strengthening of money relative to target would automatically raise required reserves relative to the nonborrowed reserves path, and *reliably* cause an automatic rise in the funds rate exactly in proportion to the increase in borrowings. In principle, the gradient could be set equal to the slope of the "optimal combination policy" of total reserves and interest rates that would minimize the expected short-run error in controlling money, given the error distributions and elasticities of the money supply and demand functions.[38] After the establishment of CRR and the phase-in of the MCA, I suspect that my preference, however, would be for somewhat more accommodation to money demand-side shocks — in other words, a gradient shallower than that.[39] The gradient should be shallower so as to permit adequate cushioning of money market conditions in the short run from the impact of transitory disturbances to money demand.[40] Nevertheless, at that time I would prefer to see a somewhat steeper gradient than is now produced on average by administrative pressure.[41] A steeper gradient than now combined with the virtual elimination of the error in the discount borrowing function also would, under nonborrowed reserves targeting, enhance the monetary control gains available from the phase-in of the MCA and the return to CRR.

In my view, nonborrowed reserves targeting with this reform of the discount window would yield far superior results in terms of the appropriate balance between monetary control precision and volatility in short-term interest rates, than any of the other competing proposals I have seen, including staggered accounting.

In conclusion, I believe that the last four proposals, taken together, would noticeably tighten the monetary control mechanism, even though one could argue that the gains from adopting any one individually might be small. Such a structure of reserve requirements and the discount window would mitigate the influence of money supply-side disturbances on the nonborrowed reserves multiplier. Remaining monetary control slippage in the short-run would predominately reflect money demand-side shocks. Those deviations in the stock of money from short-run targets that would occur despite a degree of automatic and discretionary resistance stemming from the nonborrowed reserve procedures would reflect an essentially desirable degree of accommodation to demand-side disturbances. This remaining slippage would provide breathing room for determining whether the source of the money demand disturbance was transitory noise, a response to shifting nominal spending demands, or a permanent drift in the money demand function. Each of these possibilities would have different implications for monetary policy responses over the intermediate and long run.

The odds on the occurrence of substantial drifts in the relationship between the demand for narrow money and its key determinants — real income, market interest rates, and the price level — would likely be substantially lowered by the first three proposals. While these proposals for eliminating artificial impediments to the payment of market-determined yields on all deposits and required reserve balances have other advantages — including gains in economic efficiency — as well as some transitional disadvantages for certain institutions, their potential for aiding stabilization policy to me seems of paramount importance. Taken together, my proposed reforms would, I submit, contribute to the successful conduct of monetary policy.

Notes

1. Friedman (1981). The study being referred to is Federal Reserve staff (1981).
2. For more extensive discussion of the mechanics of the new operating procedures, see Board of Governors of the Federal Reserve System (1980a); Axilrod and Lindsey (1981); Axilrod (1981); and Lindsey et al. (1981).
3. For a more detailed episodic review of the new procedures see Sternlight et al. (1981). Also see Axilrod (1981) for an overview and evaluation of the new operating procedures in their first year.
4. Brian Madigan of the Board staff has estimated a linear regression equation using weekly data. The spread of the funds rate over the basic discount rate is explained by a constant term of 17 basis points plus 82 basis points per billion of adjustment borrowing plus 78 percent of the surcharge rate. The latter two variables have t values in excess of 4 while the constant term is not significantly different from zero. The standard error of the equation is 78 basis points and the $\bar{R}^2$ is 0.91. Strictly speaking, this relationship represents a structural equation rather than the reduced-form equation in which free reserves would replace the borrowings variable so as to incorporate the excess reserves demand function. Thus, the coefficient of adjustment borrowings likely is biased downwards owing to simultaneous equations bias. Furthermore, the true function appears to be nonlinear, steepening as borrowings rise above an inflection point. See Tinsley, Fries et al. (1981).
5. See Sternlight et al. (1981) for these figures.
6. See Johnson et al. (1981) for an empirical study of the relationship between the federal funds rate and other market rates in the first year following the introduction of the new operating procedures.
7. See Enzler (1981) for an investigation of this timing.
8. Lagged reserve accounting imparts a certain recursivity to the monetary control mechanism in a weekly context. While the mechanism becomes more simultaneous when viewed over a longer horizon, the effect of the lag seems to be revealed in monthly data. The recursive structure with weekly data involves the following (simplified) causal chain. Deposits two weeks ago determine required reserves this week. Given the current week's nonborrowed reserves target, the supply of free reserves is determined. The demand for free reserves, composed of excess reserves demand minus borrowed reserves demand, interacts with the supply of free reserves (nonborrowed reserves minus required reserves) to determine the federal funds rate, given the discount rate structure. Expected levels of the federal funds rate in the near future determine other short-term interest rates. Current and lagged values of these rates and of exogenous real income and prices determine the current week's deposits and currency via their demand functions. Deposits this week then determine required reserves two weeks later, and so on. This stylized picture, of course, ignores several connections, including feedbacks in setting the nonborrowed reserve targets. For a formal modeling of this mechanism under lagged reserve requirements (LRR) and the implications

of LRR for money supply functions and the choice of operating targets see Porter, Lindsey, and Laufenberg (1975) and LeRoy (1979).

9. See Lindsey et al. (1981) and Judd and Scadding (1981) for a discussion of the large errors in standard money demand functions over these quarters, as contrasted to the performance of the "San Francisco" equation that contains a bank loan shock variable. Also see Tinsley, von zur Muehlen, et al. (1981) for a simulation of the new operating procedures with the Board's money market model suggesting that the model was subjected to errors in 1980 that were exceptional by historical standards and that short-run monetary control under the new procedures could be expected to be considerably more precise during more normal periods.

10. Two alternative theories of the impact of nationwide NOWs support this conclusion. The first is that inflows to NOWs originating from savings instruments, which were induced in part by relatively high minimum balance requirements, retain their savings function and are not used by depositors as transactions balances. Thus, observed *M1B* overstates the underlying growth of transactions balances. The second theory is that the advent of an explicit own rate on these transactions accounts has raised the marginal net return available on transactions balances on average and has shifted the transactions deposit demand function outward for given market interest rates, real income, and prices. Thus, although correctly measuring transactions balances, observed *M1B* growth in 1981 would have a less expansionary impact on economic activity than similar growth rates in the past, other things equal.

11. See Simpson et al. (1981a), and, for more detail, Simpson (1981b).

12. In terms of unadjusted *M1B*, which since June 1981 has fallen within the range for *shift-adjusted M1B*, two separate effects have worked at cross purposes. Nationwide NOWs have raised the demand for observed *M1B*, while a basic downward drift of unexpectedly large proportions in the demand for transactions balances has moved that aggregate in the opposite direction. In this regard, Weintraub (1981) has noted that the reasonable velocity behavior of observed *M1B* by historical standards in 1981 suggests that its demand function has not been subject to abnormal influences on net and that the Federal Reserve should have set an annual range for unadjusted *M1B* of 3-½ to 6 percent in the first place and never introduced the shift-adjusted series. By contrast, I believe that it is analytically useful to separate the two influences, which, fortuitously, have roughly offset one another so far this year, although they were not expected to do so when the annual growth rate ranges were established. Even so, Weintraub's conclusion that *M1B* growth has been about right on balance in 1981 does not seem farfetched.

13. This equation is described and simulated in Simpson and Porter (1980). Lindsey et al. (1981) have established that is post-sample performance compares quite favorably to the predictions of a variety of competing money demand equations.

14. The equation would have overpredicted *M1* growth *ex ante* during 1981 if the assumed five-year bond rate had been too low. In fact, this bond rate was higher in 1980 than might have been anticipated as the year began — even given perfect foresight of short-term interest rates, real income, and prices.

15. Consider the following simple demand function expressed in natural logs: $\ln M2^d = a - b(\ln i - \ln r_{av}) + c \ln Y$, where $r_{av} = pi + (1 - p)r$ is the average own rate, i is the market rate, r is the fixed ceiling rate, assumed to equal the rate paid on deposits subject to fixed rate ceilings, and p is the proportion of *M2* bearing market-related yields. Since many of these *M2* assets are nonreservable, the effect of reserve requirements on rates paid is ignored for simplicity, as is the currency component of *M2*.

16. For a more technical analysis of the monetary policy implications of a market-related own rate on money stock deposits, see Lindsey (1977).

17. A similar analysis, attempting to teach the same lesson, may be found in Board of Governors of the Federal Reserve System (1980a).

18. Even these figures are oversimplified by the inclusion of required reserves at non-member institutions against all deposits and of required reserves at members against U.S. government, net interbank, and telephone transfer deposits.

19. See Lindsey et al. (1981) for elaborations upon these relationships.

20. Balbach (1981).

21. Johannes and Rasche (1981).

22. Lindsey et al. (1981). Also see a more technical presentation in Lindsey, Farr, et al. (1982).

23. The fact that the nonborrowed reserves multiplier was less predictable in practice than these figures would suggest reflects in part the intermeeting adjustments to its reserve target path that were made to offset money demand-side disturbances. Although these adjustments brought money closer to path, they enlarged multiplier prediction errors by causing substantial misses in the direction opposite to the money disparity in the forecasts of the nonborrowed reserves in the denominator of its multiplier.

24. This phrase is, of course, taken from Milton Friedman's book of the same name, published in 1959. Indeed, he also recommended three of the seven proposals I have listed. He has since recommended a fourth: the return to contemporaneous reserve requirements, which, of course, were still in effect at the time his book was written. For another influential set of proposals for improving monetary control see Poole and Lieberman (1972). For a careful review of the monetary control literature and various proposals for reform that were extant in the fall of 1980, see Lombra (1980). For a survey of the literature on the money supply process as of 1974 that is critical of the foundations of standard models, see Dewald and Lindsey (1974).

25. For an analysis of proposals for permitting interest on both demand deposits and required reserves, see Axilrod et al. (1977). For a theoretical discussion of implications for monetary policy, see Lindsey (1977).

26. Kopecky, Parke, and Porter (1980), Lindsey, Hadjimichalakis, and Grupe (1980), Lindsey et al. (1981) and Tinsley, Fries, et al. (1981).

27. Once the phase-in of the new reserve requirements has proceeded for several years, consideration might well be given to imposing the interest-bearing supplemental reserve requirement on transactions accounts, so as to raise the proportion of aggregate transactions deposits subject to binding reserve requirements. See Lindsey, Hadjimichalakis, and Grupe (1981).

28. See, for example, Greenbaum (1979) and Kanatas and Greenbaum (1979).

29. I also favor the elimination of both the reservability of deposits due to banks and the deductibility of deposits due from banks combined with changed procedures for booking cash items in process of collection, due from's and due to's. See Board of Governors of the Federal Reserve System (1980b) for the description of this proposal when it was put out for comment (but received no support from academic economists).

30. In three studies involving stochastic model simulation, the gains under a nonborrowed reserves operating regime, even in combination with full phase-in of the Monetary Control Act (MCA) are estimated to be small. See Lindsey et al. (1981), Tinsley (1981), and Jones (1981). By contrast, Tinsley, Fries, et al. (1981) reach a different conclusion in a recent simulation of a more elaborate monthly model than used in the first two studies just cited. They find that after full MCA phase-in, the standard error of controlling monthly *M1* growth

falls from 9 percentage points at an annual rate to about 4 percentage points owing to a switch to CRR, a decline in the standard error similar in size to their estimate under the pre-MCA reserve requirement structure, though from a lower level. Their simulation exercise necessarily assumes, contrary to fact, that no intermeeting adjustments are made to reserve paths. My considered opinion is that, in practice, the gain from switching to CRR might be about one-half as large as these last estimates suggest.

31. For earlier analysis of these issues, which also are addressed in the papers referenced in the previous footnote, see Porter, Lindsey, and Laufenberg (1975) and Board of Governors of the Federal Reserve System staff (1977).

32. See Pierce (1981) for quantitative estimates of the degree to which transitory noise falls off as the interval of measurement lengthens. At present under LRR, the weekly nonborrowed reserve paths are adjusted week-by-week to equalize over the remaining weeks of the intermeeting period the expected weekly borrowing levels implied by the average nonborrowed reserve targets: this procedure tends to damp week-to-week funds rate movements in a way that would be less effective under CRR.

33. See Lindsey et al. (1981) and Tinsley, Fries, et al. (1981) for estimates from model simulations leading to this conclusion.

34. Unlimited carryover with penalties was proposed by Poole (1975). Variants of staggered accounting systems have been supported over the years by Friedman, the Shadow Open Market Committee, and Representative Henry Reuss.

35. See Morgan Guaranty Trust Company (1981a, 1981b).

36. See theoretical studies by Laufenberg (1978), Poole (1978), and Trepeta and Lindsey (1979) for the derivation of these results. Laufenberg noted that perpetual cycles are generated in a textbook model of earning asset adjustment by settling banks with total reserves fixed: Poole pointed out that damped cycles are a possible outcome, and Trepeta and Lindsey noted that no cycles could arise under certain assumptions, such as perfect foresight, about the adjustment process.

37. Refer to note 4 for one estimate of this error.

38. For examinations of variants of this proposal see Quick (1979) and Keir (1981). For an empirical estimate of the implied improvement in monetary control precision with nonborrowed reserve targeting, see Lindsey et al. (1981).

39. The required reserve balance on a lagged basis is used to give the Federal Reserve advance knowledge of each institution's (and hence the aggregate) borrowing schedule in dollar terms. Such a procedure is not inconsistent with contemporaneous reserve requirements for reserve maintenance purposes. Institutions that have not opened either of these accounts would not be eligible for adjustment borrowing, but this criterion would not preclude eligibility for the seasonal, special, and other extended credit programs.

40. See Poole (1970), LeRoy (1975), LeRoy and Lindsey (1978) and LeRoy (1979) for a discussion of the optimal combination policy, which has received undue neglect in the money control literature.

41. Indeed, after the institution of these other reforms reduces the importance of money supply-side shocks, the optimal combination policy curve may assume a negative slope. This means that if the federal funds rate rises unexpectedly given the level of reserves (that was initially thought consistent with the money target in the absence of errors in the money supply and demand functions), then the level of reserves should be *reduced, amplifying* the upward funds rate movement. Such a reaction is based on the likelihood that the initial increase in the funds rate arose predominately from an as yet unobserved positive error in the money demand function. See LeRoy (1976).

42. Proposals for floating the discount rate at a penalty level involve virtually foresak-

ing this cushioning function of the discount window. I would therefore only consider instituting a floating discount rate if it were to be set *below* a moving average federal funds rate so that adjustment borrowing would normally be above a fractional level and thus would have room both to rise and fall.

43. Recall once again note 4.

References

Axilrod, S.H. "Federal Reserve Staff Study of the New Monetary Control Procedures: Overview of Findings and Evaluation." In *New Monetary Control Procedures,* Vol. I. Federal Reserve Staff. Board of Governors of the Federal Reserve System, February 1981.

Axilrod, S.H., and Lindsey , D.E. "Federal Reserve System Implementation of Monetary Policy: Analytical Foundations of the New Approach." *American Economic Review, Papers and Proceedings* (May 1981). Paper delivered at the American Economic Association Meetings, September 6, 1980.

Axilrod, S.H., et al. "The Impact of the Payment of Interest on Demand Deposits." Unpublished staff study, Board of Governors of the Federal Reserve System, January 31, 1977.

Balbach, A.B. "How Controllable is Money Growth?" *Federal Reserve Bank of St. Louis Review* (April 1981).

Board of Governors of the Federal Reserve System (1980a). "The New Federal Reserve Technical Procedures for Controlling Money," January 30, 1980. Also appearing as "Appendix B: Description of the New Procedures for Controlling Money," appended to "Monetary Policy Report to the Congress Pursuant to the Full Employment and Balanced Growth Act of 1978," February 19, 1980.

Board of Governors of the Federal Reserve System (1980b). Federal Reserve press release and attached "Notice of Proposed Rulemaking: Reserve Requirements of Depository Institutions," June 4, 1980.

Board of Governors of the Federal Reserve System Staff. "Analysis of the Impact of Lagged Reserve Accounting," unpublished manuscript, October 6, 1977.

Dewald, W.G., and Lindsey, D.E. "Alternative Views of the Money Supply Process: A Critical Survey." Unpublished paper, delivered at the Econometric Society Annual Meetings, December 29, 1974.

Enzler, J. "Economic Disturbances and Monetary Policy Responses." In Federal Reserve Staff, *New Monetary Control Procedures*, Vol. I. Board of Governors of the Federal Reserve System, February 1981.

Federal Reserve Staff. *New Monetary Control Procedures*, Vols. I and II. Board of Governors of the Federal Reserve System, February 1981.

Friedman, M. *A Program for Monetary Stability*. Fordham University Press, 1959.

Friedman, M. "Monetary Policy: Theory and Practice." Lecture delivered July 5, 1981. *Journal of Money, Credit and Banking* (February 1982).

Greenbaum, S., Testimony, House Committee on Banking, Finance, and Urban Affairs, March 5, 1979.

Johannas, J.M., and Rasche, R.H. "Can the Reserve Approach to Monetary Control Really Work?" *Journal of Money, Credit, and Banking* (August 1981).

Johnson, D., et al. "Interest Rate Variability Under the New Operating Procedures and the Initial Response in Financial Markets." In Federal Reserve Staff, *New Monetary Control Procedures*, Vol. I. Board of Governors of the Federal Reserve System, February, 1981.

Jones, D. "An Empirical Analysis of Monetary Control under Contemporaneous and Lagged Reserve Accounting." Unpublished manuscript, Board of Governors of the Federal Reserve System, October 11, 1981.

Judd, J.P., and Scadding, J.L. "Liability Management, Bank Loans, and Deposit 'Market' Disequilibrium." *Federal Reserve Bank of San Francisco Economic Review* (Spring 1981).

Kanatas, G., and Greenbaum, S. "Bank Reserve Requirements and Monetary Aggregates." Working Paper No. 55. Banking Research Center, Northwestern University, 1979.

Keir, P. "Impact of Discount Policy Procedures on the Effectiveness of Reserve Targeting." In *New Monetary Control Procedures*, Vol. I. Federal Reserve Staff. Board of Governors of the Federal Reserve System, February 1981.

Kopecky, K.J., Parke, D.W., and Porter, R.D. "Interbank Deposit Flows and Money Stock Control." Unpublished manuscript, Board of Governors of the Federal Reserve System, January 1980.

Laufenberg, D. "Staggered Reserve Periods." Unpublished manuscript, Board of Governors of the Federal Reserve System, July 6, 1978.

LeRoy, S. "Efficient Use of Current Information in Short-Run Monetary Control." *Special Studies Paper*, No. 66. Board of Governors of the Federal Reserve System, September 1975.

LeRoy, S. "Optimal Interest Rate Smoothing." Unpublished manuscript, Board of Governors of the Federal Reserve System, 1976.

LeRoy, S. "Monetary Control Under Lagged Reserve Accounting." *Southern Economic Journal* (October 1979).

LeRoy, S., and Lindsey, D. "Determining the Monetary Instrument: A Diagrammatic Exposition." *American Economic Review* (December 1978).

Lindsey, D.E. "The Implications of Removing the Demand Deposit Rate Prohibition for Monetary Control and the Conduct of Monetary Policy." *Special Studies Paper*, No. 104. Board of Governors of the Federal Reserve System, March 1977.

Lindsey, D.E., Hadjimichalakis, K., and Grupe, M. "The Monetary Control Act of 1980: The Choice of a Reserve Operating Target." Unpublished manuscript, Board of Governors of the Federal Reserve System, March 1981, delivered at the Eastern Economics Association Meetings, April 9, 1981.

Lindsey, D.E., Farr, H.T., et al. "Short-Run Monetary Control: Evidence Under the New Operating Procedures." Unpublished manuscript, Board of Governors of the Federal Reserve System, February 1982.

Lindsey, D.E., et al. "Monetary Control Experience Under the New Operating Procedures." In *New Monetary Control Procedures*, Vol. II, Federal Reserve Staff. Board of Governors of the Federal Reserve System, February 1981.

Lombra, R. "Monetary Control: Consensus or Confusion?" In *Controlling Monetary Aggregates III*. Federal Reserve Bank of Boston Conference series, No. 23, October 1980.

Morgan Guaranty Trust Company. "Interest Rate Volatility: A Way to Ease the Problem." *Morgan Guaranty Survey* (July 1981).

Morgan Guaranty Trust Company. "Summary of Reader Comments on Proposal for Four-Week Reserve Settlements . . . and Morgan Guaranty Responses." Unpublished manuscript, Morgan Guaranty Trust, September 4, 1981.

Pierce, D. "Trend and Noise in the Monetary Aggregates." In *New Monetary Control Procedures*, Vol. II., Federal Reserve Staff, Board of Governors of the Federal Reserve System, February 1981.

Poole, W. "Optimal Choice of Monetary Policy Instruments in a Simple Stochastic Macro Model." *Quarterly Journal of Economics* (May 1970).

Poole, W. "The Making of Monetary Policy: Description and Analysis." *New England Economic Review* (March/April 1975).

Poole, W. "Letter to Representative Henry Reuss," July 25, 1978.

Poole, W., and Lieberman, C. "Improving Monetary Control." *Brooking Papers on Economic Activity*, No. 2, 1972.

Porter, R., Lindsey, S.E., and Laufenberg, D. "Estimation and Simulation of Simple Equations Relating Reserve Aggregates and Monetary Aggregates." Unpublished manuscript, Board of Governors of the Federal Reserve System, September 24, 1975.

Quick, P.D. "Federal Reserve Discount Window Procedures and Monetary Control: Two Modest Proposals." Unpublished manuscript, Board of Governors of the Federal Reserve System, 1979.

Simpson, T.D., and Porter, R.D. "Some Issues Involving the Definition and Interpretation of the Monetary Aggregates." In *Controlling the Monetary Aggregates III*, Federal Reserve Bank of Boston Conference Series, No. 23, October 1980.

Simpson, T.D., et al. (1981a). "Recent Revisions in the Money Stock: Benchmark, Seasonal Adjustment, and Calculation of Shift-Adjusted *M1B*." *Federal Reserve Bulletin* (July 1981).

Simpson, T.D., et al. (1981b). "Recent Revisions in the Money Stock: Benchmark, Seasonal Adjustment, and Calculation of Shift-Adjusted *M1B*." Unpublished manuscript, Board of Governors of the Federal Reserve System, July 1981.

Sternlight, P.D., et al. "Monetary Policy and Open Market Operations in 1980." *Federal Reserve Bank of New York Quarterly Review* (Summer 1981).

Tinsley, P.A. "A Field Manual for Stochastic Money Market Impacts of Alternative Operating Procedures: Unpublished manuscript, Board of Governors of the Federal Reserve System, June 1981.

Tinsley, P.A., von zur Muehlen, P., et al. "Money Market Impacts of Alternative Operating Procedures." In *New Monetary Control Procedures*, Vol. II, Federal Reserve Staff. Board of Governors of the Federal Reserve System, February 1981.

Tinsley, P.A., Fries, G., et al. "Estimated Monetary Policy Consequences of Reserve Accounting Procedures." Unpublished manuscript, Board of Governors of the Federal Reserve System, September 10, 1981.

Trepeta, W., and Lindsey, D.E. "The Reuss Proposal to Stagger Reserve Accounting Periods." Unpublished manuscript, Board of Governors of the Federal Reserve System, April 25, 1979.

Weintraub, R. "Current Monetary Policy." *Wall Street Journal Transcript* 62, (August 3), 531, 1981.

Appendix: Simple Theoretical Model of the Money Supply Process Under Nonborrowed Reserves Targeting

Money demand function:

$$M^d(\overset{-}{i}, \overset{-}{r}_{\text{av}}, \overset{+}{y}, \overset{+}{P}) + e_{M^d} = D^d(\overset{-}{i}, \overset{-}{r}_{\text{av}}, \overset{+}{y}, \overset{+}{p}) + C^d(\overset{-}{i}, \overset{+}{y}, \overset{+}{P}) + e_{D^d} + e_{C^d} \quad (1A.1)$$

Money "supply" function:

$$M^s(\overset{+}{i}, \overset{+}{\overline{NR}^s}, \overset{-}{r}_{\text{dis}}, \overset{-}{r}_{\text{av}}, \overset{-}{y}, \overset{-}{P}) + e_{M^s}$$

$$= D^s(\overset{+}{i}, \overset{+}{\overline{NR}^s}, \overset{-}{r}_{\text{dis}}, \overset{-}{r}_{\text{av}}, \overset{-}{y}, \overset{-}{P}) + C^d(\overset{-}{i}, \overset{+}{y}, \overset{+}{P}) + e_{D^s} + e_{C^d}$$

$$= \frac{\overset{+}{\overline{NR}^s} + \overset{+}{BR(i - r_{\text{dis}})} - ER^d(\overset{-}{i}, \overset{+}{r}_{\text{dis}}) - \rho_T T^d(\overset{-}{i}, \overset{+}{r}_{\text{av}}, \overset{+}{y}, \overset{+}{P})}{\rho_D}$$

$$+ C_d(\overset{-}{i}, \overset{+}{y}, \overset{+}{P}) + \frac{e_{BR} - e_{ER^d} - \rho_T e_{T^d} + \rho_D e_{C^d}}{\rho_D} \quad (1A.2)$$

where

M	=	narrow money
D	=	transactions deposits
C	=	currency
NR	=	nonborrowed reserves
BR	=	borrowed reserves
ER	=	excess reserves
T	=	total time and savings deposits
ρ_D	=	average required reserve ratio on transactions deposits
ρ_T	=	average required reserve ratio on total time and savings deposits
i	=	nominal short-term interest rate
r_{dis}	=	discount rate
r_{av}	=	average own rate on total time and savings deposits
y	=	real income
P	=	average price level
e	=	error term

and d superscript represents "demanded," s superscript represents "supplied," and contemporaneous reserve requirements are assumed.

Figure 1–9 presents a graphical interpretation of this model in terms of money demand and supply functions.

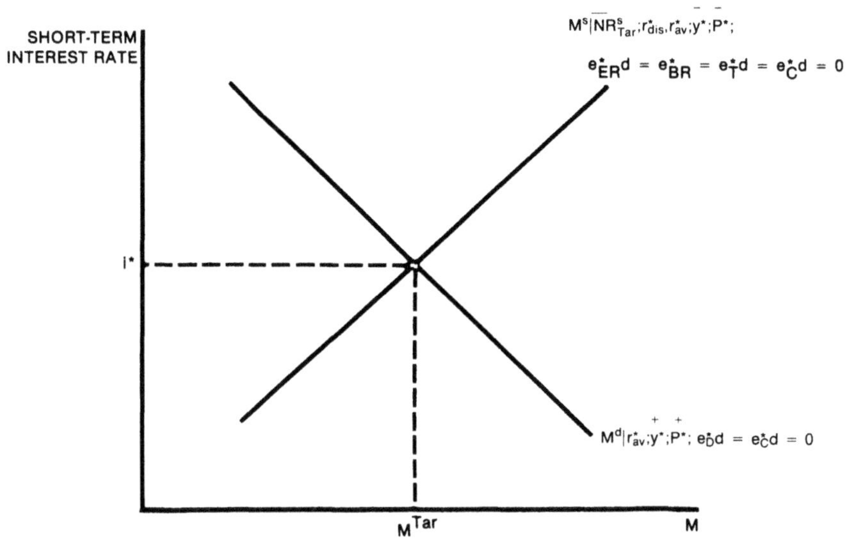

Note: * = initially expected values; $BR(i^* - r^*_{dis})$ = initial borrowing assumption; M_{Tar} = intermeeting money stock target; NR^s_{Tar} = initial nonborrowed reserves target; TR_{Tar} = initial total reserves target = $NR^s_{Tar} + BR(i^* - r^*_{dis})$.

Figure 1–9 A Graphic Interpretation of the Money Supply Process under Nonborrowed Reserves Targeting

Technical adjustments to NR and TR target paths restore the estimated M^s schedule to its initial position at i^* and M_{Tar}, other things equal, following recognition of realizations of e_{ER^d}; e_{T^d}; e_{C^d}; ρ_D; ρ_T; r_{av}; y; P; and, upon occasion for the NR target path only, e_{BR}.

Discretionary adjustments to the NR target path move the estimated M^s schedule away from its initial position at i^* and M_{Tar} in the opposite direction of recognized shifts of M^d schedule owing to realizations of e_{D^d}, e_{C^d}, r_{av}, y, and P.

DISCUSSION 1

R. Alton Gilbert

Before turning to the comments I prepared for this session, I wish to comment on Lindsey's interpretation of fluctuations in short-term interest rates and the money supply during the past two years. Lindsey interprets the movements of interest rates and the money supply as evidence that the money demand schedule has been unstable. In his view, the Federal Reserve has been resisting the full impact of unstable money demand on the money supply by targeting on nonborrowed reserves and permitting short-term interest rates to fluctuate. The results of using this operating procedure when money demand is unstable are sharp fluctuations in interest rates and a positive association between changes in short-term interest rates and the money supply. Under this interpretation, an argument could be made that Federal Reserve policy has been optimal for stabilizing the economy in the past two years, given the instability in money demand.

There is an alternative explanation for the pattern of short-term interest rates and the money supply that makes more sense to me. In my view, the demand curve that has been unstable is demand for bank credit as a function of short-term interest rates. A shift in demand for bank credit will affect the rate of money creation, unless the Federal Reserve uses the nonborrowed reserves operating procedure aggressively to limit deviations of total reserves from levels consistent with objectives for money growth. As I will demonstrate in my comments, the Federal Reserve has not used its current operating procedure aggressively to control money growth. As a result, shifts in demand for bank credit have caused short-term interest rates and the money supply to fluctuate in the same direction.

Having made these preparatory remarks, I should note that, because Lindsey discusses such a wide range of issues in his paper, it is hard to choose where to start my comments — and perhaps even harder to tell where to stop. I have chosen to focus on his analysis of the movements in the various reserve aggregates and their reliability as operating targets.

Lindsey's basic contention is that we cannot determine the variability of the money supply that would result from targeting on the monetary base (*MB*) or total reserves (*TR*) by examining the past relationships between the money supply and the *MB* or *TR*. If the Federal Reserve had been targeting on the *MB* or *TR*, their respective money multipliers might have been more variable than those that were actually observed in the past.

Lindsey discusses the results of simulations designed to remove this bias in measuring errors in control of the money supply that would result from targeting on the *MB* or *TR*, simulations that are based on the Board's money market model. In those simulations, errors in controlling the money supply turn out to be smaller under a policy of targeting on nonborrowed reserves (*NR*), than those associated with targeting on the *MB* or *TR*.

I think it is relevant to consider the nature of these simulations in some detail, since they illustrate difficulties in simulating monetary control under alternative procedures for conducting monetary policy. Results of these simulations are also relevant for the choice of the reform proposals presented at the end of Lindsey's paper. In examining the simulations, it is important to note that depository institutions are implicitly subject to lagged reserve accounting. Under lagged reserve accounting, required reserves are predetermined each week. The Board's model is estimated over a period during which the Federal Reserve has had a policy of supplying reserves each week that are at least as large as required reserves. Also, representatives of Federal Reserve Banks have continually told member bankers that allowing their reserves to be deficient is not an acceptable practice in reserve management. As a result, few member banks have chosen to hold deficient reserves, even when the penalty rate on reserve deficiencies has been less than the federal funds rate. Equations in the Board's model, in particular the equations for excess reserves and borrowings, reflect these practices.

Now, behavior underlying the equations in the Board's model would be altered if the Federal Reserve began targeting on the *MB* or *TR*, irrespective of required reserves, but retained lagged reserve accounting. Under such a policy, excess reserves would tend to be negatively related to short-term interest rates. Since, in some weeks, reserves supplied would be less than required reserves, the Federal Reserve would have to permit depository institutions the option of holding deficient reserves under some penalty arrangement.

Simulations of the Board's model do not adjust for these changes in behavior that would result from targeting on the *MB* or *TR*. In the simulations, the factor that produces the relatively large errors in monetary control under *TR* targeting is the error in predicting the average reserve requirement on demand deposits. If, for instance, the average reserve requirement on demand deposits is underestimated, the amount of money that can be supported with a given amount of reserves would be overestimated. With the Federal Reserve targeting on *TR*, there is no mechanism in the simulations that would keep the error in estimating the average reserve requirement on demand deposits from depressing the money supply below the projected level, even though the federal funds rate would be projected to rise sharply. In simulations with the Federal Reserve targeting on *NR*, the federal funds rate rises if the average reserve requirement on demand deposits is underestimated. The rise in the federal funds rate induces banks to borrow more reserves and, therefore, the deviation of the money supply from the projected level would be less than in the case of targeting on *TR*.

If excess reserves were interest sensitive, however, a change in excess reserves would serve the same role as a change in the supply of reserves through the discount window in dampening the errors in projecting the money supply, due to errors in estimating required reserves on demand deposits. For these reasons, I think that simulations of the Board's money market model *overstate* errors in monetary control and *overstate* fluctuations in interest rates that would result from targeting on the base or *TR*, even under lagged reserve accounting.

These observations illustrate a general principle: It is difficult to demonstrate empirically the effects of policies that have not been implemented. These observations are also relevant for Lindsey's choice of financial reforms. He would prefer to continue targeting on *NR*, even under contemporaneous reserve accounting, because of concern that fluctuations in interest rates would be larger if the Federal Reserve targeted on the *MB* or *TR* instead. His perception of the fluctuations in interest rates that would result from targeting on the *MB* or *TR* may be based on his simulation of the Board's money market model. I think that those simulations overstate the fluctuations in interest rates that would occur under such policies, because they do not allow for dampening effect of variations in excess reserves that would develop. However, I cannot prove it; we have not pursued such policies. I would prefer to have the Federal Reserve target on the *MB* or *TR*, and depend on the banking system to develop practices that would dampen fluctuations in interest rates.

My final comments are concerned with the following issue: during 1980 and 1981, there have been large deviations of *M1B* from the short-term and annual objectives of the Federal Open Market Committee (FOMC). Do these deviations of *M1B* from stated objectives reflect problems with using the current procedure for monetary control, or do they reflect policy actions based on objectives other than controlling money growth? Statements in the second section of Lindsey's paper indicate that the largest deviations of growth in *M1B* from stated objectives reflect decisions of the Federal Reserve to allow such results, rather than technical problems with monetary control under the current operating procedure. Lindsey indicates that the Federal Reserve chose to have rapid growth of *M1B* in the second half of 1980, and has decided to keep *M1B* below its annual range during most of 1981. I would agree with those interpretations of the events. Information on the conduct of monetary policy in 1980, presented in table 1–3 and figure 1–10 support this interpretation.

The first column of table 1–3 presents periods between FOMC meetings. Periods between meetings longer than five weeks are divided into two periods for purposes of setting *TR* paths. The staff of the Board of Governors estimates the average level of *TR* over periods between FOMC meetings that are consistent with growth of the monetary aggregates voted by the FOMC in the last meeting. The first specification of the *TR* path is generally made on the Friday after an FOMC meeting. At the same time, the staff projects what they think the average level of *TR* will actually be over the intermeeting periods. Projections and path levels of *TR* are generally respecified each Friday. The last two columns of table 1–3 indicate the dates that projections and path levels of *TR* were specified, and the difference between the projection and path level of *TR* as of each date.

The center column presents the difference between the actual level of *TR* over the intermeeting periods and the final specification of the path levels. These differences between average reserves and final path levels

Table 1–3. Difference Between Total Reserves and Path Levels over Intermeeting Periods, and Projections of the Differences Made during the Periods, February 1980 to December 1980 (millions of dollars)

Period	Actual Total Reserves Less Final Path Level	Projection of Total Reserves Less Path Level		
		Set as of		*Amount*
3 weeks ending February 27	$ 264	February	7	$ −38
			15	313
			22	541
3 weeks ending March 19	662	February	29	626
		March	7	644
			14	724
5 weeks ending April 23	−483	March	21	26
			28	62
		April	4	−313
			14	−295
			18	−432
4 weeks ending May 21	−888	April	25	−588
		May	2	−802
			9	−821
			16	−854
4 weeks ending June 18	−65	May	23	0
			30	0
		June	6	−6
			13	0
3 weeks ending July 9	79	June	20	0
			27	0
		July	7	0
5 weeks ending August 13	151	July	11	0
			23	0
			28	33
		August	1	57
			8	159
5 weeks ending September 17	362	August	15	128
			19	128
			22	282
			29	362
		September	5	285
			12	380

Table 1–3. (continued)

Period	Actual Total Reserves Less Final Path Level	Projection of Total Reserves Less Path Level		
		Set as of		Amount
5 weeks ending October 22	380	September	19	382
			26	495
		October	3	323
			10	442
			17	438
4 weeks ending November 19	349	October	24	209
			31	201
		November	7	219
			14	300
5 weeks ending December 24	343	November	21	297
			25	403
		December	1	341
			5	261
			12	210
			23	224

are closely related to deviations of *M1B* from the levels voted by the FOMC. To verify this observation, compare deviations of *TR* from path levels over the various periods to movements of *M1B* relative to level implied by votes of the FOMC in the chart.

The issue I will consider concerning use of the *NR* operating procedure is whether projections of *TR* relative to path levels made early in the intermeeting periods indicated the nature of policy actions that would have been appropriate to keep *TR* close to the path levels, and therefore, appropriate for controlling money growth. Deviation of the projection of *TR* from the path level provides a guide for policy actions that are appropriate for monetary control. If *TR* are projected to be above path, for instance, the appropriate policy actions are to reduce the supply of *NR*, raise the discount rate, or both.

In the first period listed, the three weeks ending February 27, 1980, the initial projection of *TR* and specification of path level did not indicate the nature of policy actions appropriate to keep *TR* on path. The problem with use of the procedure in that period was that the path level was

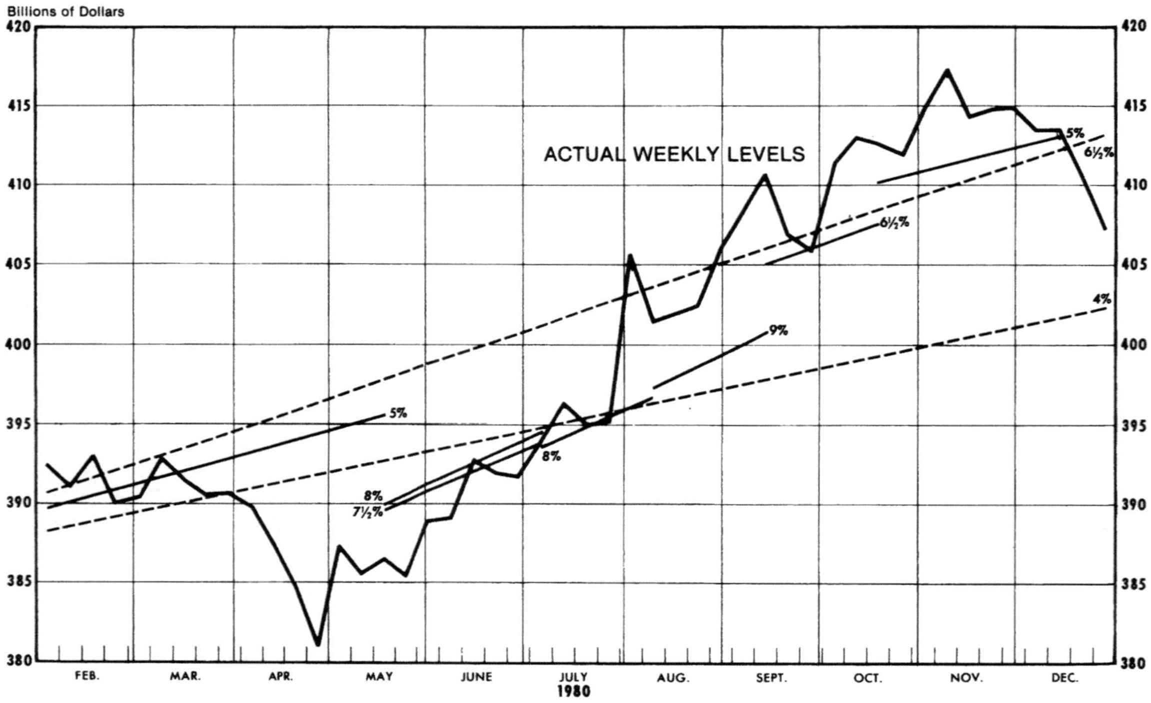

Note: The dashed lines represent growth of *M1B* from the average level of IV/1979 at annual rates of 4 and 6.5 percent. The continuous line is the weekly average levels of *M1B*, revised as of January 1981. The short lines represent the levels of *M1B* implied by the short-term objectives of the Committee. In specifying short-term objectives for growth of the monetary aggregates at each meeting, the Committee specifies an initial period, a terminal period, and desired growth rates for each aggregate. The short lines indicate levels of *M1B* derived by extrapolating growth from the initial periods at the rates desired by the Committee. Levels of *M1B* derived by such extrapolation are plotted for only those weeks between Committee meetings to which they apply. Levels of *M1B* in the initial periods from which *M1B* is extrapolated are as of the January 1981 revision.

Figure 1–10 Growth Objectives for *M1B*

initially too high. By February 15, when this problem was recognized, it was too late in that period to reduce *TR* to the lower path level, because of lagged reserve accounting and the commitment of the Federal Reserve to supplying required reserves.

In the second period, however, the three weeks ending March 19, the large deviation of *TR* from path was projected accurately in the first week, but policy actions were not taken to narrow the gap between *TR* and the path level. The third period, the five weeks ending April 23, indicates how the credit control program hampered monetary control. The Federal Reserve did not project the large declines of *TR* below path that resulted from declines in demand for credit until late in the period.

For the rest of the year, the Federal Reserve projected large deviations of *TR* from path early in the periods in which there were, in fact, large deviations of *TR* from path. The Federal Reserve was able to project deviations of *TR* from path, but did not take the actions that would have been appropriate, based on information available at the time, to keep money growth closer to FOMC objectives.

This observation about the use of the current procedure has implications for the conditions that are most important for improving monetary control. There are several proposals being discussed that would improve the technical ability of the Federal Reserve to achieve short-term monetary control, including contemporaneous reserve accounting and a discount rate tied to or above market interest rates. I support adoption of these proposals. Such reforms might do little to improve the conduct of monetary policy, however, since the Federal Reserve is not now exploiting the potential of the current procedure, under current institutional arrangements, for monetary control. The greatest problems with monetary control are not the technical problems associated with the current operating procedure; instead they are the lack of agreement on which monetary aggregate to control, and lack of determination to keep other considerations from interfering with the control of that aggregate.

DISCUSSION 2

W. Lee Hoskins

David Lindsey's paper provides a detailed description of how he, and perhaps the Federal Reserve, perceives nonborrowed reserve targeting working to control money growth. However, I doubt that this is the perception of participants in the money and credit markets. Nor is it the perception of those who sought to change the old operating procedures to a true reserve targeting procedure. I suspect both of these groups perceive little substantive change from the old procedures other than increased volatility of both interest rates and money growth.

My comments are confined to three areas. First, why the new procedures, from the market participants' perspective, represent nothing more than the old procedures with a wider federal funds band. Second, why the new procedures are a disappointment to those seeking a true reserve targeting procedure. Third, how the change in procedures raises some issues for monetary control.

The Market Perception

Prior to the change in procedures in October 1979, money market analysts focused on the actions of the Fed to derive estimates about the future course of the funds rate. They watched the time of day the Desk entered the market and the level of the funds rate when the Fed did match sales or repos. They charted net borrowed reserves as well as borrowing and scrutinized the weekly money numbers. They do the same today. What is different is the magnitude of the change in the funds rate. Despite the greater volatility in the funds rate, there is a belief that the Fed is still operating with an interest rate constraint (in terms of either an operating or intermediate target). Why? Because the Fed behaves as if it does.

Under the new procedure, the Fed retained a target federal funds band but widened it substantially. In the second quarter of 1980, with *M1B* falling below target, the Fed increased nonborrowed reserves sharply, as figure 1–2 in the Lindsey paper indicates, and the funds rate fell sharply. However, there was a wide-spread suspicion that the Fed was more interested in halting the decline in rates than in sticking to a reserve path that would bring money growth back to target. The concern over the level of interest rates was centered on the declining exchange value of the dollar. In an August 8, 1980, *New York Times* article, Governor Wallich confirmed that suspicion. The Governor stated that "had we stayed rigorously on the money supply track after being forced off it in a downward direction we would have pushed interest rates down a good deal more than they went."

Another example that interest rate movements were of primary concern came in October of 1980. Adjusted *M1B* growth had rapidly climbed above the upper limit of its target band. Lindsey's figure 1–2 shows that the federal funds rate, after moving up sharply in September, held steady for most of the month of October. Correct or not, the speculation in credit markets at that time was that the Fed was holding the funds rate in order to avoid being part of the election fray. An alternative view, and a more likely one in my opinion, was that the Fed was not aggressively curtailing money growth by letting the funds rate rise because of fear of aborting the recovery. This theme of rising interest rates aborting recoveries has been played many times by the Fed. It wasn't until shortly after the election that the Fed reimposed a surcharge on the discount rate, halted total reserve growth, and curtailed the sharp six-month acceleration in money growth.

An indication that money market participants viewed the Fed funds rate as a significant element in the Fed's operating target came in March 1981. The funds rate had dropped from a high of 20 percent in January to below 14 percent by mid-March. When the minutes of the February meeting were released in early April, the market was "surprised" that the lower end of the funds range was 15 percent — not the generally presumed 13 or 14 percent. The funds rate shot up 100 basis points the day the minutes were released and within a week or so settled in a half point above the presumed floor of 15 percent.

The aggressiveness of the moves to reduce nonborrowed reserves and curb money growth in May and June 1981 caused some second thoughts about the notion that the Fed was operating with interest rate constraints. These second thoughts were somewhat dispelled by this summer's experience. With adjusted *M1B* substantially below target, the Fed announced that it would accept a shortfall in *M1B* in order to keep *M2* from exceeding its upper bound. Many market participants viewed this shift in emphasis from *M1B* to *M2* as a rationale for slowing the decline in the funds rate. Large reserve injections would be necessary to push *M1B* to the lower end of its target range. Such large reserve injections would likely cause a precipitous decline in the funds rate. Thus, a sharp drop in the funds rate was avoided by focusing on *M2*.

While the validity of this view of the market's perception is certainly debatable, the fact is that anytime the Fed funds rate is trading at either the ceiling or floor of its band, or is being pegged for another reason, the old operating procedures are in force and money growth is the residual. Moreover, when money growth is off target and discretionary adjustments to the reserve path are nonexistent or small, interest rate considerations (either to smooth fluctuations or to temporarily maintain rate levels) would appear to be the reason. To the extent that this occurs, little has changed except greater week-to-week interest rate and deposit volatility associated with a wider funds band.

A True Reserve Target

In Lindsey's reading of this history, quite a lot has changed. He cites four episodes of strengthening in the aggregates and three of weakening. In each case, borrowings moved in the expected direction indicating counteraction by the Fed. The same is true for the change in the spread between the funds rate and the discount rate. This is given as evidence that the nonborrowed targeting procedures responded appropriately to increases or decreases in money growth. However, much the same could be said for the old interest rate targeting procedure. Under it, a sufficiently large increase in money above target ultimately prompted FOMC action to raise the funds rate by altering its provision of nonborrowed reserves. In both cases, better monetary control probably could have been achieved with more aggressive use of the operating target, despite its technical limitation.

Lindsey also describes these periods of strengthening in the aggregates as a result of increases in the demand for money. He argues that the variation in short rates primarily represents Federal Reserve resistance, through nonborrowed targeting, to shifts in the position of the money demand schedule. The instability of observed money in the last three quarters of 1980 is attributed to the credit control experiment, although the credit control program ended for all practical purposes in July. The explanation of shift adjusted *M1B* running below target for most of 1981 is attributed to a large downward drift in money demand caused by innovations in cash management induced by high interest rates.

These interpretations are not surprising since he uses a demand-oriented model of money stock determination. An alternative view can be found in the analysis of Robert Laurent in a recent working paper of the Chicago Fed (*A Critique of the Federal Reserve's New Operating Procedure,* Staff Memoranda, April 1981). He argues that such models incorrectly attribute movements in the supply of money to shifts in money demand. Part of the problem is lagged reserve accounting which inhibits and delays bank portfolio adjustments to changes in the spread between the funds rate and yields available on credit market assets. As Laurent demonstrates, the new procedures during the first year generated increased weekly funds rate volatility which in turn generated greater deposit volatility. A true reserve operating procedure requires the Fed (1) to provide the targeted reserves and (2) to permit contemporaneous reserve accounting. Under such an arrangement, the funds rate automatically guides current deposits to match current required reserves.

In short, the new operating procedure, as Laurent succinctly states, "is not a shift to what advocates mean by a reserve operating procedure, but actually a change in how the Fed determines a federal funds rate." In my view, the way in which the funds rate is determined is unnecessarily complicated and does little other than enhance the demand for Federal Reserve economists by private financial institutions.

Some Monetary Control Issues

As Lindsey points out, there is substantial room for discretionary and technical adjustments to the nonborrowed reserve path. Many proponents of reserve targeting felt that one improvement would be a more stable or consistent adjustment of reserves when money growth was off-track. The current process leaves considerable discretion in terms of the size and timing of the reserve path adjustments. A concern of mine is who is making these discretionary adjustments. The concern is that once the FOMC chooses its money growth target, the problem of how to get there and how fast to adjust the reserve path rests with the staff. Perhaps Lindsey can enlighten us as to how these discretionary adjustments are determined. Has there been a shift in who makes policy? If so, then maybe the Senate should confirm staff appointments as it does for governors.

Another issue has to do not with the method by which money growth is controlled, but with the resolve to do so. Is nonborrowed reserve targeting just one more diversion causing the focus to be on the method rather than the result? After all, money market participants have seen a host of "new" procedures starting with the announcements of targets for money growth, the RPD experiment, quarterly money targets, annual targets, multiple aggregate targets, and now nonborrowed reserve targeting. Through all of these, money growth (*M1B*) has generally exceeded announced targets. Promises were not matched with performance. The underlying reason has been a persistent concern by the Fed with interest rate movements because they might impact the exchange value of the dollar or alter real economic activity. To date, market participants have seen little to alter expectations that the same won't hold for the future. Thus, the question boils down not to whether nonborrowed reserve targeting will work better than some other form of monetary control, but rather to the issue of whether or not there is a political constituency to support anti-inflationary monetary policy. The test will come when the economy is recovering from the current recession and upward pressures on interest rates mount. Will the Fed attempt to dampen the rise in rates in order to "help" the recovery and in so doing permit another round of excessive money growth?

DISCUSSION 3

William Poole

I am very pleased to be able to discuss Dave Lindsey's paper. We have a similar outlook on the issues involved. I think that Lindsey's paper contains a few mistakes, but suspect that, after several iterations, we will come to an agreement on the technical issues, with each of us backtracking somewhat on views that may be stated with excessive certainty.

My comments are divided into sections on monetary targets, monetary control, optimal combination policy, and some concluding comments.

Monetary Targets

I emphatically and wholeheartedly agree with Lindsey that adjustments to the definitions of monetary aggregates and to their targets are unsatisfactory in the present environment. In talking of the Porter-Simpson money demand equation, Lindsey says that "Such an approach really represents only a band-aid cure for a serious malady. The basic problem lies with the incentive structure built into the regulatory framework that, in an inflationary environment, virtually guarantees the kind of innovations in cash management techniques and in transaction-type instruments that have made targeting on narrow money so problematic since the mid-1970s. In my view, radical surgery to the regulatory structure to remove the artificial impediments to a market-related return on all transactions balances offers the only reliable hope over the long run. . . ." Let me emphasize Lindsey's use of the term "radical surgery." That term is not too strong.

I have a question, however. Is this view put to the Congress regularly and consistently? I have read pages and pages of congressional testimony by Federal Reserve officials explaining why monetary targets should not be taken too seriously, why the monetary measures are confusing, and why the Federal Reserve must retain a large degree of discretion in monetary management. Perhaps I missed the relevant passages in my hasty reading of recent testimony, but I do not remember ever seeing a clear Federal Reserve statement to the Congress that interest rate ceilings and prohibitions had gone far to destroy the certainty and predictability of monetary management.

Monetary Control

The fourth section of Lindsey's paper discusses the relative advantages of the monetary base and nonborrowed reserves as control instruments; in the fifth section are the various regulatory reforms that might make monetary control more exact. I will divide the topic somewhat differently. First, I will discuss purely technical control issues; second, the political aspects of these matters; and third, expectational issues.

Technical Issues

In this discussion let us accept in strict form various alternative assumptions about Fed control of particular variables under different regulatory arrangements, and treat the problem as one of deriving the consequences of these assumptions for variables of interest.

At this stage, I want to assume that the goal is to minimize the variance of deviations of the money stock from its target path. I will discuss interest rate and money control trade-offs later.

The analysis by Lindsey, and others, of the relative advantages of Fed control of the monetary base and total reserves is incomplete and misleading in that there has been an undue concentration on the stability of money multipliers. To illustrate this point, consider the following conventional textbook model:

$$B = C + R \tag{1.1}$$

$$M = C + D \tag{1.2}$$

$$C = qM \tag{1.3}$$

$$R = kD \tag{1.4}$$

$$\frac{1}{M} = \frac{1}{B}[q + k(1 - q)] = \frac{m_B}{B} \quad \text{(base exogenous)} \tag{1.5a}$$

$$\frac{1}{M} = \frac{1}{R}[k(1 - q)] = \frac{m_R}{R} \quad \text{(total reserves exogenous)} \tag{1.5b}$$

where:

B = monetary base
C = currency
R = reserves
M = money supply
D = demand deposits
q = currency ratio
k = reserve ratio
m_B = money multiplier (with monetary base exogenous)
m_R = money multiplier (with reserves exogenous)

Suppose q, the currency ratio, is nonstochastic but that the reserve ratio, k, is variable; then the variance of the inverse of the base multiplier, denoted here by m_B, equals the variance of the inverse of the reserves multiplier, denoted by m_R. Equation 1.5a shows that the variance of $1/M$ will be lower when the monetary base is exogenous than it will be in equation 1.5b when the level of bank reserves is exogenous since $1/B$ is less than $1/R$. We must pay attention not only to the variance of the multiplier but to the size of what is being multiplied. This objection, of course, does not apply if the problem is formulated in terms of percentage rates of change.

My second point is more important and cannot be disposed of through the growth rate transformation. The covariances are as important as the variances. In the simple model presented above, the variance of $1/M$ depends importantly on the covariance between the multiplier and the base in equation 1.5a and the multiplier and total reserves in equation 1.5b. This elementary point is especially important when considering regulatory changes, since these changes will affect not only the multiplier and base or reserves variances but also the covariances.

Consider Lindsey's discussion of three alternative arrangements to provide reserve adjustment. The first is Lindsey's discount window proposal; the second is staggered reserve accounting; and the third is penalty carry-over. Suppose, first, that there is a given change in the money stock which is, by assumption, to be temporarily accommodated.

With Lindsey's discount window, the accommodation leaves the multiplier unaffected but changes the reserve base. In comparison, under both staggered reserve accounting and penalty carry-over, the reserve base is unaffected but the multiplier changes. The fact that the multiplier changes rather than the reserve base is of *no* consequence whatsoever at this stage of the analysis.

Lindsey, however, emphasizes the predictability of the multiplier: "More importantly, staggering would impair monetary control by lessening the predictability of the reserve multiplier." I would replace that sentence with the following two sentences. "It is almost irrelevant that staggering would lessen the predictability of the reserves multiplier. We know that, while staggering will increase that variance, it will also change both the covariance of the multiplier with the level of reserves and the variance of reserves."

Instead of assuming that a given monetary disturbance is fully accommodated, now consider the more fundamental issue of the effects of various disturbances on the money stock under the three adjustment mechanisms being analyzed. To be specific, suppose there is a random decline in reserves supply due to operating factors or an increase in reserve demand due to an increase in the average reserve requirement caused by a shift in deposits from small banks to large banks. I assert that the impact effect on the money stock will be about the same under all three systems depending, of course, on the exact design of each system. Part of the disturbance will be accommodated and part will produce a decline in the money stock.

While the impact effects under the three adjustment arrangements are about the same, the lagged effects are somewhat different. Under either the staggered or carry-over systems, the banking system in effect borrows future reserves from itself; a reserve deficiency one week must be offset by excess reserves in the future. For the disturbance being analyzed, the impact effect is to reduce the money stock, and the lagged impact is also a reduced money stock. After several periods, though, the money stock can return to its target level. Under the Lindsey discount window approach, the impact effect is a reduced money stock, but there are no lagged effects tending to reduce the money stock. For the disturbance being analyzed, the Lindsey discount window technique provides an adjustment mechanism that is superior to the other two.

But, of course, the catalog of effects is much larger than discussed so far because there are other types of disturbances than those analyzed above. Any disturbance that raises interest rates permanently, relative to the short-run adjustments being analyzed, will generate permanently higher borrowing under the Lindsey discount window procedure and, therefore, result in a permanently higher money stock. This effect will not exist under the other two arrangements. However, the systems would be about the same if, under these other two, the Fed supplied nonborrowed reserves along a function with some interest elasticity, or if Lindsey's discount window had a basic discount rate that was a moving average of past market rates. From the discussion so far there is not a strong reason to prefer one of these institutional arrangements over another.

As a final comment on the technical issues, I must say that one of Lindsey's arguments for his penalty discount window strikes me as peculiar. He argues that his discount window proposal "would yield far superior results in terms of the appropriate balance between monetary control precision and volatility in short-term interest rates. . . ." Just prior to this he had argued that this discount window would produce a reliable relation between the level of borrowings and the level of the federal funds rate. I fail to see that even a perfectly reliable relation between borrowing and the funds rate tells us anything about the precision of monetary control. The discount rate gradient can pin down the degree of interest rate volatility, but so also can the penalty rate in the carry-over proposal.

Political Issues

The technical examination of various competing proposals to ease reserve adjustment suggests that there are a variety of ways of accomplishing about the same thing. No doubt, depending on the sources of disturbances, some arrangements have some advantages over others. Some may also have administrative advantages.

But my real concern is what I call, for want of a better term, political issues — the viability and understandability of alternative arrangements in the political market place. Compare the probability of market failure and political failure.

Lindsey objects to staggered reserve accounting on the market failure ground that banks may make mistakes which feed into the system in such a way as to generate some avoidable instability. I think his argument here is weak, but I am certainly willing to accept the position that institutional arrangements should be robust with respect to private market mistakes.

Reasoning in the same vein, let me ask some questions about possible political failure of the Lindsey discount window. Is it reasonable to believe that the Fed will eliminate all administrative pressure, given that it has operated through administrative pressure since 1913? Will the Fed either set a steeply graduated discount rate or adjust the base rate in timely fashion to prevent the money stock from being so highly interest elastic as to be destabilizing? Assuming that the Fed wants to continue to permit problem banks to borrow at a subsidy rate for assistance purposes, can the Fed really separate assistance borrowing from adjustment borrowing?

The answers to these questions do not depend merely on the competence and good will of the Federal Reserve but also on the nature of the political pressures on the Fed. I am well aware that the Fed does many things because it has little political leeway, but what it can do is to be sensitive to the way in which its regulations affect the probability of success of these pressures.

These matters are of considerable importance for the general issue of reserve adjustment mechanisms. To some observers, a big advantage to maintaining an open discount window for adjustment borrowing may be that the adjustment and assistance borrowing are indeed mixed up together. If all adjustment borrowing were eliminated by providing for reserve adjustment through staggered accounting or penalty carry-over, then any bank that borrowed from the Fed would be obviously tagged as a weak bank.

There is a genuine problem in reporting the identity of weak banks. In Australia the central bank does not report even total loans to banks on its balance sheet, consolidating this account for reporting purposes with a number of other accounts. And the banks in their published balance sheets do not break out borrowings from the central bank. That solution probably is not possible in the United States; I do not believe that it is desirable either.

To my mind, one of the advantages of staggered accounting (or penalty carry-over) is precisely that it makes assistance borrowing highly visible and reduces the incentive to provide such borrowing. Central bank lending to individual banks at subsidized rates is not necessary for the stability of the banking system except at rare and exceptionally disturbed times, but is subject to considerable abuse because of the subsidy involved. And the discount window obviously complicates money stock control.

In sum, when I consider U.S. monetary history and look at the continuing pressures to misuse the window, I doubt that Lindsey's proposed discount window is politically viable. It is far more probable that his discount window will come unstuck than it is that serious instabilities will arise from mistakes by banks operating under staggered reserve accounting.

Expectational Issues

A continuing problem for the Federal Reserve is to reestablish its credibility — to generate market confidence in its willingness and ability to carry through on its announced monetary policies. At present the announcement of money growth targets is not enough, given the history of those targets and the money growth realizations since 1975.

I believe that Lindsey's discount window reform is unlikely to have a favorable impact on the expectations upon which credibility depends. The reform is too easily undone by changes in the discount rate gradient, by failure to move the base rate, and by subtle resort to administrative pressure that was supposed to disappear. I wouldn't trust the Federal Reserve on this one even if Dave Lindsey himself were Chairman of the Board of Governors!

Staggered accounting or penalty carry-over is much more robust from this perspective. If the Federal Reserve has a genuine interest in reducing some of the political pressures that contribute to monetary policy mistakes, it can distance itself to some extent by introducing one of these two regulatory changes. I may be wrong, but I don't see how pressures from Congress or from the financial industry can warp either of these arrangements to the point that they undermine the objective of obtaining better monetary control. Assuming that market participants reach the same conclusion, at least after a little experience, their expectations about the avenue for political undermining of monetary control should change.

The Optimal Combination Policy

I am, of course, very pleased to see Lindsey take up the issue of optimal combination policy; but flattery will get him nowhere! He says that there is a *prima facie* case that recent observations showing a positive covariance between money growth and interest rate changes arise from a positively sloped money supply function being traced out by an unstable money demand function. The argument is not, in fact, so easy, as I will demonstrate.

First, what matters is instability in the money demand function itself when that function has in it both interest rate and income arguments. Lindsey's observation refers only to a money demand function with an interest rate argument. It certainly could be the case that what is driving *that* function is variation in the income argument.

Moreover, the possible role of money supply instability in generating this result is not examined in Lindsey's paper. Consider another simple model for purposes of illustrating the point.

$$Y_t = -ai_{t-1} \tag{1.6}$$

$$M_t^D = b_1 Y_t - b_2 i_t \tag{1.7}$$

$$M_t^S = ci_t + e_t \tag{1.8}$$

$$M_t^D = M_t^S \tag{1.9}$$

The variables are all measured as deviations from their means. The only disturbances driving the system are the disturbances in the money supply function (1.8), the e_t. The solution for the interest rate is

$$i_t = -\left(\frac{1}{b_2 + c}\right)e_t + \sum_{k=1}^{\infty}\left(\frac{-ab_1}{b_2 + c}\right)^k e_{t-k} \tag{1.10}$$

where:

Y = income
i = interest rate
M^D = demand for money
M^S = supply of money

This solution assumes, of course, that

$$\left|\frac{ab_1}{b_2 + c}\right| < 1$$

From equation 1.10 we can derive the following expressions for the variance of the interest rate and the covariance of the interest rate with the money stock.

$$\text{var}\,(i_t) = \sigma_e^2\left[\left(\frac{1}{b_2 + c}\right)^2 + \frac{ab_1^2}{(b_2 + c)^2 - a^2b_1^2}\right] \tag{1.11}$$

$$\text{cov}\,(M_t, i_t) = \left(\frac{\sigma_e^2}{b_2 + c}\right)\left(\frac{c}{b_2 + c} - 1\right) + \sigma_e^2\, c\left[\frac{a^2b_1^2}{(b_2 + c)^2 - a^2b_1^2}\right] \tag{1.12}$$

The variance of the interest rate is higher, the higher is the variance of the disturbance in the money supply function and the higher is the size of the parameter c which reflects accomodative policy. The covariance is positive if c is large enough, but negative if c is zero or small. The message is that we should worry as much about reducing σ_e^2 as about finding the optimal accommodative parameter, c.

My real world instincts on accommodation are these. First, over the business cycle the optimal policy is to have a reserves supply with a zero or possibly negative interest elasticity. Second, the shorter the interval the less negative and then the more positive should be the interest elasticity of reserves supply. On a daily basis the reserve supply might best be quite highly interest elastic to offset short-run disturbances due to operating factors and other similar disturbances.

It is very difficult to write down an equation for reserves supply that has these properties. Functions with lags look satisfactory, but only superficially. The interactions of the lags in a reserves supply function with other lags in the economy make such a reserves supply unattractive.

The advantage of a staggered accounting system or a penalty carry-over is that the high short-run elasticity is built into the regulations rather than into the reserves supply itself. Moreover, these two regulatory arrangements would produce interest rate smoothing relative to expected *future* short-term interest rates rather than relative to past rates. That property has a big advantage in stabilizing the macro system because it allows discrete adjustments in the entire level of interest rates — both current and expected future rates.

Discrete interest rate adjustments in response to new information help to equilibrate the system in the face of many different kinds of disturbances. At the same time, these two regulatory approaches provide a stabilizing mechanism against disturbances which the market judges to be temporary. Finally, by building the short-run accommodation into the regulations the problems of political interference and of long-run accommodation are reduced.

Concluding Comments

Several times in his paper, Lindsey comments on matters ignored by academics. Since Lindsey has tossed a brick, I'll toss it back.

The fact is that academics were concerned about money supply issues long before the Federal Reserve was. Until very recently the Federal Reserve Board has been unwilling to give much weight to these issues. Reflecting this inattention, to my knowledge — and I hope Lindsey will correct me if I am wrong — before the policy changes of October 1979 there was no careful staff work whatsoever on the operational details of reserves control except for what could be done over a relatively few days on a crash basis. Despite years of talk the Fed was not prepared with a contingency plan for introducing reserves control.

Over the years, of course, the Board staff has worked on money control issues. Major effort was devoted to modeling an unsatisfactory system of reserve regulations, but relatively little effort to studying reforms of those regulations. And the work that was done had little or no effect on the regulations determined by the Board.

I feel an obligation to push this unfortunate point further. It has been two years since the Federal Reserve adopted its new money control procedures. Over this period the Fed has made little use of its administrative discretion to improve regulations affecting monetary control. Contemporaneous reserve accounting is still being studied. Existing administrative authority permitting the Fed to move to a greater uniformity of reserve requirements on different size banks is unused. The Fed has not pushed to raise Regulation Q ceilings; in the recent vote on passbook account ceilings, the Fed voted against the proposed ceiling increase. In a note, Lindsey mentions his suggestion for changed treatment of due from's, due to's, and cash items. Academics may have ignored his suggestion, but has the Board implemented it?

The discount rate surcharge has been an innovation. But since administrative pressure and arbitrage restrictions remain, this innovation is of minor importance. In fact, I regard the innovation to be a backward step because it makes possible a larger differential between the base discount rate and money market rates, thereby increasing the subsidy to small banks that borrow and widening the role for administrative pressure. Perhaps the discount rate surcharge has improved matters — I am willing to listen to arguments and to be persuaded. There have been regulatory changes to reduce float. But have there been any other improvements to the regulatory arrangements over the last two years?

In short, the Federal Reserve has shown no sense of urgency over reforming regulations that cause money control problems, either before October 1979 or since. Lindsey knows that the problem is not that academics have ignored the issue but that the Board has been unwilling to give any priority to money control in shaping Federal Reserve regulations. I know that Lindsey himself has been interested in regulatory reform, but I cannot let stand the implication that some may read into his paper that the Board and its staff have been out front on this issue.

II MONEY STOCK CONTROL IN EUROPE: SWITZERLAND AND THE UNITED KINGDOM

2 TARGETING THE MONETARY BASE: THE SWISS CASE

Kurt Schiltknecht

The subject of the present paper, the conduct of Swiss monetary policy by means of a base target, has, as is probably well known, been of continued research and policy interest to the Swiss National Bank. Several papers on the issues involved have appeared, in particular an article by Georg Rich and myself (1979). I shall summarize the latter in the first part of this presentation; readers familiar with its ideas should immediately proceed to the second part of the paper, where I evaluate our most recent experiences with a monetary base target. In the third part of this paper, I shall discuss a problem that has increasingly come to preoccupy us, namely the relative inefficacy of changes in the monetary base that are likely to be perceived as merely transitory by financial markets. This part of my presentation leaves more questions open than it answers, but represents, so I hope, a first step toward a theoretical justification for the Swiss National Bank's increasing unwillingness to depart from a present money growth target and to engage in short-term activism.

Money Stock Target and Method of Control — The Period 1975–1978

Model of the Money Multiplier

When Switzerland adopted a floating exchange rate in January 1973, the stage was set for conducting an effective anti-inflationary monetary policy. The switch to a floating exchange rate allowed the Swiss National Bank to conduct such a policy on the basis of a money stock target. This policy approach, inaugurated in 1975, has become an important feature of the Swiss financial scene. Until 1978, the target referred to *M1* narrowly defined, comprising currency and sight deposits held by the nonbank public.[1] From the beginning, our money stock policy was viewed as a medium- or long-term one, although, in the short run, the Swiss National Bank was prepared to depart from its target in order to dampen excessive fluctuations in the exchange rate. Contrary to most other central banks, we decided to adopt the monetary base, rather than an interest rate, as an instrument to control money stock growth. This decision was, at least at the beginning, not motivated by a well-defined view of the money supply process, but reflected a long-standing tradition in Swiss monetary policy.[2]

A monetary base approach made necessary regular forecasts of the money multiplier. While such longer-term forecasts (up to one year) were largely based on the cyclical pattern of the multiplier and its components, short-term multiplier forecasts were derived from a simple mechanistic procedure. The starting point was the following naive model.[3]

$$m_t = m_{t-1} + m_{t-12} - m_{t-13} + E_t \qquad (2.1)$$

where

m_t = M_t/B_t
m_t = money multiplier in month t
M_t = money stock *M1* in month t
B_t = adjusted monetary base (= monetary base net of window dressing operations)
E_t = disturbances

The error term E_t is negatively correlated with the difference between the variation in the monetary base over one month and its change over one year. With this naive model, it was possible to forecast the money multiplier rather accurately for the next three months. The Swiss National Bank used this approach from the beginning of 1975 to the autumn of 1976, whereas for the next two years, we controlled the money supply by means of an econometric money multiplier model. This model[4] is based on an important assumption concerning cash reserve management of the Swiss banks.[5] As a result of the balance of payments fluctuations, the behavior of the Swiss monetary base has been extremely volatile. For this reason, banks do not adjust instantaneously their earning assets in response to shifts in the monetary base. An instantaneous reaction would be sensible only if the banks knew that the change in the monetary base was going to be a permanent affair. Considering the volatility of the monetary base, the banks face a difficult decision problem. They have to evaluate the extent to which a change in the monetary base is transitory or permanent. As far as this decision problem is concerned, the model incorporates the assumption that the money supply only adjusts to changes in the monetary base banks regard as permanent. Alternatively, changes that are considered to be transitory are absorbed by shifts in the free reserve ratio of the banking system. This hypothesis is formalized in the following way.

$$\frac{\dot{B}}{B} = \frac{\dot{B}^p}{B^p} + \epsilon \qquad E(\epsilon) = 0 \tag{2.2}$$

where

$\dot{B}/B$ = actual growth rate of the monetary base
$\dot{B}^p/B^p$ = growth in the permanent component of the monetary base
ϵ = transitory term

Similarly, the growth rate of the money stock is defined as

$$\frac{\dot{M}}{M} = \frac{\dot{M}^p}{M^p} + \mu \qquad E(\mu) = 0 \tag{2.3}$$

where

$\dot{M}/M$ = growth rate of the money stock
$\dot{M}^p/M^p$ = growth in the permanent component of the money stock
μ = transitory term

The actual growth rate of the money stock can be approximated by

$$\frac{\dot{M}}{M} = \frac{\dot{m}}{m} + \frac{\dot{B}}{B} \tag{2.4}$$

where $\dot{m}/m$ = growth rate of the money multiplier. Similarly, the relationship for the permanent parts is given by

$$\frac{\dot{M}^p}{M^p} = \frac{\dot{m}^p}{m^p} + \frac{\dot{B}^p}{B^p} \tag{2.5}$$

Combining equations 2.3 to 2.5, the actual growth rate of the money multiplier is obtained:

$$\frac{\dot{m}}{m} = \frac{\dot{m}^p}{m^p} + \frac{\dot{B}^p}{B^p} - \frac{\dot{B}}{B} + \mu \tag{2.6}$$

With regard to bank behavior, it is assumed that banks form their expectations about the permanent parts of B on the basis of past and current information. The rate of growth in B^p_t is determined by a linear combination with variable coefficients.

$$\left(\frac{\dot{B}^p}{B^p}\right)_t = \sum_{j=0}^{l} \beta_j \left(\frac{\dot{B}}{B}\right)_{t-j} \tag{2.7}$$

If equation 2.7 is a minimum-variance estimator, it can be shown that the weights and, therefore, the speed of adjustment depend on the relative variance of the permanent and transitory increments of the monetary base.[6] Since the fluctuations of the monetary base were large, long adjustment periods were expected and also found.

Using an analogous combination for the change in the permanent money multiplier (with γ_i standing for the respective weights), substituting equation 2.7 into equation 2.6 and rearranging terms, an equation is obtained that can be estimated using a generalized form of a Box-Jenkins transfer function model.

$$\frac{\dot{m}_t}{m_t} = \sum_{i=1}^{k} \frac{\gamma_i}{1-\gamma_0} \frac{\dot{m}_{t-i}}{m_{t-i}} + \sum_{j=1}^{l} \frac{\beta_j}{1-\gamma_0} \frac{\dot{B}_{t-j}}{B_{t-j}} - \frac{1-\beta_0}{1-\gamma_0} \frac{\dot{B}_t}{B_t} + \frac{\mu_t}{1-\gamma_0} \tag{2.8}$$

The best forecasting properties were obtained by using $i = 1, 6$, and 12 months and $j = 0, 3, 6, 9$, and 12 months. Analysis of the estimated model has shown that the prediction process is stable and that the confidence region is quite narrow. The model further seems to indicate that the changeover from a fixed to a flexible exchange rate system has not affected the money supply process.

Application of the Model

The usefulness of the money multiplier model for monetary policy depends not only on the accuracy of the forecasts, but also on the stability of the money supply process, as well as on the degree to which the adjusted monetary base can be controlled. In theory, the monetary base is under the full control of the monetary authorities. In practice, however, the control of the monetary base is complicated by the need to soften the impact of various disturbances on the money and foreign exchange markets. Therefore, the money multiplier model can not be applied in a simplistic and mechanistic way. In the following, we describe the role of the model in the conduct of monetary policy, at least as it was practiced by the Swiss National Bank until 1978.

In order to determine the desired growth in the adjusted monetary base, the money stock target is employed as a point of departure. The decision as to the size of the target is normally taken by the governing board of the Bank at the end of a calendar year. After fixing the money stock target, the money multiplier model is used to derive an annual growth target for the adjusted monetary base. The calculation is based on the assumption that the adjusted monetary base will be increased gradually over a given year. However, the Bank does not follow a rigid approach to monetary policy. For this reason, the Bank does not necessarily aim at a steady increase in the adjusted monetary base over the year. On the contrary, short-term deviations from the monetary base target frequently occur as a result of official intervention in the foreign exchange market. In order to decide whether the monetary base target must be revised in the light of current developments in the money and foreign exchange markets, the Bank has instituted a set of weekly meetings. At these meetings, decisions as to the size and duration of deviations from the monetary base target are taken.

Ideally, the money multiplier model should be reestimated after a deviation from the monetary base target has occurred, since that deviation itself affects bank behavior and the size of the multiplier. This implies that the growth in the adjusted monetary base required to achieve a given money stock target should be recalculated whenever such deviations take place. In practice, however, monetary base targets are not often altered within the year. Generally speaking, the Swiss National Bank merely seeks to correct deviations from the monetary base target at a later stage so that the target is met for the year as a whole. If deviations lead to significant shifts in the money multiplier, this procedure will cause the actual growth in the money stock to depart from its target. The Bank is prepared to tolerate such departures from the money stock target.

There are two reasons why we are reluctant to reestimate too frequently the money multiplier model. First, Switzerland possesses only monthly data on the money stock, precluding weekly revisions of the multiplier forecasts. Second, we are of the opinion that the model should not be reestimated whenever prediction errors arise. Our experiments with the model suggest that prediction errors are frequently random events and do not necessarily point to systematic deficiencies in the parameter estimates of equation 2.8. So long as prediction errors are random, the use of the latest available observations does not systematically improve the quality of forecasts. On the contrary, we know from a few cases that the forecasts tend to deteriorate if the prediction error for the last observation covered by the sample period is quite large.

Except for periods with seasonal liquidity problems (e.g., at the end of the year), the adjusted monetary base has seldom deviated from the target because of money market problems. This is due to the fact that, in general, the Bank believes that short-run fluctuations in money market interest rates do not affect the economy as long as the level of these rates is not altered permanently.

On the other hand, the extensive fluctuations in the exchange rate of the Swiss franc have been of considerable concern to the Swiss National Bank. The Bank has taken advantage of the sluggish adjustment in the money stock to a change in the adjusted monetary base in order to dampen exchange rate fluctuations. Official intervention in the foreign exchange market has little impact on the money stock as long as these interventions are reversed within the following two to three months. Therefore, short-run operations in the foreign exchange market can be conducted without jeopardizing the money stock target. It can be seen from table 2–1 that this short-run flexibility in the control of the monetary base has been widely used. Monthly changes of 2 to 6 percent in the adjusted monetary base have been quite normal.

As can be seen from table 2–2, our approach to monetary policy has produced satisfactory results, despite the unstable pattern of the adjusted monetary base. Moreover, the huge overshooting of the *M1* target in 1978 was not due to erroneous control procedures, but reflects a shift in monetary policy in response to the strong appreciation of the Swiss franc in that year.

An examination of the month to month results provides further insights into the forecasting properties of the model. Table 2–3 presents, as examples, the forecasts for the growth in *M1* made on October 22, 1976, and January 7, 1977. As indicated by the table, the forecasts are fairly accurate. In the case of the first date, the biggest forecasting error (1.8 percent) can be observed for December 1976. The January 1977 forecasts are more interesting than those made on the first date. At first sight, they also look rather good. However, a more thorough inspection of table 2–3 suggests that the growth in *M1* was seriously underestimated for the period from

Table 2–1. Percentage Change in the Adjusted Monetary Base Compared to the Level in the Previous Month

	Year			
Month	*1975*	*1976*	*1977*	*1978*
January	2.0	5.0	0	6.0
February	2.3	−5.8	−4.5	1.3
March	−1.6	−0.6	−2.8	1.2
April	−1.0	1.1	−0.4	1.9
May	2.8	0.8	0.8	−4.8
June	1.9	5.9	0.7	−3.1
July	−1.2	−6.0	3.1	5.0
August	2.2	−6.2	−0.4	0.4
September	0.4	7.9	0.4	5.8
October	0.4	−2.1	1.9	18.3
November	−0.6	1.7	−1.5	5.6
December	1.9	6.0	6.3	3.2
Average	1.5	4.1	1.9	4.7

June to August 1977. During this period, the observed level of the adjusted monetary base was much higher than the assumed level used to carry out the forecasts. Considering the prediction error, one might conclude that the quality of the multiplier forecasts starts to deteriorate after three or four months. Such a conclusion, however, would be misleading. The reason for the prediction error was the so-called Chiasso fiasco of the Swiss Credit Bank. Since the episode sheds interesting light on the practical problems of monetary management, we shall briefly discuss the Chiasso affair.

As a result of the difficulties faced by the Swiss Credit Bank in May 1977, the Swiss financial community became concerned that the public

Table 2–2. Comparison of Target and Actual Growth in *M1* (percent)

Calendar Year	*Target*	*Actual*
1975	6	4.4
1976	6	7.7
1977	5	5.5
1978	5	17.3

Table 2–3. Forecasts of the Growth Rates of the Money Stock

Month	Actual Annual Growth Rates of M1	Forecast of October 22, 1976		Forecast of January 7, 1977		Adjusted Monetary Base (in billion SFr.)		
		Predicted	Error (%)	Predicted	Error (%)	Actual	Assumed 10/22/1976	Assumed 7/1/1977
July 1976	9.5	9.6*	+0.1			24.7		
Aug.	9.7	9.0*	−0.7			24.5		
Sept.	9.1	9.4*	+0.3			24.6		
Oct.	8.6	8.1	−0.5			24.1	24.6	
Nov.	6.9	7.1	+0.2			24.5	24.6	
Dec.	8.1	6.3	−1.8			26.0	24.6	
Jan. 1977	7.1			6.2	−0.6	25.9		24.2
Feb.	9.6			7.8	−1.8	24.8		24.2
March	7.1			7.3	0.2	24.1		24.2
April	6.3			6.4	0.1	24.0		24.2
May	4.7			6.5	−1.8	24.2		24.2
June	3.7			6.2	−2.5	24.4		24.2
July	3.1			6.7	−3.6	25.2		24.2
Aug.	3.6			7.2	−3.6	25.1		24.2
Sept.	4.5			6.2	−1.7	25.2		24.2
Oct.	6.0			4.7	1.3	25.6		24.2
Nov.	5.5			4.9	0.6	25.3		24.2
Dec.	4.1			2.5	1.6	26.9		24.2

* Forecast, using actual figures for the adjusted monetary base.

would lose confidence in the banking system and that large-scale deposit withdrawals would ensue. These concerns prompted the commercial banks to augment their demand for precautionary reserves. If the Swiss National Bank had refused to supply additional base money to the banking system, the scramble for reserves would have caused a sharp contraction in the money supply. In order to forestall such a contraction, the Bank decided to increase the monetary base at a faster rate than it had planned originally. Despite the flexibility displayed by the Swiss National Bank, however, the expansion in bank reserves was not sufficient to accommodate fully the shift in demand. For this reason, short-term and medium-term interest rates increased markedly. The rise in interest rates induced a shift from demand to time deposits, resulting in slower growth of *M1*. Later in the year, it became known that the Swiss Credit Bank would be able to absorb, without major difficulty, the losses of its Chiasso branch. Since the commercial banks no longer faced the prospect of large-scale deposit withdrawals, they gradually restored their normal levels of reserves. Thus the growth rates of *M1* began to accelerate again.

This episode shows once again that targets for the money stock and monetary base must be handled in a flexible manner if the Swiss National Bank is to prevent unexpected disturbances from exerting harmful effects on the economy.

The Shift to a Monetary Base Target

In October 1978, the Swiss National Bank decided to drop temporarily the money stock target. Instead, it began to intervene massively in the foreign exchange market in order to counteract an excessive revaluation of the Swiss franc. After the switch to an exchange rate policy the money multiplier model was no longer employed to forecast the growth in the money stock. Since the situation in the foreign exchange market improved quickly, the Bank, in the spring of 1979, was able to return to a policy of actively controlling the monetary base, although it did not make a public announcement to this effect. The system of monetary control introduced in the spring of 1979 differed from the earlier approach insofar as the Bank did not fix a target for *M1*, but determined directly a target for the monetary base.

Upon the introduction of a monetary base target, the money multiplier model was once again used for forecasting purposes. However, when forecasts were made for the period from early 1978 to July 1979, it turned out that the predictive power of the model had deteriorated substantially compared with the pre-1978 period. This result was independent of the estimation period underlying the model. Thus it appears that the predictive power of the model was adversely affected by the exchange rate disturbances as well as by the substitution of an exchange rate for a money stock target.

The reasons for deterioration in the quality of the forecasts are not entirely clear. In order to get more insight into the forecasting properties of the model, we carried out long-term dynamic forecasts.[7]

The prediction errors are heavily correlated with the dollar/Swiss franc exchange rate. This result indicates that the money stock is affected by exchange rate expectations, and this was confirmed by a study of the demand for money.[8] During the years of flexible exchange rates, the expectations of a permanent appreciation of the Swiss franc with respect to the dollar had induced Swiss residents to repatriate part of their foreign cash balances and to increase their demand for money denominated in Swiss francs. Moreover, even an expected temporary depreciation of the dollar may lead to an increase in the demand for money.

If these findings are correct, a meaningful short-run money stock target can be formulated only if the influence of exchange rate expectations on the money stock can be accurately predicted. As long as this is not possible, it is difficult to know whether a deviation from the money stock target is due to a change in exchange rate expectations or an inappropriate monetary policy. In the event of an inappropriate monetary policy, the monetary base must be adjusted in order to push the money stock back to the target. If, on the other hand, the deviation reflected a change in exchange rate expectations, an adjustment in the monetary base would be undesirable. An expected appreciation of the Swiss franc would increase the demand for money and subject the Swiss economy to deflationary pressures. The money stock, in turn, would rise above its target. If, under such conditions, the Swiss National Bank were to contract the monetary base, monetary policy would reinforce the deflationary effect of the shift in exchange rate expectations.

In retrospect, this scenario would appear to explain certain events observed in the early summer of 1978. At that time, the Swiss National Bank was faced with a large positive deviation of the money stock from its target. In order to correct that deviation, the Bank reduced the monetary base. Later on, the Bank realized that the tightening of monetary policy had been inappropriate since it contributed to the exchange rate crisis in the autumn of 1978. It is likely that the deviation was not due to a policy error, but reflected the influence of exchange rate expectations on the demand for money.

Monetary Base Target — The Period 1980 until Today

In the light of the experience of autumn 1978, the Swiss National Bank decided, at the end of 1979, to modify its approach to monetary policy and to set a target for the monetary base rather than for *M1*. A monetary base target has both advantages and disadvantages. On the one hand, a base target reduces the risk of an inappropriate central bank response to shifts in the demand for Swiss francs. On the other hand, such a target increases the danger that an acceleration in the growth of the money stock resulting from, say, a rise in the inflation rate will not be offset immediately. Considering the vulnerability of the Swiss economy to externally induced shifts in the demand for Swiss francs, we believe that the advantages outweigh the disadvantages. A monetary base target was accordingly set for 1980 and for 1981; most likely another base target will be set at the end of 1981 for 1982. The Swiss National Bank's objective for 1980 (mid-November 1979 to mid-November 1980) was to let the monetary base grow by 4 percent on average; for 1981 the same 4 percent target has been chosen.

These targets are derived as follows. We start with the idea that the yearly growth rate of *M1* should be stabilized around 3 percent over a medium term of several years. Next, we forecast the money multiplier under the assumption that growth of *M1* is not influenced by exchange rate expectations; the method used to predict the multiplier is similar to the one employed from 1975 till 1977 for longer-term forecasts, i.e., we predict the cyclical pattern of the multiplier and its components. Finally, on the basis of this multiplier forecast, we derive the target for the monetary base.

By targeting the base, the Swiss National Bank allows temporary fluctuations in the money supply to occur. As long as these fluctuations are due to temporary shocks or changing exchange rate expectations they are not of great concern to us. However, if economic activity or inflation unexpectedly starts to accelerate or decelerate, the Bank is ready to deviate from its target. Since such action takes place only when the initial assumptions used to predict the money multiplier turn out to be wrong, there exists a risk that corrective measures are taken too late. We do not consider this risk to be very serious, since induced fluctuations in the money supply can only be temporary as long as the monetary base is strictly controlled over the medium term.

The Swiss National Bank uses different instruments for controlling the monetary base. In the postwar period until 1979, increases in the monetary base were mainly due to intervention purchases in the foreign exchange market. The creation of base money through open market purchases has been negligible. On the other hand, base money was, at least until the spring 1979, rarely removed through selling of foreign currency; instead excess liquidity was reduced by selling sterilization subscriptions issued by the Treasury, by imposing minimum reserve requirements on the banks, or by means of a regulation obligating commercial banks that raise Swiss-franc loans on behalf of nonresidents to convert them into dollars directly at the Swiss National Bank.

Since the spring of 1979, the method of monetary base control has been changed. As a first step, excess liquidity created to stabilize the exchange rate in autumn 1978 was mopped up by selling dollars. Secondly, we started to use swaps as the principal instrument to control the monetary base. A swap operation couples two transactions, a spot and a forward one, the latter being exactly the opposite of the former. (For example, a bank buys spot francs against dollars from the Swiss National Bank, and simultaneously sells to the Bank forward — the term is variable — an equivalent amount of Swiss francs against dollars.) Given the amount of international activity of Swiss banks, use of swaps enables the Swiss National Bank to easily control the monetary base at any moment.

Table 2–4. Percentage Change in the Adjusted Monetary Base Compared to the Level in the Previous Month

	Year		
Month	*1979*	*1980*	*1981*
January	7.5	−3.1	−3.3
February	−5.8	−3.4	−4.1
March	−7.1	−1.7	−0.7
April	−12.7	1.0	−0.1
May	−3.1	−0.9	−0.6
June	3.5	0.2	1.4
July	1.5	1.4	2.1
August	−5.3	−0.1	−1.6
September	3.0	0.7	
October	−1.0	−0.5	
November	−1.8	−0.4	
December	6.3	7.7	
Average in absolute terms	4.9	1.8	1.7

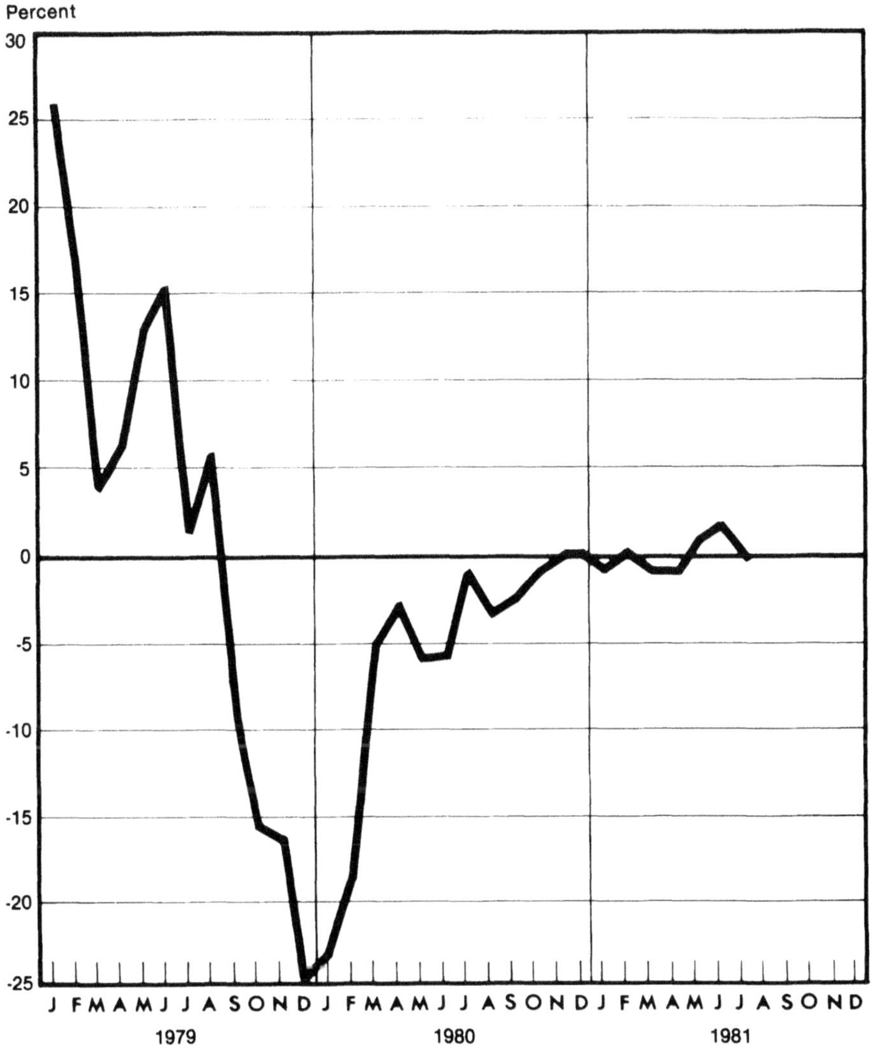

Figure 2–1 Growth Rates of the Monetary Base (year over year)

As I have already explained, we are, despite this possibility, not inclined to control the base day by day or week by week; instead our aim is to control trend growth of the monetary base. As can be seen from table 2–4, month-to-month changes are, given the removal of excess liquidity in 1979, rather low by Swiss standards. This impression is confirmed by figure 2–1, which shows the annual growth rate (year over year) of the monetary base. Greater stability in monetary base growth during the past two years was achieved not only by a better control strategy, but also by a change in our perception as regards the nature of short-term fluctuations in the exchange rate.

In fact, we feel it is not possible to dampen exchange rate fluctuations through short-term variation of the money supply.[9] As a result, our sales or purchases in the foreign exchange market have become more and more infrequent and, when such operations have taken place, their effects on the monetary base have been neutralized almost immediately. On the other hand, we abandoned the restrictions that were imposed for several years on capital inflows in order to keep the appreciation of the Swiss franc under control and to prevent it from becoming a reserve currency. The efficacy of such restrictive measures are very limited. The only way to influence the exchange rate trend is a permanent change in the money supply.

Despite the improvement in monetary base control and our relative absence from the foreign exchange market, we did not reach our monetary base target in 1980 nor will we attain it in 1981. The 1980 target (4 percent on average) was undershot to some extent since the average growth rate of the monetary base (compared to mid-November) amounted to only 2 percent. This target undershooting is mainly explained by two factors. First, during the first half of 1980, the National Bank still intervened heavily in the foreign exchange market in order to support a relatively weak Swiss franc. Although we strove to neutralize the restrictive effect of these interventions on the money supply by offering swaps to commercial banks, the monetary base did not rise significantly. Second, after we lifted the restrictions on the inflow of foreign capital, the circulation of one-thousand-franc notes began to shrink considerably, contributing further to the slower than expected growth in the monetary base. We suspect that foreigners kept a substantial volume of such notes in bank safes in an effort to get around the commission levied by the Swiss government on foreign-held deposits. It appears that in 1980 these notes were gradually winding their way back to the banks.

Since 1980, the growth rates (over twelve months) in the money stock, *M1*, have been negative. When the monetary target was set for 1980, it was expected that the growth rates in *M1* would stay negative until the early part of the summer and then turn positive again. This forecast was not borne out by subsequent developments. The persistent decline in *M1* mirrors the influence of exchange rate expectations on the demand for Swiss money. This experience indicates that the decision to shift from an *M1* target to a monetary base target was appropriate.

In 1981, the situation has been different. The 4 percent growth target for the monetary base was set under the assumption that the Swiss economy would be likely to suffer from a cyclical downturn during the year and that inflation would not increase further. This assumption turned out to be wrong. Switzerland has not yet been affected by the worldwide downturn in economic acitivity. At the same time, the rate of inflation has continued to accelerate. Consequently, we have pursued a more restrictive monetary policy, with growth of the money base fluctuating around zero. We believe that this policy stance is sufficiently restrictive to bring the actual inflation rate of 7 to 8 percent under control, and we are looking forward to a return to the low level of inflation recorded during the first years of money stock control.

Transitory Changes in Monetary Policy and Their Implications for Money Stock Control — A Sketch

The activity of a central bank is reflected in the monetary base. When banks, business firms, and other market participants have rational expectations, they will try to distinguish between the permanent, the transitory, and the random part of the monetary base.

The random component (ϵ_t) is characterized by the fact that at any moment in time the expected value of ϵ_t is zero [$E(\epsilon_t) = 0$]. The expected value of the transitory component is zero over a long period, but might be positive or negative over a shorter period. A typical transitory component of the monetary base is, for example, the change in the monetary base due to intervention purchases in the foreign exchange market, which the market expects to be offset within the next few months. The permanent component is the part of the base related to the long-term trend of monetary policy.

In the following, the random elements of the monetary base are neglected. It is assumed that banks are able to deal with the effects of these random components on their reserve position and that they are handling the corresponding cash problems along the lines explored by Miller and Orr.[10] The market not only makes a distinction between permanent and transitory parts of the monetary base but it also guesses how long a transitory part will remain in the base at time t. Let us denote the component of the monetary base that is expected to be removed after i periods by ${}_iB_t$; then ${}_i\beta_t = {}_iB_t/B_t$ is the temporary share of the monetary base regarded in existence until i, $i = 1, \ldots, n - 1$. If $i \geq n$, these elements of the monetary base are treated as permanent. ${}_iB_t$ can also be negative, indicating that the permanent monetary base is assumed to be greater than the actual base and that an increase in the base is expected to take place after i periods. The probability of the temporary share of the monetary base can be defined as

$$P_t({}_i\beta_t) \qquad i = 1, \ldots, n - 1$$

If an increase in the monetary base is regarded as temporary until j, ${}_j\beta_t$ rises and we can write

$$\frac{\delta P_t}{\delta_j\beta_t} > 0 \qquad \delta_j\beta_t > 0$$

If such an increase is considered permanent, we have a decrease in the temporary share, ${}_j\beta_t$, and then

$$\frac{\delta P_t}{\delta_j\beta_t} < 0 \qquad \delta_j\beta_t < 0$$

Since there are no objective probabilities available for ${}_i\beta_t$, market participants will have to formulate subjective ones. Assuming that the market disposes of all information available at time t (ϕ_t), the probability P_t can be written under the conditional form,

$$P_t({}_i\beta_t|\phi_t)$$

Before turning to the question as to what and how information affects P_t, I would like to elaborate a bit on the implications of P_t for decisions in the monetary sector. To investigate this problem, I will use a simple framework, assuming that interest rates are determined in the credit market. The credit market is divided into low-risk securities (S) (short-term market) and loans (L) (long-term market).[11] The transaction costs for loans, which include all costs involved with a loan, are higher than the transaction costs for securities. Let S_B and L_B denote the aggregate desired loan and securities portfolios of commercial banks. S_B and L_B can be expressed as a proportion to total demand (D) and time deposits (T):

$$S_B = \alpha_1(D + T) \qquad (2.9)$$

$$L_B = \alpha_2(D + T) \qquad (2.10)$$

Assuming that α_1 and α_2 depend (among other variables) on P_t,

$$\alpha_1 = \alpha_1(i_S, i_L, \ldots, P_t) \qquad (2.11)$$

with

$$\left.\frac{\delta\alpha_1}{\delta P_t}\,\frac{\delta P_t}{\delta_j\beta_t}\right|_{\delta_j\beta>0} >> \left.\frac{\delta\alpha_1}{\delta P_t}\,\frac{\delta P_t}{\delta_j\beta_t}\right|_{\delta_j\beta_t<0}$$

and

$$\alpha_2 = \alpha_2(i_S, i_L, \ldots, P_t) \tag{2.12}$$

with

$$\frac{\delta\alpha_2}{\delta P_t}\frac{\delta P_t}{\delta_j\beta_t} = \begin{cases} <0 & \text{if} \quad \delta_j\beta_t > 0 \\ >0 & \text{if} \quad \delta_j\beta_t < 0 \end{cases}$$

where i_S is interest rate on securities and i_L is loan interest rate.

The balance sheet of commercial banks implies that

$$r + \alpha_1 + \alpha_2 = 1 \tag{2.13}$$

where $r = R/(D + T)$ and R is reserves.

Assuming for simplicity that banks have no access to central bank credits and using a credit multiplier approach, the demands of banks for securities or for loans is

$$S_B = \alpha_1 \cdot a \cdot B = \alpha_1(i_S, i_L, \ldots, P_t)a(i_S, i_L, \ldots)B \tag{2.14}$$

$$L_B = \alpha_2 \cdot a \cdot B = \alpha_2(i_S, i_L, \ldots, P_t)a(i_S, i_L, \ldots)B \tag{2.15}$$

where

$$a = (1 + t)/[r(1 + t) + k] \tag{2.16}$$

$a = a(i_t, \ldots, P_t)$
t = time deposit ratio
k = currency ratio
i_t = interest rate on time deposit

The public's supply of loans to commercial banks (L_p) and the public's stock demand for securities (S_p) can be expressed by the following two equations:

$$S_p = s_1(i_S, i_L, \ldots, P_t) \tag{2.17}$$

$$L_p = s_2(i_S, i_L, \ldots, P_t) \tag{2.18}$$

with

$$\frac{\delta s_1}{\delta P_t}\frac{\delta P_t}{\delta_j\beta_t} \approx 0 \quad \text{if} \quad \delta_j\beta_t > 0$$

and

$$\frac{\delta s_2}{\delta P_t}\frac{\delta P_t}{\delta_j\beta_t} > 0 \quad \text{if} \quad \delta_j\beta_t < 0$$

since

$$S_B + S_p = S \tag{2.19}$$

S being the outstanding stock of securities, and since

$$L_B = L_p \tag{2.20}$$

equations 2.14 to 2.18 proximately determine the interest rates i_L and i_S and the allocation of the outstanding stock of securities:

$$\alpha_1(i_S,i_L,\ldots)a(i_S,i_L,\ldots)B + s_1(i_S,i_L,\ldots) = S \tag{2.21}$$

$$\alpha_2(i_S,i_L,\ldots)a(i_S,i_L,\ldots)B = s_2(i_S,i_L,\ldots) \tag{2.22}$$

In figures 2–2 and 2–3 the initial equilibrium interest rates in the credit market are given by i_{L0} and i_{S0}. They are the proximate result of the supply and demand equations $S_{B0} + S_{p0}$, L_{B0}, L_{p0}, and S_0. Now let us assume that the monetary base is increased through open market purchases; that is, the outstanding stock of securities is reduced to S_1. In case 1 the market regards the change as transitory, in case 2 as permanent, although in both cases the same monetary base will apply. The effect on probability $P_t({}_j\beta_t)$, however, will be different; in case 1, $\delta P_t/\delta_j\beta_t$ is greater than zero, while in case 2 this derivative is negative.

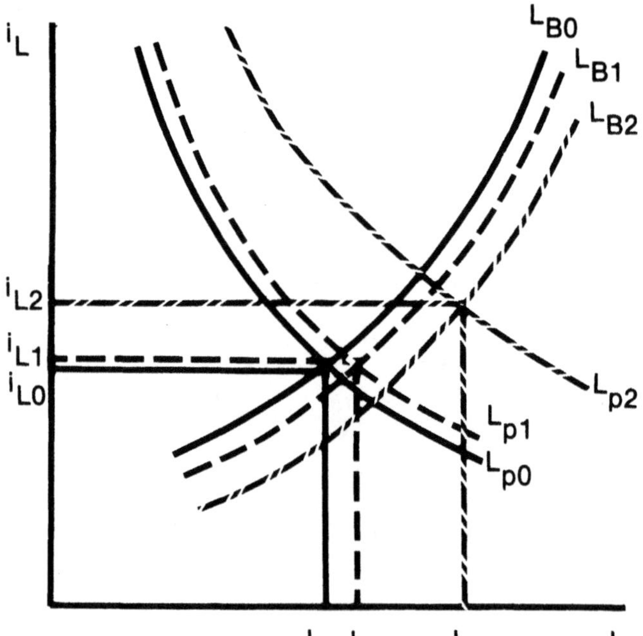

Figure 2–2 Loan Market

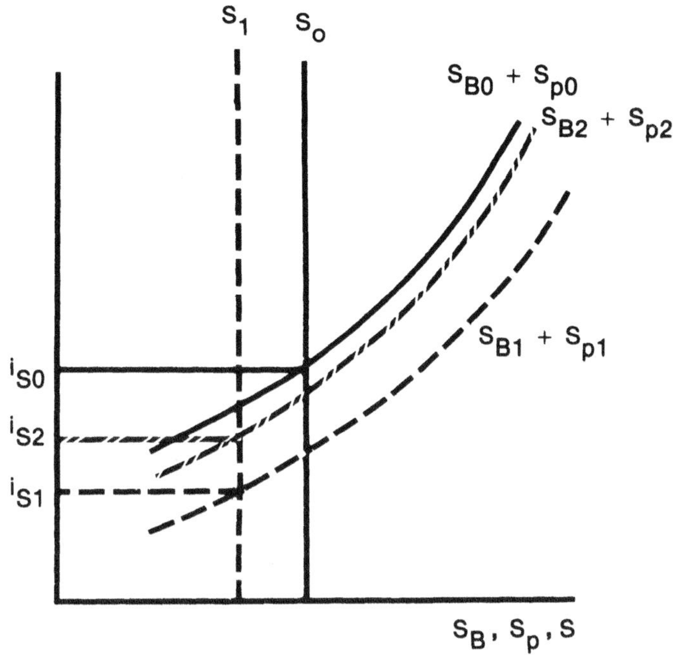

Figure 2–3 Securities Market

To make the point clear, I am not dealing with the question of what will happen after a permanent or a transitory change takes place. I am primarily interested in what kind of implications arise in the short run, if the market alters for one or another reason the subjective probability function of the monetary base. The results of the analysis will have a crucial bearing on such matters as the method of controlling monetary aggregates or the time period for which a monetary target should be set.

Let us assume that in case 1 the market expects the increase in the monetary base, which takes place at t, to be offset at $t + j$, so that j denotes the length of the expected transitory change. j will be so short that the market will alter neither its expected rate of inflation nor its expected interest rates for the period $t + q$, $q > j$. Also, the real sector of the economy will not be influenced substantially by the transitory change. Therefore, it can be assumed that banks and the public plan to restore their original portfolio structure after $t + j$. Meanwhile, banks can use the transitory increase in the monetary base to expand their supply of loans, to increase their demand for securities, or to hold more reserves.

The reaction of the banking system depends on, among other things, the expected interest rates during the period $t + 1$ to $t + j$. The formation of these short-run expectations is strongly influenced by the probability $P_t({}_i\beta_t)$; that is, by the expectations of when the transitory component of the money base will be removed. This assumption is based on the hypothesis that, in the short run, changes in the reserve position of the banking system are among the most important factors determining short-term interest rates, and that banks and the public are aware of this fact. Another crucial factor explaining portfolio adjustment to a transitory change is that of transaction costs. Given the rather high costs of acquiring information about loans, it seems obvious that an increase in the supply of credits would not be profitable, if the additional loans will have to be reduced shortly afterwards in order to restore the original portfolio structure. Therefore, it might be more profitable for banks to expand primarily their demand for short-term securities, because the transaction costs involved with buying or selling securities are much smaller. It might even be the case that, for very short holding periods, the net of transaction-costs yield of a loan or a security becomes negative.

Even if it is not possible to derive the optimal portfolio solution for banks in a general form, the direction of response is clear. The shorter is the expected transitory change, the more banks will expand their demand for securities, shifting S_B to the right (S_{B1}). As a result, the initial reduction in the interest rate following the open market purchases is magnified. The interplay between the loan and the securities market is weak ($|\delta\alpha_2/\delta i_s|$ decreases as j decreases) and the banks' demand for loan is shifted only slightly to the right (L_{B1}).

The response of the public to a transitory change is similar. In the short run, arbitrage between securities, loans, and goods is negligible. Therefore, neither the public's demand for securities nor the supply of loans to banks is altered significantly. It might be that the supply of loans will rise slightly (to L_{p1}). As a result, a new temporary equilibrium is established at the rates i_{L1} and i_{S1}.

The outcome is totally different if the increase in the monetary base is regarded as a permanent change and as indicative of a rise in the trend growth rate. While, in the first case, only the expected interest rates for the period t to $t + j$ are altered, all expected values are altered after a permanent change. As a result of the rise in expected interest rates and rate of inflation, the public increases the supply of loans to banks (shifting the L_p curve to the right, to L_{p2}). Because the change is regarded as permanent, the interplay between loan and securities markets is stronger than in the transitory case:

$$\left|\frac{\delta\alpha_2}{\delta i_S}\right|_{\delta_j\beta_t>0} < \left|\frac{\delta\alpha_2}{\delta i_S}\right|_{\delta_j\beta_t<0}$$

and

$$\left|\frac{\delta\alpha_1}{\delta i_L}\right|_{\delta_j\beta_t>0} < \left|\frac{\delta\alpha_2}{\delta i_S}\right|_{\delta_j\beta_t<0}$$

Therefore, the short-term increase in the banks' and public's demand for securities will be smaller than in the first case; thus i_S will not fall as much. On the other hand, banks expand their demand for loans from the public (shift to L_{B2}). The new equilibrium interest rates will be at i_{L2} and i_{S2}.

This crude analysis shows that a change in the monetary base has different implications for the interest rate structure depending on whether the change is perceived as transitory or permanent. While in the first case the short-term interest rate falls much more than in the second one, the long-term interest rate remains quasi stable in the former and rises in the latter. This analysis indicates that the interest rate structure is heavily influenced by probability function P_t.

I will now derive the implications of the preceding analysis for money stock growth, assuming that the structure of deposit interest rates is similar to the interest rate structure in the credit market. Using a multiplier approach, the money stock can be defined as

$$M_0 = m_0 B_0 = \frac{1 + k_0}{r_0(1 + t_0) + k_0} \cdot B_0 \tag{2.23}$$

As soon as interest rates and the probability P_t change, k_0, r_0, and t_0 change too. The ratios k, r, and t depend on P_t for the same reason as do the equations in the credit market. In general terms it can be said that the degree of substitutability between different forms of deposits decreases if the transitory component of the monetary base increases; that is, $\delta t/\delta i_t$ will be smaller if $\delta_j\beta_t > 0$. Assuming that the elasticities of the k-, r-, and t-ratios with respect to interest rates are the "normal" ones[12] (i.e., $\delta k/\delta i > 0$, $\delta r/\delta i < 0$, and $\delta t/\delta i > 0$), I get the following implications of a monetary base change for the multiplier. In case 1, both interest rates (long term and short term) fall. As a result, the reserve ratio increases ($r > r_0$) and the t-ratio and the k ratio decrease slightly. While it is assumed that the interest elasticity of the currency ratio is rather small in numerical terms, the slight decrease in the t-ratio results directly from the assumption that the possibility of substitution among different deposits is negligible when the change in the monetary base is regarded as transitory. Under this assumption, the multiplier will fall. In case 2, the long-term interest rate increases, while the short-term rate will drop. On average, the interest rate level might be slightly higher. Therefore, the reserve ratio decreases ($r_2 < r_0$) and the t-ratio increases. It is then quite possible that these two moves offset each other, leaving the multiplier more or less unchanged.

The crucial problem in this analysis is to find out what kind of impacts the term structure of interest rates has on the different ratios. It is obvious that the implication of a change in an interest rate is different depending on whether such a change is due to a transitory or to a permanent money base variation. Friedman (1977) has developed a way of dealing with this kind of problem in his article on time perspective in the demand for money: he explains why the whole term structure affects the demand for money and what weight should be given to various interest rates. Without elaborating this point further, it can be said that the effect of a change in the monetary base on the term structure and on the monetary aggregates will be different according to whether the change in the monetary base is interpreted by the market as being transitory or permanent.

Some Conclusions

The preceding approach seems to be helpful in understanding some peculiarities of financial market behavior in Switzerland. Many analysts have found it hard to understand why the sharp increase in the monetary base in the autumn of 1978, which was necessary to stop the enormous appreciation of the Swiss franc, did not lead for quite some time to a rise in long-term interest rates. In view of the analysis presented above, the behavior of the market was rational. Based on the past "anti-inflationary record" of the Swiss National Bank, the assumption made by the market, that a large part of the monetary base increase would be only transitory, was rational. Under such circumstances it was not surprising to observe short-term interest rates approach zero and to see even long-term ones falling.

Similar observations could apply to intervention purchases or sales in the foreign exchange market. After a certain time, the market learned that the impact of these operations on the monetary base was purely transitory. Therefore, no significant restructuring of portfolios took place and the effects of these operations were entirely absorbed in the money market. Neither the long-term interest rates nor the exchange rate reacted in a significant way.

Similar problems arise if the monetary authorities set short-term monetary targets. Let us assume that, under such a system, the target is missed for whatever reason, and that the central bank tries, in order to keep or to restore its credibility, to bring the monetary aggregate back on track. Banks and the public will then make an effort to figure out whether the correcting action of the central bank implies a permanent shift in the trend of monetary policy or whether it is just a transitory change to offset the deviation from the target. When the market interprets the change as transitory, the impact on the money stock will be small; that is, the change in the monetary base will be partially neutralized by a reduction in the multiplier. Therefore, the target could be hit only if the change is big enough. But such a huge variation might, in the short run, disrupt the money and foreign exchange markets and, in the longer run, induce an overshooting in a direction opposite to the intended one. Thus, the more changes in monetary policy are viewed as transitory phenomena, the less monetary aggregates are controllable in the short run. In Switzerland, our own efforts to control monetary targets in the short run did not bring the expected result, but only a greater variability in short-term money market rates. The conclusion we have drawn from this experience is that the best course of action is to set long-term targets for the monetary aggregates and to abstain from fine tuning.

Notes

1. From 1979, the target is stated in terms of the monetary base.
2. On this point, see Rich and Schiltknecht (1979).
3. See Schiltknecht (1979).
4. The following discussion is quoted from Rich and Schiltknecht (1979).
5. For a full discussion of the model, see Büttler et al. (1979).
6. See Lucas (1976).
7. For a more detailed analysis, see Rich and Shiltknecht (1979).
8. See Roth (1981).
9. The reasons for this behavior are given in the following section.
10. See Miller and Orr (1968) and Orr (1970).
11. The lines of Brunner and Meltzer (1966) are being followed here.
12. See Burger (1971).

References

Brunner, K., and Meltzer, A. "A Credit Market Theory of the Money Supply." *Rivista internazionale di scienze economische e commerciali* (1966).

Burger, A.E. *The Money Supply Process*. Belmont, CA: Wadsworth, 1971.

Büttler, H.J., et al. "A Multiplier Model for Controlling the Money Stock." *Journal of Monetary Economics* (July 1979).

Friedman, M. "Time Perspective in Demand for Money." *Scandinavian Journal of Economics,* Vol. 79 (1977).

Lucas, R.E. "Econometric Policy Evaluation: A Critique." In K. Brunner and A. Meltzer, eds., *The Phillips Curve and Labor Markets,* vol. 1 of the Carnegie-Rochester Conference on Public Policy. New York: North-Holland, 1976.

Miller, M., and Orr, D. "The Demand for Money by Firms: Extensions of Analytic Results." *Journal of Finance* (December 1968).

Orr, D. *Cash Management and the Demand for Money.* New York: Praeger, 1970.

Rich, G., and Schiltknecht, K. "Targeting and the Monetary Base — The Swiss Approach." In *The Monetary Base Approach to Monetary Control.* Bank of International Settlements, 1979.

Roth, J.P. "The Demand for Money Under Flexible Exchange Rates: The Swiss Case." Zurich, 1981, mimeo.

Schiltknecht, K. "Monetary Policy Under Flexible Exchange Rates, the Swiss Case." In K. Brunner and J.M. Neumann, eds., *Inflation, Unemployment and Monetary Control.* Berlin: Duncker und Homblot, 1979.

DISCUSSION

John Wenninger

Switzerland has often been pointed to as a country with a good record on inflation and a country that follows a monetarist approach to policy. However, Schiltknecht's paper raises many important practical policy issues and one cannot help but wonder whether the Swiss approach to monetary policy is so much in the monetarist tradition that it should be considered a model in some sense for other countries to follow.

Schiltknecht's paper was interesting in several respects — particularly from the point of view of some of the common problems the central banks of Switzerland and the United States appear to be having. In particular, if the demand for conventionally defined narrow money is not stable in the sense of money being difficult to measure or conceptualize on a consistent basis over time — for whatever the reason, be it financial innovation in the United States or exchange rate expectations in Switzerland — what course should the central bank follow? In the Swiss case, the approach seems to be to place even more emphasis on the monetary base, with the view that in the long run this will result in the desired growth of money and thereby keep inflation under control. Since month-to-month or even quarter-to-quarter control of the money stock is not pursued under such an approach, short-run forecasts of the money multiplier are not at all important. Hence, the first part of Schiltknecht's paper, which deals with short-run mechanical multiplier forecasts — which apparently were used by the Swiss National Bank prior to this new approach to policy — would not be considered an important part of the paper to focus on in discussion.

But it would seem that longer-run forecasts of the multiplier are still very important, and it would have been interesting to learn more detail, rather than just generalities, about how the Swiss National Bank formulates long-run multiplier forecasts in light of the instability in the demand for money in Switzerland. Over and beyond that, of course, is the consideration that the multiplier is not independent of the target set for the monetary base; that is, a very restrictive base target is likely to be accompanied by a higher multiplier than is a more expansionary base target. It would have been very interesting to learn in some detail how the Swiss National Bank deals with that problem, given that the Swiss National Bank normally does not impose a reserve requirement on banks and that reserve balances largely represent excess reserves or clearing balances.

All that is mentioned about the long-run multiplier forecasts is that they are based on the historical pattern of the multiplier over the business cycle. This seems to suggest an attempt to get at the problem of the multiplier increasing when the base target is restrictive, but it also seems to suggest that the multiplier forecast is somehow based on a forecast of economic activity — and, given the accuracy of GNP forecasts in the United States, for example, one cannot help but wonder how accurate these multiplier forecasts are.

But, in a sense, there does not appear to be any way to evaluate the accuracy of the Swiss National Bank's long-run multiplier forecasts even *ex post,* because if one reads between the lines — in 1980 and 1981 — what seems to be the intermediate target is not *M1,* but "*M1* adjusted for shifts in the demand for money due to changes in exchange rate expectations." That is the concept of money the Swiss National Bank wants to grow at 3 percent. At first glance, that sounds like the Federal Reserve setting an *M1B* target adjusted for NOW accounts, but I think a closer parallel would be a target adjusted for the extent to which the demand for money might shift as a result of financial innovation — and there would never be any agreement on how to measure that. In general, one would expect the exchange-rate-related errors from the money demand equation to average to zero over some longer-run time period, since exchange rate expectations can change in either direction. But again here, Schiltknecht does not give us much detail on this important practical problem — do these errors in fact average to zero in the long run? Whatever the answer, however, over the course of a one-year target period, the error could well be largely in one direction or another, making it difficult to evaluate the multiplier forecasts, because money demand equations are certain to have errors stemming from sources other than just the one the Swiss National Bank is attempting to adjust for. In any event, in the approach used by the Swiss National Bank, the multiplier forecast is based on a forecast of the business cycle, and the long-run monetary base target is derived from that multiplier forecast and the desired growth of a nonobservable monetary aggregate.

While this may or may not work out in practice to be meaningful or even accurate, it does seem at first glance to be monetary policy being conducted under what appears to be on the surface "the rational expectations version of monetarism." In other words, monetary policy doesn't matter for the real economy — unless the central bank does something truly surprising — so the multiplier forecast can be based on a forecast of the business cycle, and given that forecast of the multiplier, the monetary base and the money supply can be expanded at noninflationary rates. But if one stops and thinks about this approach a while longer, it turns out to be almost equivalent to reacting directly to movements in income from a desired or expected path — not the monetarist fixed growth rate rule for the base — and this comes out clearest in the discussion of Swiss monetary policy in 1980 and 1981.

For example, if the economy turns out to be stronger than expected, the multiplier will be higher than projected and the money stock greater than desired, and hence, monetary base growth must be reduced — the same reaction a central bank would have if it simply was attempting to offset an upward deviation in GNP from a desired or expected path. And the same analysis applies on the downside as well, with the central bank increasing the growth of high-powered money to speed up *M1* growth when the economy is weaker than expected and the multiplier lower than projected. But rather than just simply calling it counter-cyclical monetary policy, the Swiss National Bank seems to call it "adjusting base growth for cyclical misses in the multiplier forecast."

In other words, with the multiplier forecast conditional on the business cycle, the central bank ends up having to vary the growth of the monetary base in reaction to unexpected swings in economic activity more or less the same way it would if it did not have a base target at all — or for that matter a money target — and was simply reacting to economic developments. An intermediate money target would seem to make sense in the Swiss case only if a case can be made that the 3 percent money target the Swiss National Bank now has in some sense limits the size of the response of the monetary base to deviations of income from the expected path. But with the multiplier and the money stock data distorted by exchange rate expectations, this is not a very convincing argument. And if this is not the justification, why not just vary the base directly in response to deviations in income from a desired path, and eliminate the confusing intermediate targeting process altogether?

Because clearly, in the Swiss case with the multiplier dependent on the level of economic activity, the growth of money is not adding anything, *on a more timely basis,* to the information already available for policy making, unless a case can be made that the errors in the multiplier forecast give a clear-cut indication that the economy is stronger or weaker than expected before the business statistics do. But, since the GNP data would be necessary before the extent to which the money data are being distorted by exchange rate expectations could be determined from the money demand equation, it is hard to imagine how the multiplier or money stock has any informational value in this approach. The central bank would be better off looking directly at the income data. Only if a case can be made that the effect of the business cycle on the multiplier and the money stock is so much stronger than exchange rate expectations, could one argue that money and the multiplier have some informational value under such an approach.

In the final section of Schiltknecht's paper, a lot of effort is devoted to justifying short-run misses in the monetary base target — misses intentionally made, at times, for the sake of exchange rate objectives. Thus, this part of the paper appears to be an attempt to develop a case for a nonrigid approach to base control. The thrust of the argument here appears to be that if the central bank has a high degree of anti-inflationary credibility, then the market will not overreact to temporary deviations of the base from the target because the market will trust the central bank to make the necessary offsetting correction later.

This credibility argument is all right as far as it goes, but one cannot help but wonder whether the Swiss National Bank's credibility has not suffered somewhat. How can the market be sure that temporary deviations in the monetary base will be offset when the National Bank announces that it will miss its base targets for both 1980 and 1981 — in 1980, because it was not successful in offsetting later in the year a foreign exchange rate-related reduction in base growth earlier in the year, and in 1981, because the economy is stronger than expected. Granted the Swiss National Bank is undershooting its base targets during an inflationary period, but the justification given is "because the economy is stronger than expected," and this sounds like monetary policy in which the central bank is reacting directly to bad news on the inflation front, and it does not sound like strict adherence on a year-to-year basis to money or monetary base targets. In other words, if it is true — as Schiltknecht suggests in his paper — that the money supply and multiplier statistics are quite distorted by exchange rate expectations, at least in the short run if not in the long run, then it would seem that the Swiss National Bank — as it seems to be doing already — is left in a position of varying base growth directly in response to changes in economic conditions and exchange rates. So, it is not altogether clear that Switzerland is all that good an example of how to use monetary targeting to control inflation.

Moreover, it is not obvious that the reason that the Swiss *in the past* have had a good record on inflation is because of a strict adherence to a monetarist approach to policy. True, they tend to discuss their policy in terms of a monetarist paradigm. But the Swiss government does not run a deficit of a size that would put any pressure on the central bank to monetize it. The Swiss, in general, tend to adhere to very strict fiscal discipline. Moreover, the Swiss authorities do not face the same type of policy trade-offs other nations do. Recessions typically do not result in sharply rising domestic unemployment, but rather in a reduction in the use of foreign workers. In addition, in a small open economy like Switzerland — with a large volume of both imports and exports — the temptation to run an expansionary monetary policy is greatly reduced, not only because it will add directly to inflation as the exchange rate declines, and the prices of imports increase, but also because, since much of Switzerland's imports are raw materials, the relative price of its exports would not improve very much. Thus, most of the effect of an expansionary monetary policy is in terms of inflation. Despite the different policy trade-offs faced by the Swiss National Bank, as compared to the trade-offs in a larger, more closed economy, the recent record of the Swiss National Bank in attaining monetary targets is not all that good. The *M1* target was overshot somewhat in 1976, again in 1977, and in 1978, by a very large margin; there was no target in 1979, but *M1* grew at a rate of 8.5 percent on a year-over-year basis, as compared to the 5 to 6 percent targets the central bank had been setting. The inflationary consequences of that rapid money growth seem to have caught up with Swiss monetary authorities now, and they are running a rather restrictive policy in 1980 and 1981. But it is not clear that the record would be all that different if the Swiss National Bank did not claim to follow a monetarist approach. It appears from the past record that the Swiss National Bank uses monetary targets only when they do not conflict with exchange rate objectives. Thus, the Swiss case should be characterized perhaps as monetary targeting with, at times, binding exchange rate constraints. But with exchange rate expectations apparently affecting the money supply data so strongly now, it is not clear that the Swiss case could be characterized as such any longer — and certainly not as a model of how to use monetary targets to control inflation. The *level* of *M1* has been declining for quite some time now, for example, yet the Swiss National Bank has announced additional restrictive policy actions in light of continued inflation problems.

In the final analysis, it appears that while monetary targeting can contribute greatly to curbing inflation, the reverse is not necessarily always true: a country like Switzerland might have a low inflation rate simply because of a very conservative attitude about fiscal and monetary matters in general, and because of the degrees of freedom to maintain restrictive policies with only limited effects on the domestic labor market. Such a country would probably have a good record on inflation even if it had never heard of setting monetary targets. Consider, for example, how well the Swiss National Bank handled the oil shock in 1974 and 1975 without monetary targets. The Swiss National Bank appears to fully recognize the inflationary consequences of excessive money growth. But the nature of its approach seems to be highly discretionary rather than a strong emphasis on monetary targets — its record in terms of attaining monetary targets is not good.

3 RECENT DEVELOPMENTS IN MONETARY CONTROL IN THE UNITED KINGDOM

William A. Allen

The monetary authorities in the United Kingdom have, since mid-1976, made a practice of announcing in advance target ranges for the growth of the money stock. This paper discusses some of the issues that have arisen in the practice of money stock targeting, including the question of the central bank's operational techniques. In particular, the recent changes in the Bank of England's open market operations are described and explained.

Choice of Target Aggregate

One of the most important decisions that has to be made in setting a monetary target is which aggregate is to be used for targeting purposes.

In principle the decision is straightforward. The use of money supply targets rather than interest rate targets as guidelines for monetary policy is based on the supposition that the relationship between money and income is more stable than the relationship between real autonomous expenditures and nominal income, partly because of the difficulty of estimating real interest rates. Accordingly, it makes sense to target that monetary aggregate which has the most stable statistical relationship with income.[1]

The main monetary and liquidity aggregates are defined in table 3–1. In practice, in the U.K., it has proved difficult to establish as a matter of fact which of the monetary aggregates has the most stable relationship with income. The existence of a relationship between money and income is normally interpreted as a consequence of the public having a determinate demand for money balances; and consequently, the focus of research on the relationship between the monetary aggregates and nominal incomes has been the demand functions for the various monetary aggregates.

The demand for *M3* (which differs from sterling *M3* in that it includes foreign currency deposits with banks in the U.K.)[2] has been the subject of extensive research in the Bank of England.[3] The conclusion drawn by the Bank from this research is that the demand for *M3*, regarded as a function of income or some other measure of transactions, and of interest rates, appeared to shift sharply upward by as much as 25 percent in 1972–73, and down again in 1974–75. This shift is thought to have been the result of two main influences.

The first of these influences arose from the fact that the package of reforms to the financial system implemented in 1971 ("Competition and Credit Control") freed the banks from ceilings on their lending. Immediately following these reforms, the desire of the banks to increase their lending rapidly led them to bid aggressively for deposits, and this in turn led to changes in the differentials between the yields on bank deposits and on other liquid assets. Much of the extra lending was to property (real estate) companies; and the rapid fall in property prices in 1974–75 caused some banks to suffer serious losses. These losses led an abrupt shift toward greater conservatism in the banks' lending policies and thus reduced the banks' need to bid aggressively for deposits.

The second influence was that it was frequently possible in 1972–73 for companies to make a profit by borrowing from banks on fixed rate overdraft and depositing the proceeds of the borrowing in the wholesale money markets. This was known as "round-tripping." It occurred in particular when the authorities were using their open market operations to reduce the amount of reserve assets outstanding;[4] the banks reacted to reserve asset squeezes by bidding for additional deposits to finance purchases of reserve assets from nonbanks ("liability management") rather than by selling assets, as in the textbook case. This practice led to money market rates rising well above the rather inflexible rates charged by banks for overdrafts, so that round-tripping became profitable.

In practice, neither of these influences can be adequately captured in the specification of demand-for-money functions. The interest rate differentials that made switching between bank deposits and other short-term assets profitable, as well as those that made round-tripping profitable, existed for so short a time in many cases that they were not recorded. In addition, the estimates of the amount of round-tripping available are not reliable.

More recently there appeared to be another upward shift in the demand for sterling *M3*. During the financial year 1980–81 sterling *M3* increased by nearly 18 percent, while nominal GDP rose by only 11½ percent. In some degree, the fall in the income velocity of sterling *M3* was the result of the ending of the Supplementary Special Deposits scheme in June 1980 (see the following section). That scheme has created an incentive for banking business to be "disintermediated" from the banking system — that is, for it to be carried on in such a way as to prevent its appearing in the banks' balance sheets. When the scheme was ended, bank business was "reintermediated" into the banks' balance sheets and sterling *M3* increased accordingly.

However, this rather artificial development did not explain by any means all of the reduction in velocity in 1980–81. The perhaps more fundamental cause was that the severe recession of that year put an acute strain on corporate finances, and forced many companies to look for external finance in order to be able to sustain operations. Borrowing by means of debenture (long-term fixed-interest debt) issues was unattractive because the prospect of a sharp reduction in the rate of inflation implied the prospect of a crippling increase in the real cost of servicing the debt. And poor profit prospects made equity (common stock) issues unattractive. The most attractive form of borrowing was from banks.

At the same time, personal incomes were booming, and the savings ratio was unusually high. The banks thus found themselves recycling a large volume of savings from the surplus personal sector to the deficit corporate sector, and one result of this was that sterling *M3* grew very rapidly. It was clear that the demand for sterling *M3* was not being determined simply by nominal national income and interest rates, but also by the financial imbalances between different sectors of the economy.

To conclude, the experience of the last decade does not provide strong grounds for belief in a stable short-term relationship between movements in *M3* or sterling *M3* and contemporaneous movements in nominal incomes.

The demand for *M1* has also been extensively researched, and in 1978

Table 3–1. Definitions of the Monetary and Liquidity Aggregates

Aggregate	*Definition*	*Size (mid-June 1981) (£ billions)*	
Monetary base (*MO*)	There are various definitions. The most commonly used one — the "wide monetary base" — consists of bankers' balances at the Bank of England, notes and coin held by the banks, and notes and coin in circulation with the public.	Bankers' balances	.5
		Notes and coin held by the banks	.9
		Notes and coin in circulation with the public	10.3
		"Wide monetary base"	11.7
M1	Notes and coin in circulation with the public plus private sector sterling sight deposits with banks in the U.K.	Notes and coin in circulation with the public	10.3
		Private sector sterling sight deposits	20.8
		M1	31.1
M2	Notes and coin in circulation with the public plus "retail deposits" held by the private and overseas sectors. Please see the section on Possible New Techniques for full definition.	Figures not yet available.	
Sterling *M3*	Notes and coin in circulation with the public plus all resident sterling deposits with banks in the U.K. (including certificates of deposit).	*M1*	31.1
		Private sector time deposits	36.3
		Public sector deposits	1.3
		Sterling *M3*	70.7

M3	Sterling *M3* plus resident foreign currency deposits with banks in the U.K. (including certificates of deposit)	Sterling *M3*	70.7
		Foreign currency deposits	9.6
		M3	80.2
PSL1	Private sector holdings of sterling *M3* but excluding deposits with an original maturity of over two years, plus private sector holdings of Treasury and commercial bills, private sector deposits with local authorities and finance houses and holdings of certificates of tax deposit, less finance houses' holdings of sterling *M3* and other instruments included in *PSL1*.	Private sector holdings of sterling *M*	68.5
		Private sector holdings of Treasury and commercial bills	.9 0.6
		Private sector deposits with local authorities and finance houses	4.0
		Certificates of tax deposit	1.2
		less finance houses' holdings of sterling *M3* and other instruments	−1.0
		PSL1	74.2
PSL2	*PSL1* plus private sector savings deposits and securities with nonbanks (mainly building societies) less savings institutions' holdings of instruments included in *PSL2* but not *PSL1*.	*PSL1*	74.2
		Private sector savings deposits and securities with non-banks	56.8
		less savings institutions' holdings of instruments included in *PSL2* but not *PSL1*	−3.6
			127.4

Table 3–2. Shifts in the Demand for *M1* Function

Financial Year	*Predicted Growth in M1 (% during year)*	*Actual Growth in M1 (% during year)*	*Difference*
1976–77	16.7	8.9	−7.8
1977–78	20.1	24.6	4.5
1978–79	12.2	13.3	1.1
1979–80	7.5	6.5	−1.0
1980–81	4.8	8.4	3.6

it appeared that a stable demand function for *M1* had been identified.[5] However, more recently *M1* has tended to wander away from the predictions of the equation. This is illustrated in table 3–2, which compares actual growth in *M1* over financial years since 1976–77 with the growth rates that the best equations available at the beginning of each financial year would have forecast, given perfect foreknowledge of all the explanatory variables in the demand equation.[6] It seems that there have been shifts in the demand for *M1* function, which have at times been much larger than the 2 percent margin between the middle and the outside of the target ranges for money supply growth. Of course, the band could be widened to accommodate possible shifts in the demand for money function, but the figures in the table suggest that a margin of as much as 7½ percent on either side of the middle of the target range might be needed.

In addition, the data for *M1* are less reliable in a number of respects than those for the monetary base and sterling *M3*. The figures depend more heavily, in percentage terms, than those for sterling *M3* on an arbitrary allocation of checks in the course of collection between deposits and loans; they are particularly subject to temporary effects arising from the timing of new issues on the capital market, and the seasonal adjustments are prone to larger revisions in percentage terms.

Finally, there remains the problem that the demand for *M1* is liable to be affected in the future by two unpredictable developments — the spreading practice of paying interest on *M1* balances (which tends to increase the demand for *M1* at given levels of income and interest rates), and the development of new payments techniques (which tends to reduce the demand for *M1*, other things being equal, if the balances out of which payments can be made under the new techniques are not included in *M1*).

More recently, the monetary base has been suggested as a possible target variable. The most commonly used definition of the monetary base — the "wide monetary base" — consists of bankers' balances at the Bank of England, notes and coin held by the banks, and notes and coin in circulation with the public.[7] Roughly 85 percent of the wide monetary base is accounted for by the third item, notes and coin in circulation with the public, so the stability of the demand for wide base depends largely on the stability of the demand for notes and coins. The control of the monetary base under alternative definitions is discussed in the third section.

Research conducted in the Bank has shown that the estimated interest elasticity of demand for notes and coin has appeared to increase as the estimation period has lengthened.[8] Equations estimated over the period 1964–1979 show no significant interest elasticity, but when the estimation period is extended to include 1980, an interest elasticity that is statistically significant at the 95 percent level appears. The statistical explanation of this fact is that high interest rates coincided with slow growth of the public's currency holdings in 1980, but it is not certain that the latter was caused by the former rather than by other factors (e.g., increased use of credit cards and checks for payment purposes).

It would, in principle, be possible to include the use of noncurrency media of payment as an explanatory variable in the demand equation. However, if targets were to be set for the monetary base, they would have to be constructed using assumptions about the future values of this variable.

Table 3–3, which is analogous to table 3–2, shows shifts in the public's demand for currency over financial years since 1976–77. As in the case of *M1*, it appears that the shifts in the demand function have been too great to be accommodated within a target band with a margin of 2 percent on either side of the midpoint of the range.

Because these demand-for-money studies have not given a clear answer to the "which aggregate?" question, a slightly different approach to

Table 3–3. Shifts in the Demand for Notes and Coin

Financial Years	*Predicted Growth in Notes and Coin (% during year)*	*Actual Growth in Notes and Coin (% during year)*	*Difference*
1976–77	9.9	11.3	1.4
1977–78	11.1	16.4	5.3
1978–79	12.5	16.4	3.9
1979–80	12.6	6.9	−5.7
1980–81	10.8	5.9	−4.9

the question has been adopted. This, inspired by the work of Tinsley, Spindt, and Friar (1980), is to investigate the degree to which shifts in the various monetary aggregates and their components contain information about future inflation and nominal income growth. The results of work on this approach, reported by Mills (1981), indicate that the broader aggregates contain more information about future prices and nominal incomes than do the narrow ones. Figure 3–1 shows that there was indeed in 1971–75 a very close relationship between movements in the growth rate of sterling *M3* and movements in the rate of inflation two years later. No similar lead relationship existed in the case of *M1*, or notes and coin in circulation with the public, as is shown by figure 3–2. The dramatic nature of the events of 1971–75 and the closeness of the correlation between sterling *M3* and future inflation were important influences, though not the only influences, in the decision that *M3* or sterling *M3* should be the target monetary aggregate. However, the events of 1971–75 appear to have been unique: there is no other episode in U.K. monetary history in the last century in which broad money gave so accurate a prediction of future inflation (see figure 3–3).

One theoretical basis of this alternative approach may be regarded as a generalization of the theoretical basis for the demand for money approach. If it is assumed that money acts as a buffer stock, and that agents do not react immediately to excesses or deficiencies in their actual money holdings in relation to demand, then it will not necessarily be possible to estimate a demand for money function in the normal way. However, in spite of this, if it is assumed that the demand for money reasserts itself in the longer run, then changes in money balances may nevertheless be expected to have a delayed effect on nominal incomes.[9]

Given the lack of any clear indication either from demand for money functions or from the relationships between the growth rates of the various aggregates and subsequent inflation, the factor that turned the decision about the target aggregate in favor of a broad aggregate was that it is possible to account for changes in sterling *M3* — the total domestic sterling deposit liabilities of the banking system — in terms of changes in the various categories of assets of the banking system and of nondeposit liabilities — the latter item generally being small and stable. The accounting framework is set out in table 3–4. Monetary growth has as its counterpart on the assets side of the banks' balance sheets three main elements: that part of the budget deficit not financed by sales of public sector debt to the nonbank private sector (lines 1 and 2), sterling lending by the banking sector to the private sector (line 3) and the influence of external transactions (line 4).

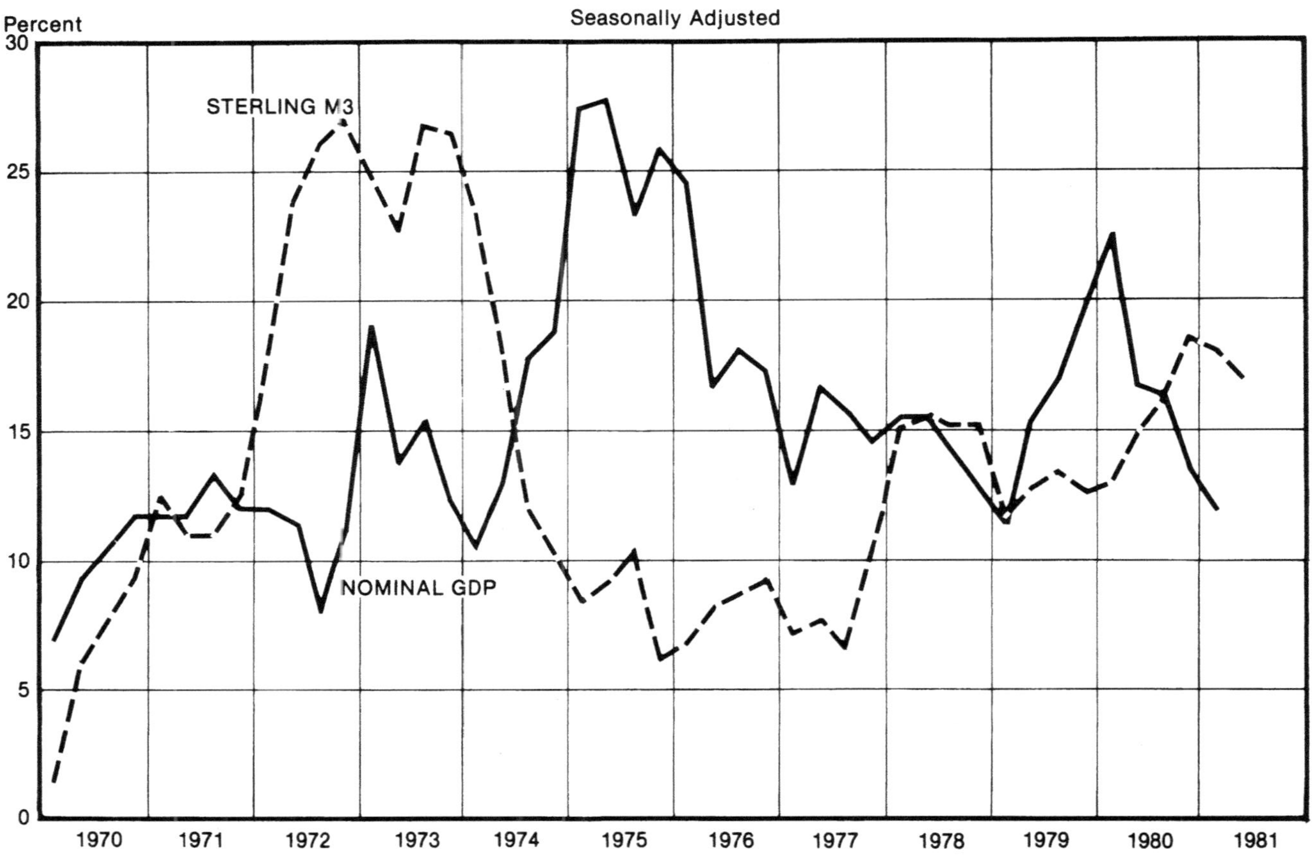

Figure 3–1 Annual Percentage Changes of Sterling *M3* and GDP (seasonally adjusted)

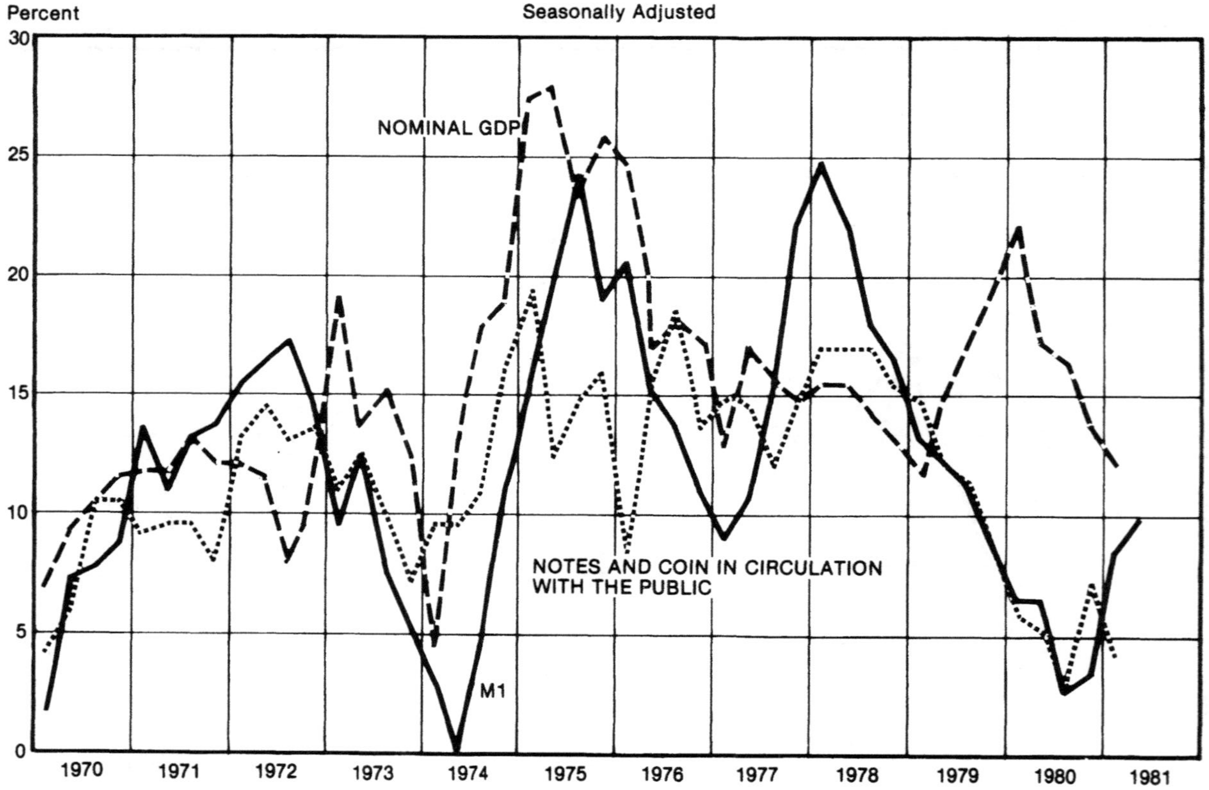

Figure 3–2 Annual Percentage Changes of *M1* and Notes and Coin in Circulation with the Public (seasonally adjusted)

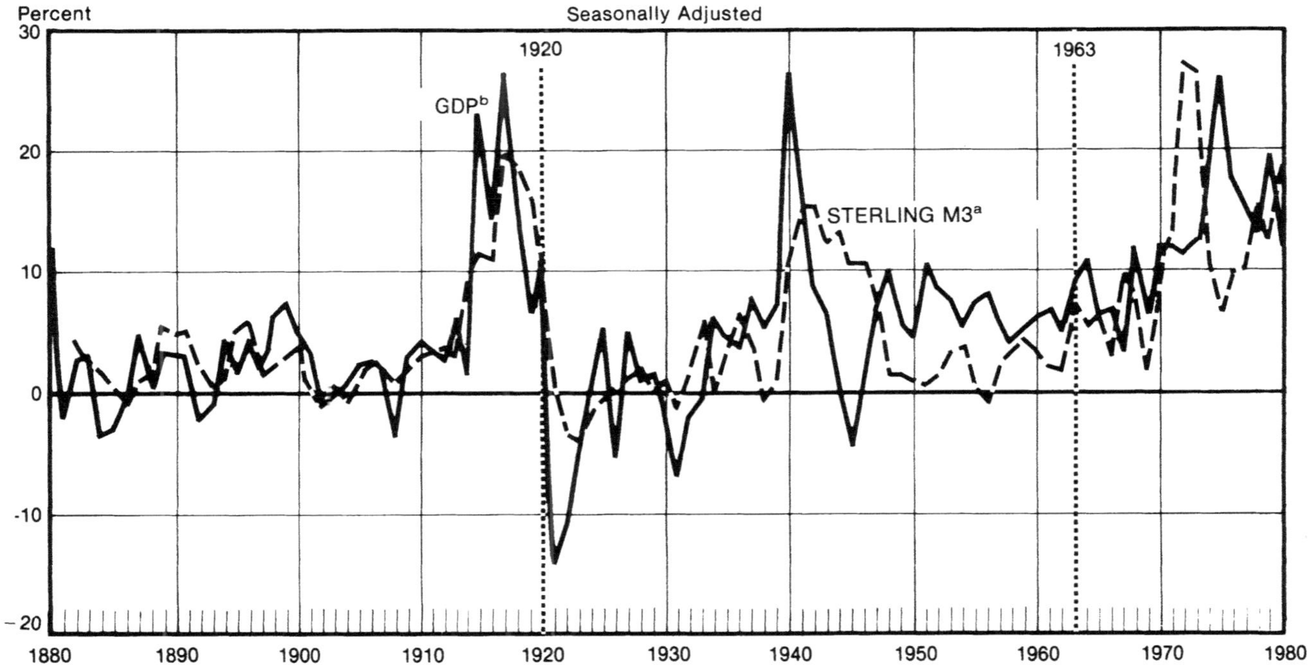

[a]1880–1962: Notes and coin in circulation, plus total bank deposits (annual averages), from Sheppard (1971), table 3.3; end of 1962–end of 1980: sterling *M3* (end-of-year figures, seasonally adjusted) statistics published by Bank of England.
[b]GDP (at market prices); 1880–1955.

Figure 3–3 Annual Percentage Changes of Broad Money and National Income — 1880–1980

Table 3–4. Counterparts to Growth in Sterling *M3* (in sterling billions)

	Financial Year 1980–81
1. Public sector borrowing requirement (budget deficit)	13.2
2. Sales of public sector debt to non-bank private sector (increase −)	−10.9
3. Sterling lending by banking sector to private sector	9.3
4. External influences[a]	0.4
5. Nondeposit liabilities (increase −)	− 1.3
6. Total = increase in sterling *M3*	10.7

[a] Equals the sum of the following items:

Change in reserves (increase +)

Public sector foreign currency borrowing (increase −)

Overseas purchases of public sector debt (increase −)

Overseas residents' sterling deposits (increase −)

Banks' sterling lending overseas (increase +)

Banks' foreign currency deposits, net of foreign currency loans (increase −)

This description does not, of course, imply that the three main elements are independent influences on sterling *M3*. Indeed, it is quite clear that they are interdependent. Nevertheless, it can, in some circumstances, indicate what policy measures are most appropriate if the growth of sterling *M3* is off target. For example, if there is a large unfunded budget deficit, and sterling *M3* is overshooting, then in the short run it is natural to try to find ways of funding more of the deficit, perhaps by issuing new kinds of government debt. Moreover, the evolution of the counterparts can give an early impression of general economic developments — in particular the financial position of the private sector, and the balance of payments.[10]

Techniques of Control

The classic weapon central banks have at their disposal is the discount rate; and, until recently, announced variations in the Bank of England's minimum lending rate (MLR) had a central role in monetary policy. After the adoption of monetary targets, the authorities aimed to set MLR in such a way as to be consistent with the achievement of the monetary target. When judgments made at the beginning of the financial year were proved wrong by unexpected developments, the authorities were ready to change MLR in response to the unexpected developments.[11] However, the effects of changes in interest rates on sterling *M3* have proved slow and uncertain. Some 60 percent of sterling *M3* is interest bearing, and that part of sterling *MS* that is noninterest bearing is most easily switched into interest bearing sterling *M3* when interest rates rise. Rather, the effects of interest rate changes on sterling *M3* have to work indirectly. If increases in interest rates reduce loan demand, then the banks may bid less aggressively for deposits. The interest differential between wholesale bank liabilities and other short-term assets then moves against bank deposits, and the growth rate of sterling *M3* will be dampened. And, if increases in interest rates stimulate government debt sales, the banks will lose deposits. If the banks have spare liquidity, they may accept this loss of deposits — that is, they may not attempt to replace the lost deposits through the wholesale money markets. However, it is not clear that increases in interest rates do succeed in reducing loan demand in all circumstances — in any case, the effect is slow.

In addition, the announced MLR attracted a degree of public attention that had become detrimental to monetary control. Declared changes in MLR tended to be political events of considerable significance for the government. This carried the risk that the actual timing and amount of changes in MLR would not be the ones most appropriate to the needs of the monetary situation. Of course, it was possible for the authorities, without changing MLR, to exert some influence, through open market operations, on market interest rates; but there were difficulties with this, as follows. First, MLR was taken by the markets as a benchmark for interest rates at maturities much longer than the longest maturity (7 days) at which it was customary for the Bank to lend at MLR to the discount houses. Second, the banks relate their overdraft charges to their base rates, which, in general, they change only when MLR changes, so that changes in money market rates with MLR left unchanged had no effect on overdraft borrowers (overdrafts account for about a third of bank loans). Finally, if money market rates rise above base rates by enough, the round-tripping operations already described become profitable — companies borrow on overdraft and redeposit the proceeds in the wholesale markets. In these circumstances, a rise in interest rates may have the effect of increasing sterling *M3*, at least for a while. As is explained in the section on "Changes in the Monetary System," it is hoped that the suspension of MLR will lead to a greater market influence on the determination of the term structure of interest rates, and specifically that it will cause the banks to charge more flexible rates for overdraft borrowing.

The object of the Supplementary Special Deposits scheme (the "corset") introduced for the first time in December 1973, was to eliminate the scope for liability management and round-tripping by imposing harsh penalties on the banks if their interest-bearing eligible liabilities grew at more than a certain rate. The scheme was withdrawn in January 1975, but was reimplemented in December 1976 (until June 1977) and in June 1978 (until June 1980). In practice, although the scheme probably had certain favorable announcement effects on the first two occasions, it represented a severe constraint on the normal activities of the banks only in the third of these episodes. Even then, the banks were able to circumvent the constraint quite easily, for example, by persuading borrowers to issue commercial bills, accepting (i.e., guaranteeing) the bills, and offering them to depositors.

It would, of course, have been fairly simple for the authorities to close some of the loopholes in the scheme — for example, by making acceptances part of the aggregate subject to control. But, after the removal of exchange controls in October 1979, it would not have been possible to prevent disintermediation via the Euro-sterling market. In other words, there would have been no way of preventing banking business whose conduct was inhibited in London by the corset scheme from being done in financial centers in continental Europe. Bearing in mind that, in the absence of exchange control, nothing could be done to close this loophole permanently, the authorities saw no point in closing the other loopholes. The commercial bill loophole at least had the virtue that the extent of its use was regularly measured.

Possible New Techniques

In November 1979, the Chancellor of the Exchequer in the new Conservative government, which had been elected in May 1979, announced that he had set in hand a review of methods of controlling the money supply. Accordingly, in March 1980, a consultation paper entitled "Monetary Control" was issued by the Bank of England and the Treasury. The debate that followed the publication of the consultation paper was mainly focused on the issue of monetary base control. The debate ended in the autumn of 1980 and was followed by the announcement of certain changes in the Bank's methods of operation in the short-term money markets.

The purpose of the remainder of this section is to describe the conclusions drawn by the Bank of England from the debate on monetary base control and to explain the changes in methods of operation.

Monetary base control means the use of open market operations to aim at a target for some subset of the liabilities of the central bank. One possible form of monetary base control involves setting a target for the wide monetary base, as described in the first section of this paper. The discussion in this section, however, is about forms of monetary base control in which variations in the monetary base are intended to exert their influence mainly by affecting the behavior of the banks. In other words, it relates to forms of monetary base control in which the base is defined in such a way that the reserves held by the banking system represent a quantitatively important part of the base.

It is assumed that the demand for the monetary base is related predictably to the size of the banks' liabilities, or to nominal incomes, or to both. This requires that the marginal yield of these liabilities is markedly lower than the market rate of return, because, if it were not, the demand for the monetary base would become highly sensitive to the interest rate differential between the monetary base and other short-term assets, and there would be no predictable relationship between the size of the monetary base and the banks' liabilities and/or nominal incomes.

The mechanism of control is as follows. The size of the monetary base indicates the tightness or ease of monetary policy. A reduction in the supply of the monetary base can be achieved only through sales of securities by the monetary authorities. These sales will drive up interest rates, both nominal and real, by some finite amount, and that in turn will exert contractionary effects on bank deposits and on the economy generally. In addition to this, some advocates of monetary base control have suggested that there is a second mechanism, which works through the effect of the announcement of targets for the monetary base on the behavior of the banks. The suggestion is that the knowledge that the quantity of the monetary base will be strictly limited, and that the cost of borrowing will therefore rise if the demand for monetary base increases, will induce the banks to adjust their lending strategies in such a way that they conform more nearly with the official targets for money and inflation. Only experience can tell whether or not this mechanism is effective, though most of those consulted on this in the U.K. have expressed skepticism about it.

Considered in its pure form, monetary base control is a polar opposite to interest rate targeting, in that it involves attaching no weight to interest rate changes in conducting open market operations while pure interest rate targeting involves attaching no weight to the monetary base. Any move toward monetary base control must therefore be a move away from interest rate smoothing. An important question for policymakers is how much interest rate volatility is likely to be induced by moves toward monetary base control.

It is perhaps worth reviewing briefly the reasons why this question is important. The most general reason is that interest rates are prices, and the function of prices in market economies is to give signals to the economy that can influence behavior in a socially desirable way. Other things being equal, more-volatile prices give less clear signals than less-volatile prices. Second, more-volatile interest rates increase the risks involved in maturity transformation. This may mean either more severe stress on financial institutions — something undesirable in itself since the smooth running of the financial system depends on depositors' faith in the soundness of financial institutions — or else a curtailment of the supply of financial services involving maturity transformation offered to the economy. Both these alternatives, considered by themselves, involve some reduction in welfare. In other words, the authorities are obliged to regard interest rate volatility as a cost, to be set against the benefits that may accrue from monetary base control. Finally, recent experience has been that exchange rate movements have tended to follow nominal interest rate differentials. If this were to continue, it might be feared that monetary base control would induce exchange rate volatility as well as interest rate volatility. Insofar as interest rate volatility is regarded as having adverse consequences, the second mechanism described above through which monetary base control might work, by affecting the behavior of the banks, is potentially very important. However, as already mentioned, only experience can tell whether it is effective.

The points made in the preceding paragraphs apply to monetary base control in general. However, as the consultation paper pointed out, monetary base control can be either mandatory or nonmandatory. The two forms raise different issues, which are discussed in turn in the following two subsections.

Mandatory Monetary Base Control

Under mandatory monetary base control, the banks are obliged to observe a minimum reserve ratio against either all, or some subset, of their deposits. The authorities use open market operations to affect the reserve base of the system, and thereby hope to influence the total of deposits against which the reserve requirement is levied.[12]

The conclusions of the Bank from the debate as regards mandatory monetary base control were as follows. The first conclusion was that a mandatory reserve requirement amounts in some degree to a tax on banking. This applies even if a market rate of interest is paid on required reserve holdings, since, as already noted, submarket rates must be paid on marginal reserve holdings. The requirement therefore offers an incentive to the banks to disintermediate their business. While it is possible, as it was with the corset, for the authorities to prevent some forms of disintermediation, since the removal of exchange controls in October 1979, there have been no means by which the authorities can permanently prevent a shift of wholesale banking business from London to the Eurosterling centers.

The second conclusion is that, even if the problem of disintermediation could be ignored, it would be imprudent to use mandatory monetary base control with reserve requirements levied against a set of deposits as wide as the set included in sterling *M3*. The reason is that, as already mentioned, the effects of interest rate changes on sterling *M3* are slow and uncertain. This remark applies as well to aggregates broader than sterling *M3*. If monetary base control works by means of induced changes in interest rates, then it is likely that the application of base control to sterling *M3* or a broader aggregate would result in frequent upward or downward spirals in interest rates. The induced changes in the monetary aggregate or the demand for reserves would be weak because these aggregates are not very responsive to interest rate movements in the short run. If the second of the above mechanisms — the effect of monetary base control on the behavior of the banks — could be relied upon to ensure that the growth of the broad target aggregate was held in line with the preannounced growth of the monetary base without interest rate instability, then no problem need arise. However, this mechanism has not been tested and it would be imprudent to rely on it alone to secure the success of a new system of monetary control. In practice, the result of the attempt to use base control on a broad aggregate would almost certainly be disintermediation of banking business by some means, probably combined with greater volatility of interest rates.

Nevertheless, these two points do not rule out mandatory monetary base control. They do indicate, however, that the technique should be used only on an aggregate that is interest sensitive and represents deposits created by banking business that is capable of being disintermediated only at considerable cost. As already explained, sterling *M3* and broader aggregates are not suitable for mandatory monetary base control; and neither is *M1*, since a substantial proportion of *M1* consists of wholesale interest bearing sight deposits which could be disintermediated without great difficulty. The idea of using noninterest-bearing *M1* as an object for mandatory monetary base control was rejected because of the uncertainty and unpredictability of the speed with which the practice of paying interest on demand deposits will spread. Indeed, if mandatory base control related to noninterest-bearing *M1* were introduced, the banks might choose to offer interest payments on sight deposits in order to avoid the tax implicit in the minimum reserve requirement.

Partly because neither *M1* nor noninterest-bearing *M1* provide a clear and satisfactory measure of transactions deposits, the authorities have asked the banks to start supplying statistics of "retail deposits," which, when added to the public's currency holdings, will comprise a new aggregate to be known as *M2*.[13] It is hoped that the figures will provide some idea of the size of retail transactions balances, and that there will prove to be a stable relationship between the *M2* aggregate on the one hand, and nominal incomes and the level of interest rates on the other. The definition of retail deposits is to be as follows:

1. all noninterest-bearing sight deposits
2. all other checkable accounts up to £100,000
3. all accounts up to £100,000 from which standing orders, direct debit mandates, or other regular payments may be made
4. all accounts of up to £100,000 with a residual maturity of 14 days or less
5. accounts up to £100,000 that can be withdrawn in cash, or used automatically or on the holder's instruction to make frequent transfers of funds to an account covered by 1, 2, 3, or 4 above without significant penalty. Loss of interest for 14 days or less would not normally be considered significant. Accounts are included only if three or more withdrawals or transfers per month are permitted, legally or by common practice, but inclusion should not depend on the number of withdrawals or transfers actually made.

Apart from the considerable intrinsic interest of these statistics, collecting them will enable the authorities to learn something about the effectiveness of a possible mandatory monetary base control scheme aimed at control of *M2*, by investigating the stability of the demand function for *M2*, and estimating the size of the interest elasticity of demand for *M2*. If the interest-elasticity were to prove to be very small, then there would be a danger that monetary base control applied to retail deposits would cause violent fluctuations in interest rates, while a very large elasticity would imply that other assets were such close substitutes for *M2* that control of *M2* alone was pointless.

Nonmandatory Monetary Base Control

In nonmandatory systems of monetary base control, such as that in use in Switzerland, the banks are left free to hold noninterest-bearing reserves in whatever amount they think appropriate. Again, the authorities use open market operations to keep the reserve base of the system on or close to some desired path. They may regard control of the base as sufficient by itself to secure control of the rate of inflation (as in Switzerland); or, alternatively, they may regard control of the base as a means of controlling broader monetary aggregates, *M1*, *M2*, or *M3*, control of which is necessary and/or sufficient for adequate control of the rate of inflation. The difference between these two approaches is that in the latter case, but not the former, the target for the growth of the monetary base would presumably be altered if the broader aggregates were to grow at a rate significantly different from that which had previously been expected.

It is reasonable to suppose that, if the banks had a stable nonzero demand for reserves that depended on the size of some part of their balance sheets and on the level of interest rates (i.e., the marginal opportunity cost of holding reserves), then, in a nonmandatory system, control of the monetary base would achieve control of bank deposits and control of this broad aggregate would in turn be a necessary condition for control of the price level. The issue of nonmandatory monetary base control therefore hangs on the nature of the banks' demand for reserves.

In fact, there is no basis for knowledge of what reserves banks in the U.K. would want to hold if left free to choose.[14] Under the previous arrangements, the London clearing banks were required to hold 1½ percent of their eligible liabilities in the form of noninterest-bearing deposits at the Bank of England. However, this was an *average* requirement — shortfalls were permitted provided they were made up later. The behavior of the banks under the previous arrangements gave no guide to how they might behave under nonmandatory monetary base control, under which shortfalls (i.e., borrowing on overdraft from the central bank) would be heavily penalized. Banks' behavior under the arrangements recently instituted may give some clues as to how they would behave under nonmandatory monetary base control.

Of course, the example of Switzerland, where nonmandatory monetary base control has been employed by the authorities, is available. But there are reasons for suspecting that the differences in institutional structure between the financial systems of Switzerland and the U.K. may mean that banks in the U.K. would behave differently from Swiss banks under nonmandatory monetary base control, although of course, in the absence of any direct experience, it is not possible to be certain how banks in the U.K. would behave.

The reasons for this suspicion are as follows. Banks hold reserves as insurance against illiquidity. In the U.K., where the government banks with the Bank of England and accounts for by far the larger part of the Bank of England's business, it is broadly true to say that the commercial banks as a group lose cash on days when the government has a surplus and gain cash on days when it has a deficit. These daily surpluses and deficits frequently exceed the amount of clearing bank balances held at the Bank of England. The object of official operations in the money markets is to buy or sell bills or to lend money in amounts sufficient to provide just that amount of reserves that enables the banks to achieve their target balances at the end of the day. If these operations could be conducted with perfect accuracy, the sum of bankers' balances at the end of each day would be on target.

Of course, this is not the same thing as ensuring that each bank individually is able to achieve its target balance. It might be expected that, if nonmandatory monetary base control were introduced, banks would want to hold reserves against the risk of illiquidity even in conditions where they knew that enough reserves would be available for the system as a whole. In other words, Bank A would hold reserves not as insurance against a "system drain" of cash affecting Bank A along with other banks, but as insurance against a drain of cash from Bank A matched by an inflow of cash to the other banks.

However, it is impossible to be sure that banks in the U.K. would behave in this way under nonmandatory monetary base control. The tradition of large-scale interbank borrowing and lending is well established in London — there is a very active interbank deposit market — and it is entirely possible that instead of holding noninterest-bearing reserves as insurance against illiquidity, clearing banks would instead rely on their ability to borrow when they had a deficit in the clearing from the other clearing banks with the corresponding surplus, secure in the knowledge that a "system drain" would be prevented by official operations. Alternatively, the clearing banks might settle debts among themselves in Treasury bills, for example. In other words, the banks might not hold reserves in significant or stably determined amounts under nonmandatory monetary base control, and official control of the monetary base might, consequently, not imply control of any aggregate of bank deposits.

In practice, it is not possible for the authorities to offset precisely government surpluses and deficits through their open market operations, because uncertainty about the balance between the government's disbursements over the whole day and its revenues over the whole day persists right up to the end of each day. Nevertheless, if the banks were willing to rely on settlement of debts among themselves by some means not involving their balances at the Bank of England, the amount of those balances that they choose to hold would be determined by the likely size of system drains (i.e., official errors in forecasting government surpluses and deficits). It is clear that the likely size of these errors need bear no necessary relationship either to broader monetary aggregates or to nominal incomes; they are more likely to be related to the unpredictable variability of the government's daily surplus or deficit. This would be true even if the authorities abandoned their objective of preventing system drains altogether.

The preceding few paragraphs have highlighted one area of uncertainty about the demand for the monetary base under a nonmandatory system of monetary base control. The other principal uncertainty relates to the interest-elasticity of demand for the monetary base. As already mentioned, the price signal induced by a squeeze on the monetary base is a rise in the interest rate. If the demand for the base were interest-inelastic, then there would be danger that monetary base control would entail large fluctuations in interest rates.

The Changes in the Monetary System

As the previous section indicated, the authorities concluded that they did not have sufficient knowledge about the monetary system to be able to make a judgment about what the costs and benefits of monetary base control would be. Accordingly, the changes that have been made in the monetary system have been designed in such a way that the operation of the system after the changes will provide more information about how monetary base control might work. The changes do not amount to the adoption of monetary base control, nor do they imply that monetary base control will be adopted. However, they are consistent with the future adoption of monetary base control; and quite apart from the question of monetary base control, they are considered desirable in their own right.

One change has already been mentioned — that the banks are being asked to provide figures of retail deposits, in order to establish whether retail deposits would be a suitable denominator for a system of mandatory monetary base control. The nature of the cash-holding requirement placed on the banks has been altered. In the past, the requirement was on the London clearing banks alone, to maintain an average level of 1½ percent of their eligible liabilities in the form of bankers' balances at the Bank of England. The requirement has since been extended to all banks, and now specifies that banks should hold ½ percent of their eligible liabilities in the form of a nonoperational, frozen, noninterest-bearing balance at the Bank of England. In addition, the banks may hold in separate accounts whatever operational noninterest-bearing balances they wish. The purpose of the nonoperational balances is purely to provide an income for the Bank of England (which does not profit from the note issue); it has no monetary control function. The behavior of the operational balances should provide information about the banks' voluntary demand for reserves, which will be of obvious use in assessing the merits of nonmandatory monetary base control.

Important changes have been made in the Bank's technique of operating in the money markets. The object of the changes has been to secure a greater market influence on the determination of the term structure of short-term interest rates, and to a more limited extent, at least in the initial stages, on the level of rates. The nature of the changes is as follows. The Bank's dealings in the money market now overwhelmingly take the form of open market operations, that is, purchases and sales of bills (Treasury bills, eligible commercial bills, and local authority bills), rather than direct lending to the discount houses. Moreover, rather than, as in the past, declaring rates at which it was prepared to buy bills, the Bank has adopted the practice of inviting offers of bills, and of basing the decision as to which offers to accept partly at least on the estimated shortage of cash in the system. Thirdly, the authorities' objective of deliberately creating a shortage of funds in the money market every week, in order to be able to have a greater influence on interest rates, has been abandoned. These changes mean that the interest rates at which the Bank supplies cash to the market, or withdraws cash from the market, are no longer directly administered by the Bank.

It is a necessary concomitant of these changes that the Bank should abandon the practice of continuously posting a discount rate. The Bank's minimum lending rate (MLR) has therefore been suspended — although the Bank has retained the option, for use in exceptional circumstances, to announce a minimum lending rate to be maintained for a finite unspecified period. However, official interest rate objectives have not been abandoned. The authorities now aim to ensure that very-short-term interest rates are kept within a band of finite range, the position and width of which are unpublished. There is no objective for longer-term rates, however. The balance between official and market influence on the level of interest rates is capable of being varied under the new system; the aim at the outset has, for reasons of caution, been to maintain a significant official influence, but there is scope for evolution toward a greater element of market determination of interest rates. It is hoped that changes in the band, being unannounced, will not normally be important political events in the same way as changes in MLR, and this should do something to reduce the "bias for delay" in interest rate changes. Moreover, there should be some induced effects on bank behavior. Banks will no longer be able to use MLR as a guideline for their own interest rates. This may lead to more flexible pricing of overdrafts, which might help to eliminate round-tripping; and, more important, it may mean that the effects of official operations in the money markets are more quickly communicated to the economy at large. Finally, it is possible, although not certain, that heightened uncertainty about official lending rates will make the banks more cautious in their own lending operations.

Another change is the abolition of the required reserve asset ratio. As already noted, any squeeze, whether deliberately engineered by the authorities or not, on the reserve asset base simply resulted in liability management by the banks and the opening up of opportunities for round-tripping.

The Bank is, as has already been described, to concentrate its open market operations in the bill market rather than on direct lending to the discount houses. An alternative and at first sight more natural medium for official operations might be the interbank deposit market. The Bank could simply place or take deposits in whatever amounts were considered appropriate. This option was considered but was rejected, for reasons connected with the structure of the U.K. banking system. There is a small number of large clearing banks which have extensive branch networks and which account for a very large percentage of retail deposits. These few banks generally have surplus funds to lend in the interbank market, while the many other banks are normally obliged to borrow in the interbank market to fund their lending. Considering these conditions, the authorities are concerned that if they were to conduct their open market operations in the interbank market, the process of interest rate determination would not be that of a free market, but that it would be subject to undue influence from the small number of clearing banks that normally consititute the lending side of the market.

For this reason, the Bank is anxious to continue operating in the bill market through the discount houses. The problem is to ensure that the bill market remains large enough to accommodate official operations. The membership of the group of banks whose acceptances are eligible for rediscount at the Bank has been widened, and those banks that are members of the group have undertaken to hold on average a certain percentage of their eligible liabilities in the form of deposits with the discount houses,[15] subject to a fixed minimum percentage, in order to enable the houses to continue to make a market in bills. This requirement is a kind of insurance policy designed to ensure that the bill market survives. If in the light of experience it becomes clear that the bill market can survive without the requirement or with a less stringent requirement, then this aspect of the new arrangements will be modified.

What Next?

Recent discussions of monetary control in the U.K. have been remarkable for the number of unanswered questions they have thrown up. Some of the unanswered questions about monetary base control may be answered by the experience of operating the monetary system following the described changes. However, there is a fundamental question relating to money supply control that is largely unrelated to the new arrangements for official operations in the money markets. This relates to the choice of target aggregate.

The first section of this chapter described the considerations involved in choosing a suitable target aggregate. Events since monetary targeting was adopted five years ago in the U.K. have not demonstrated convincingly that a narrow aggregate would have been better as a target aggregate than a broad one. However, the difficulties of controlling an aggregate as broad as sterling *M3*, by whatever means, are formidable. There is strong evidence that the banks in the U.K. are efficient and competitive in relation to other financial institutions and that they are anxious and able to increase their share of the market in the provision of financial services, and indeed to increase the size of that market. In the field of lending to the personal sector, banks have gained share over the last few years at the expense of other financial intermediaries, and banks have had a near monopoly of corporate lending during the current recession (though it is true that the monopoly may be coming to an end). Moreover, the address by the Chairman of Barclays to the 1981 Annual General Meeting contains the following revealing passage:

> What then does the future hold in store for the clearing bankers? I believe we must be prepared to think of ourselves as universal providers of finance, at least in this country. With an extensive and expensive network of branches, we

> must make sure that we are able to offer every form of finance for all our citizens and this will certainly include a mortgage. Even more important than the provision of finance, is the ability to compete effectively for savings and we must make sure that we find means of marketing new schemes as they arise.

This extension of the scope of the activities of the banks is bound to involve a larger increase in sterling *M3* than would otherwise have occurred. In this light, it is difficult to know what should be the attitude of the authorities to the aggression, enterprise, and competitiveness of the banks. Two alternative, and diametrically opposed, attitudes are possible, as follows.

1. The accumulation of financial liabilities by banks is not inherently more inflationary than the accumulation of similar liabilities by nonbank financial institutions. The enterprise of the banks is a national asset and it would be entirely wrong to try to stifle it in the name of monetary control. Monetary control should not be synonymous with containing the size of the banking system; it should consist either (a) of controlling a narrow aggregate, or (b) of controlling a price (e.g., exchange rate or real interest rates), or else (c) of controlling an aggregate encompassing the liabilities not only of the banks, but of other institutions as well. The last of these options might, however, still cramp the bank's style somewhat, and is therefore the least desirable.
2. Research has shown that sterling *M3* is as good an indicator of future inflation as any other monetary aggregate. The overriding priority for economic policy is to reduce the rate of inflation, and this entails limiting the deposit-creating activities of the banks. It may be true that this involves stifling enterprise, but that is just too bad.

The choice is an unpleasant and difficult one, but it is one that will have to be made before a durable system of monetary control can be established.

Notes

1. Poole (1970) shows that an exception might be made if, in the *IS–LM* framework, the correlation coefficients between the shifts in the *LM* curves based on the various aggregates and the shifts in the *IS* curve were markedly different, but there is no evidence that this is the case in the U.K.

2. Until the abolition of Exchange Control in October, 1979, residents' holdings of foreign currency deposits were severely restricted by law.

3. See Goodhart and Crockett (1970); Price (1972); and Hacche (1974).

4. Under "Competition and Credit Control," the banks were required to hold "reserve assets" in amounts not less than a fixed percentage of their eligible liabilities (broadly, their total sterling liabilities plus net liabilities in foreign currencies). For most of its life, the fixed percentage was 12½ percent, but lately it was reduced to 10 percent and at times 8 percent. "Reserve assets" consisted of call money deposited with the discount houses and listed brokers, Treasury and local authority bills, commercial bills (subject to the limitation that commercial bills held in excess of 2 percent of eligible liabilities would not qualify as reserve assets) and government securities with less than a year to maturity.

5. See Coghlan (1978).

6. More information on demand for *M1* equations can be found in Appendix 1 to this chapter by J.M. Trundle, which is available from the author.

7. See the *Bank of England Quarterly Bulletin* (March 1981) for a fuller description of the monetary base and for statistics.

8. This is documented in an appendix to this chapter on the public's demand for notes and coin by P.V. Temperton, which is available from the author.

9. This approach was first suggested as an explanation of the apparent instability of the demand for sterling *M3* in the early 1970s by Artis and Lewis (1976).

10. It is, of course, possible to account equally neatly for changes in the wide monetary base in terms of changes in the various categories of assets held by the monetary authorities. At the time the decision was taken, in the mid-1970s, the idea of controlling the monetary base for its own sake had not been widely advocated in the U.K. To target monetary base would have seemed like a retreat to the doctrines of the currency school, which had long been out of favor.

11. The exception to this was in 1980–81, when MLR was reduced despite an overshooting of the target for sterling *M3*. The reason for the decision to overrule the monetary target was that the authorities believed that both the supply and the demand functions for *M3* had shifted, and, as mentioned above, that consequently the rate of growth of sterling *M3* was giving a misleading impression of the tightness of monetary policy.

12. The position is obviously more complicated in systems like those in operation in the U.S.A. and in Germany, in which different percentage reserve requirements are levied against deposits of different kinds.

13. This is not the same as the *M2* series which was introduced in 1970 (see "The Stock of Money," *Bank of England Quarterly Bulletin*, September 1970, pp. 320–326). Publication of this series ended in December 1971. A large percentage of building society shares and deposits are similar in nature to retail deposits held with banks, and it may well prove to be the case that a better relationship with incomes and interest rates will be obtained by adding these building society liabilities to *M2* rather than by looking at *M2* alone. The new *M2* series represents the first attempt in the U.K. to construct a monetary aggregate according to an economic rather than an institutional concept.

14. They were free in the interwar period, and on make-up days maintained a ratio between reserves (including till money) and deposits of about 10 percent. However, the large banks reported on different days of the week, and the figures were subject to heavy window dressing. In any case, conditions have changed so much since then that it would be unreasonable to draw any conclusions for current policy from the interwar period.

15. Also, money brokers and gilt-edged jobbers.

References

Artis, M.J., and Lewis, M.K. "The Demand for Money in the United Kingdom 1963–1973." *Manchester School* (June 1976).

Coghlan, R.T. "A Transactions Demand for Money." *Bank of England Quarterly Bulletin* (March 1978).

Feinstein, C.H. *Statistical Table of National Income, Expenditure and Output of the U.K., 1885–1965*. Cambridge University Press, 1972.

Goodhart, C.A.E., and Crockett, A.D. "The Importance of Money." *Bank of England Quarterly Bulletin* (June 1970).

Hacche, G. "The Demand for Money in the United Kingdom: Experience Since 1971." *Bank of England Quarterly Bulletin* (September 1974).

Mills, T.C. "The Informational Content of Monetary Aggregates in the U.K." Unpublished Bank of England document, 1981.

Poole, W. "Optimal Choice of Monetary Policy Instruments in a Simple Stochastic Model." *Quarterly Journal of Economics* (May 1970).

Price, L.D.D. "The Demand for Money in the United Kingdom: A Further Investigation." *Bank of England Quarterly Bulletin* (March 1972).

Sheppard, D.K. *The Growth and Role of U.K. Financial Institutions*. New York: Methuen, 1971.

Temperton, P.V. "The Demand for Notes and Coin." Appendix 2 to this chapter. Available from author.

Tinsley, P.A., Spindt, P.A., and Friar, M.E. "Indicator and Filter Attributes of Monetary Aggregates." *Journal of Econometrics* (January 1980).

Trundle, J.M. "Demand for *M1* Equations." Appendix 1 to this chapter. Available from author.

DISCUSSION

Michael Parkin

William Allen's paper does five things. First, it provides an account of the Bank of England's rationale for using sterling *M3* as an intermediate target for monetary policy. Second, it describes (rather briefly) the technique of monetary control employed in the United Kingdom from the inception of targeting in 1976 to the time when the "new" techniques of control were introduced in August 1981. Third, it discusses and evaluates, from the perspective of the requirements of policy in the United Kingdom, possible new techniques of control. Fourth, it describes and defends the recent changes in control techniques implemented by the Bank of England. Fifth, it seeks to delimit the range of possible future developments in monetary control procedures in the United Kingdom. This discussion is organized around these five issues.

The Rationale for Sterling *M3* as the Intermediate Target

Allen suggests that the choice of a target aggregate is a straightforward one and that the appropriate aggregate is the one "which has the most stable statistical relationship with income." He goes on to note that "In practice, in the U.K., it has proved difficult to establish as a matter of fact which of the monetary aggregates has the most stable relationship with income'' and, as a consequence three criteria, two of them indirectly related to the main criterion, have been employed. These criteria are, first, the stability of the demand function for the aggregate in question; second, its information content (as a predictor of future movements of income); and third, ''the factor that turned the decision about the target aggregate in favor of'' sterling *M3*, namely, the ability to account for changes in the aggregate ''in terms of changes in the various categories of assets of the banking system. . . .''

Allen's entire discussion of the criteria for choosing sterling *M3* strikes me as confused. First, the basic criterion — choosing that aggregate which has the ''most stable statistical relationship with income'' is ambiguous. Second, of the three operational criteria suggested, only one of them makes even moderate sense.

The first criterion — the stability of the demand function for the aggregate — while not totally irrelevant, does need careful interpretation and qualification. Stability is certainly a necessary condition. In addition, however, one needs an aggregate whose interest-elasticity is ''appropriate.'' The notion of the appropriate interest-elasticity can be given precision through the analytical framework developed by Poole (1970), extended by Parkin (1978), and discussed in another paper in this conference by Siegel. Clearly, an aggregate that has a very high interest-elasticity, such as one suspects sterling *M3* has, will produce an *LM* curve that is rather flat and will therefore deliver a monetary policy that is not very different from one of interest rate rather than money stock control. To select an aggregate that has a very low interest-elasticity will generate a rather steep *LM* curve and will imply that *IS* fluctuations will come out more in interest rate than in real output fluctuations. Whether one wants to go for an aggregate that has a highly elastic or a highly inelastic demand function with respect to the rate of interest depends on the joint distribution of shocks arising from the goods and money markets as worked out in Poole's analysis. Alas, there is no discussion of these matters in Allen's paper nor, one suspects, are they given much weight in the Bank of England's own evaluation.

The condition which ''turned the decision'' is utterly irrelevant. It is possible to define the change in *any* monetary aggregate in terms of changes in the various categories of assets of the banking system. The so-called counterparts to growth in sterling *M3* (table 4–4) or what in the American nomenclature is called the ''formation table'' is nothing other than an identity and plays no role either in determining what the appropriate monetary aggregate is or in achieving control of that aggregate. Much mischief has been caused by concentration on the formation table. It gives rise to specific intervention in the foreign exchange or domestic bond markets or to direct controls on bank lending when any one of these items appears to be growing at a rate that is out of line with the other two. If the logic of monetary targeting is taken seriously, what is happening to any individual credit counterpart is not a matter of concern to the monetary authorities. Interest rate and exchange rate movements can take care of *any* developments in the credit counterparts.

The one criterion that is to be taken seriously is the information content of the chosen aggregate. Indeed, I can make no sense of the notion of a stable relationship between a monetary aggregate and income other than by regarding the relationship in question as one that focuses exclusively upon the predictive content of the chosen aggregate. To be more precise, what seems to be required is that the chosen aggregate have desirable Granger causality relations with some relevant ultimate targets. I state this purposely in vague terms to avoid begging a crucial question that I now want to address.

In most exercises that have searched for the Granger causal relations between money and target variables, nominal GNP is treated as the ultimate target. This strikes me as being an inappropriate way to proceed. Classical economic theory — and the new classical economics as developed by Robert E. Lucas, Jr. and others (e.g., Lucas, 1973, and Sargent, 1976) — leads to the strong prediction that real variables are *not* Granger caused by *any* monetary variables. This is not to say that there is no contemporaneous correlation between money and real output. Indeed, it is the essence of the new classical macroeconomics that there is such a correlation and that it arises from "surprise" developments in the money stock. What is denied is that the current level of output and employment and all other real variables are affected by *past* values of the money stock. What the money stock causes (in a Granger sense) is the nominal variables (the price level and its rate of change, nominal rates of interest, and exchange rates). Traditional and the new rational Keynesian theories of macroeconomics (e.g., Taylor, 1979) predict that monetary aggregates will Granger-cause real as well as nominal variables. Those theories do *not*, however, predict that the causal relation between money and real income will be the same as that between money and prices. Thus, all theories lead to the implication that causal relations between money and prices and money and real income should be studied. What we need to find, in searching for the monetary aggregate on which to target, is that aggregate which provides the most powerful Granger causal relation with the price level. Ideally, we should like an aggregate which at the same time does *not* Granger-cause real variables. This would make it possible to pursue steady monetary policies aimed at providing the economy with a sound monetary standard while having no adverse effects upon real variables such as output and employment. This can be the only sensible criterion for the choice of a monetary aggregate. Once selected, the task of the monetary authority is clear and simple. It is to make that aggregate grow at a rock steady rate. By so doing, the monetary authority will be providing the economy with the one thing that it is uniquely charged with and capable of providing, namely a monetary standard.

Which United Kingdom monetary aggregate best fits this bill is not a settled matter. The works of Holly and Longbottom (1980); Wren-Lewis (1980); and Budd et al. (1981) have examined the Granger causal relations between sterling *M3* and inflation and found there exists such a relationship. They have not systematically explored the Granger causal relationships between other available monetary aggregates and prices, nor have they systematically studied the Granger causal relations between the various monetary aggregates and real variables. To the best of my knowledge, the Bank of England has not undertaken such studies either, except indirectly in the early 1970s (see Goodhart and Crockett, 1970).

To summarize, Allen's account of the procedure whereby the Bank of England has chosen sterling *M3* as the best intermediate monetary target is sadly lacking. The criteria used are deficient and the tests required to select the appropriate aggregate have not been formulated and performed.

A priori I suspect that sterling *M3* is a particularly bad aggregate for the purpose of monetary control. It includes three-month term deposits and certificates of deposit. It excludes three-month acceptances. From the viewpoint of asset holders, the included and excluded items must appear at the margin as almost perfect substitutes for each other. If that is so, then including the relevant opportunity cost variables in the demand for *M3* function would reveal that the relevant interest elasticities of demand were very high indeed. This would of course imply that even if sterling *M3* growth was controlled precisely the uncontrolled growth of acceptances would render that control ineffective.

Techniques of Control

Allen begins his discussion of the techniques of monetary control by noting that "The classic weapon central banks have at their disposal is the discount rate; and, until recently, announced variations in the Bank of

England's minimum lending rate (MLR) had a central role in monetary policy." It is true that the discount rate (or bank rate or, in current U.K. terminology, the minimum lending rate) is indeed the "classic weapon." What the Bank of England seems not to have noticed, however, is that the discount rate is the *appropriate* weapon for achieving monetary control only under a commodities or fixed exchange rate standard. It is emphatically not the classical weapon for achieving monetary control when the objective of monetary policy is the achievement of the steady growth rate of a monetary aggregate. Under a commodity or fixed exchange rate standard, the nominal quantity whose magnitude the central bank is seeking to hold steady is the money price of the commodity or of the foreign currency against which the domestic currency is being pegged. That being so, the proximate activity of the central bank is to deal in the market for foreign exchange or the market for the commodity in question to establish a fixed price. In order to pursue such a policy it is necessary, of course, that the central bank always have reserves with which to trade. If reserves appear to be running out too quickly then the remedy is to raise the discount rate, thereby lowering the demand for the liabilities of the central bank and raising the central bank's reserves. When the monetary standard is the quantity of money itself (or its growth rate) so that the central bank is pursuing a target growth rate for the money supply, then wholly different techniques of monetary control are required.

Until recently, the method whereby the Bank of England has sought to control the money stock appears to be as follows. First, the demand function for sterling *M3* is estimated. This is a function (with distributed lags) of real income, the price level, and a three month rate of interest. Next, the target for *M3* growth is set and forecasts of real output and prices are obtained from the official short-term forecasting model. That model is a Keynesian income–expenditure model supplemented with an expectations-augmented Phillips curve with expectations that are essentially exogenous. Having obtained forecasts of output and the price level and having a target for *M3* growth it becomes a simple arithmetical matter to solve for that rate of interest that would deliver the monetary target selected, conditional on the forecasts for output and prices being correct and conditional on the error term in the demand for money function being equal to zero (or some other nonzero forecasted value based on the autoregressive structure of that error). The bank then sets the minimum lending rate and operates in the bill markets to achieve three-month rates suitable to the attainment of the required *M3* target.

The Bank of England has not been happy with this technique of control. First, as reported by Allen, it saw the interest rate response of sterling *M3* as too "slow and uncertain." This was seen as arising partly from the lags in the demand for *M3* function and partly from its perceived low interest elasticity. The low interest elasticity is not a *ceteris paribus* but rather a *mutatus mutandus* change in interest rates. That is, allowing for the fact that the general structure of interest rates moves together, a change in the three-month rate on bills and a change in the minimum lending rate typically bring changes in rates on bank deposits (the own rate on a large component of sterling *M3*) thereby rendering the interest-elasticity of sterling *M3*, in a general equilibrium sense, very low. Second, movements in the minimum lending rate which have been viewed as necessary in order to support a particular three-month rate structure have attracted a large amount of public attention and become essentially political events. Therefore the timing of changes in the minimum lending rate have been determined as much with an eye on political as on economic requirements.

The Bank has not seen as a problem the potential for misforecasting output and price developments. At least, if it has seen this as a problem, it has not sought to emphasize it. Nor has the Bank seen as a problem the rather obvious fact that, by controlling the money stock via interest rates, any unexpected movements in output or prices require an administrative–political response and cannot be taken care of by an automatic market response. Thus, for example, if inflation turns out to be higher than had previously been anticipated, that higher inflation rate would produce a higher money growth rate than had been targeted. This is a problem inherent in the technique of control employed by the Bank of England. If conversely, the Bank had been controlling say the monetary base, then the higher than anticipated inflation would, of course, have raised interest rates. It would also, of course, have raised the money supply growth rate somewhat but by less than would occur if the interest rate was pegged.

Not for these reasons however, but for the two reasons set out above, the Bank has become increasingly concerned about its control technique and has sought to explore alternatives.

Possible New Techniques of Monetary Control

As Allen points out, there has been an ongoing debate in the United Kingdom on possible new techniques of monetary control. The main focus of that debate has been the monetary base. The Bank's conclusions from that debate are set out by Allen. They are that monetary base control would, in its pure form, be the polar opposite of interest rate targeting and would generate interest rate volatility which would be undesirable. Further, to have an effective monetary base control technique would require the establishment of required reserves and it would be imprudent to place required reserves against a set of deposits as wide as those included in sterling *M3*. The argument offered against this is that there could be a perverse reaction of the volume of sterling *M3* to a tightening of reserves. The mechanism that the Bank seems to have in mind is one whereby a cut in reserves would lead to a rise in interest rates as banks competed for the smaller volume of reserves. The higher interest rates would spread through to interest rates on time deposits. Thus, the higher interest rates would themselves induce a shifting to *M3* deposits. Such a move may be so strong as to produce a rise rather than fall in *M3*. That such a sequence of events is a theoretical possibility is clearly true. That it is even remotely likely needs a good deal of work to demonstrate, none of which is presented in Allen's paper and none of which, so far as I am aware, has been undertaken by the Bank of England or anyone else.

The entire discussion of monetary base control, reserve requirements, interest on reserves, and the role of last resort lending all show a woeful neglect of the relevant (mainly U.S.) literature on money and banking. They also show an unwillingness to learn from the experiences of others, notably Japan, Germany, Switzerland, and the United States, where monetary base control techniques have been employed, in some cases with remarkable success.

The New Control Technique

The new control technique employed by the Bank of England in an attempt to overcome its own identified shortcomings of the previous technique is emphatically not monetary base control and no commitment has been undertaken to move to such a control procedure. As described by Allen, the new techniques of control amount to the following six changes. First, the reporting of data on retail deposits is to commence with a view to establishing a new, more appropriate monetary aggregate. Second, the Bank is to obtain revenue from required balances equal to one-half a percent of commercial banks' eligible liabilities on which no interest is to be paid. (This of course has nothing whatsoever to do with monetary control and is purely the Bank of England's method of obtaining seniorage from the banking system.) Third, the minimum lending rate is to be suspended and official targets for interest rates no longer announced. Fourth, official targets for interest rates are to be restricted to short (up to fourteen day) paper and the term structure beyond fourteen days is to be determined purely by market forces. Fifth, the Bank will no longer declare rates at which it is willing to trade, but rather will invite offers and decide which offers to accept on the basis of the estimated shortage of cash of the banking system. Sixth, open market operations will be concentrated in the very-short-term bill market.

As explained and evaluated by Pepper (Pepper, 1981), although the Bank has ceased to announce official targets for interest rates, it is in fact continuing to make its rate targets known to the public. It does this through the information that it makes available twice daily on Reuter's monitor. From this source, information is made available twice daily on the spread of rates at which official deals have taken place, the types of instruments, the terms of the instruments in four bands (less than two weeks, between two weeks and two months, two to three months, and three months) so that in effect, the authorities *are* publishing their interest rate policy.

It seems to me that the new techniques of monetary control introduced last year by the Bank of England are almost identical to what they have replaced. The Bank of England is trying to control a monetary aggregate whose value as the basis of a monetary standard has not been been proven, using a technique of control for which there is neither theoretical nor empirical support.

What Next?

Allen is clearly aware that there is a danger in the current situation. He sees the existing arrangements as a halfway house between the old techniques and something to which the Bank of England will ultimately move. Since this conference took place, and since Allen wrote his paper, it has become increasingly clear that what the Bank of England is moving toward is a managed exchange rate — joining the European monetary system and, in effect, buying monetary stability from the Germans. That may well be the right thing and best thing for Britain to do at the present time. It is certainly clear that Britain is in desperate need of a monetary standard. There are, as far as is known, only two ways of achieving such a standard. One is to peg the value of the money to some other money or commodity and the other is to fix the quantity of money (or its growth rate). Since the Bank of England has shown itself both unwilling and unable to do the latter, perhaps the former is the only way to go in that country.

Overall, William Allen's paper has been a useful public airing of the thought processes through which the Bank of England goes. Observing those thought processes is not, however, a happy sight. It does nevertheless help to make sense of what has been going on in Britain in the recent past.

References

Budd, A., Holly, S., Longbottom, A., and Smith, D. "Does Monetarism Fit the U.K. Facts?" London Business School, Centre for Economic Forecasting. Paper presented at the City University Conference on "Monetarism in the U.K.," September 1981.

Goodhart, C.A.E., and Crockett, A.D. "The Importance of Money." *Bank of England Quarterly Bulletin* (June 1970), pp. 159–98.

Holley, S. and Longbottom, J.A. "The Empirical Relationship between the Money Stock and the Price Level in the U.K.: A Test of Causality." London Business School, Economic Forecasting Unit Discussion Paper No. 78, July 1980.

Lucas, Robert E., Jr. "Some International Evidence on Output-Inflation Trade Offs." *American Economic Review* (June 1973), pp. 326–334.

Parkin, M. "A Comparison of Alternative Techniques of Monetary Control Under Rational Expectations." *The Manchester School* (September 1978), pp. 252–87.

Pepper, G. "The New Bank of England System of Monetary Control." A talk given to the Lombard Association, 14 October, 1981. New York: W. Greenwell Associates.

Poole, W. "Optimal Choice of Monetary Policy Instruments in a Simple Stochastic Macromodel." *Quarterly Journal of Economics* (May 1970), pp. 197–216.

Sargent, T.J. "A Classical Macroeconometric Model of the United States." *Journal of Political Economy* (April 1976), pp. 207–38.

Taylor, J.B. "Staggered Wage Setting in a Macro Model." *American Economic Review* (May 1979), pp. 108–13.

III CONSEQUENCES OF IMPROVED MONEY STOCK CONTROL

4 MONETARY STABILIZATION AND THE VARIABILITY OF PRICES AND INTEREST RATES

Jeremy J. Siegel

The role of monetary policy has always held a central role in the theory and practice of macroeconomic stabilization. In the two decades following the Second World War, most stabilization analysis centered on the acceptance of a particular model of economic behavior, usually some variant of the Keynesian *ISLM* framework, with uncertainty playing little role. In these models, proper use of monetary and fiscal policy could exercise complete control over income and interest rates.

But even during this period there were doubts. Friedman (1953) warned that uncertain lags in policy effects, as well as uncertainty of the type of model that governs economic behavior, are reasons to shun active stabilization. Later Brainard (1967) specified the biases introduced into any optimizing policy if policymakers are not sure of the parameters of the model. However, there was a prevailing optimism that econometric models could, through time, pinpoint the true parameters, making active stabilization policy a realistic goal.

The decade of the 1970s was marked by a retrenchment in such optimism. Large-scale models did not explain macro behavior any better than did small models (neither doing very well). Rational Expectations theory shook the foundations of macro policy by questioning the efficacy of any policy rules based on known information (see Sargent and Wallace, 1975, and Barro, 1976). It soon became central to policy analysis to specify the exact nature of the uncertainty in the economy, the form of expectations, and the informational set available to economic agents.

The model analyzed in this paper specifies the effects of monetary policy in an environment where interest rates are currently known by all economic agents but complete information on prices or aggregate demand is not. This structure has its antecedents in William Poole's (1970) description of monetary rules in a simple stochastic *ISLM* model. The analysis here provides a very simple criterion for achieving the optimal policy rule for economic stabilization and broadens the results to include a disaggregated monetary sector. The costs of price and interest rate uncertainty and variability are explored in the last section to guide the monetary authority on the proper selection of the variables to stabilize.

The Model

Equilibrium in the economy is assumed to be described by a monetary sector, which equates the demand and supply for real money balances, and a real sector, which equates the demand and supply for aggregate commodities. Money market equilibrium is described in terms of the demand and supply for high-powered money, that is,

$$\frac{H(r)}{P} = L(r) + \epsilon_L \qquad L_r < 0 \tag{4.1}$$

H is the supply of nominal high-powered money, which is assumed to be deterministically controlled by the central bank without error.[1] The supply response of H may be patterned on the nominal interest rate, r, which is revealed immediately to all market participants. P is the aggregate price level, which is not known with certainty until the subsequent period. The real demand for high-powered money, L, is the sum of the demands by the banks for reserves and the public for currency.[2] Later, these demands will be specifically disaggregated. As usual, L is inversely influenced by the rate of interest. ϵ_L is the stochastic, unpredictable disturbance to the real demand for money.

The supply of commodities (consumption plus investment) is for simplicity determined exogenously to the model, but output could be dependent (as is frequently done in rational expectations literature) on the deviation of the actual from the expected price level without changing the qualitative results of the model.[3] The demand for output is negatively dependent on the real rate of interest, i, and positively dependent on real wealth W so that the excess demand for commodities A can be written

$$A(i,W) = \epsilon_A \qquad A_i < 0,\ A_W > 0 \tag{4.2}$$

Wealth is defined as $(H + B^s)/P + K$, where B^s is the nominal supply of government debt held outside the central bank, and K is the real capital stock. The inclusion of government interest-bearing debt into a demand function implies either imperfect discounting of future tax liabilities by the public, or the imperfect substitutability with private debt instruments (see Barro, 1974). Without one of these assumptions, open market operations would not affect real rates of interest or aggregate demand in the economy, although nominal interest rates and prices might be influenced. $A_W = 0$ allows for this total discounting possibility, although in general the model assumes positive wealth effects. ϵ_A represents the disturbance term to the excess demand function for commodities.

To simplify the analysis of the model, it is assumed that ϵ_A and ϵ_L behave over time as trendless random walks, so that the best estimate of next period's prices and interest rates, given the values of all known variables, is identical to this period's values. In other words, the shocks ϵ_A and ϵ_L are perceived as permanent in nature, and therefore there are no inflationary expectations in the system and the nominal and real rates of interest are equal.

Equations 4.1 and 4.2 close the system and determine P and r, the endogenous variables, which are stochastic due to the stochastic nature of the system. If the supply of high-powered money from the central bank is linked to the interest rate, it too is a random variable, although not an independent one in the system.

The equilibrium conditions can be linearized around the equilibrium values r^* and p^* as

$$(h_r - L_r)\tilde{r} - \left(\frac{H}{P^*}\right)\tilde{p} = \tilde{\epsilon}_L \tag{4.3}$$

and

$$A_i\tilde{r} - A_W\left(\frac{H + B^s}{P^*}\right)\tilde{p} = \tilde{\epsilon}_A \tag{4.4}$$

where p is log P, $h_r = [\partial H(r^*)/\partial r](1/P^*)$, and $\tilde{r}$ and $\tilde{p}$ represent deviations (disturbances) around the equilibrium values. Since the endogenous variables are random walks, $\tilde{r}$ and $\tilde{p}$ can be interpreted as the unanticipated changes from the last period's values, and r^* and p^* as last period's interest rate and price level. Note that nominal government liabilities $(H + B^s)$ are exogenous since changes in high-powered money are affected through open market operations and offset by identical changes in the opposite direction in government bonds. h_r is the real value of the Fed's reaction function and a policy parameter chosen by the central bank.

The disturbances to the interest rate, prices, and nominal high-powered money can be solved as[4]

$$\tilde{r} = \frac{\tilde{\epsilon}_A - A_W\tilde{\epsilon}_L}{(L_r - h_r)A_W + A_i} \tag{4.5}$$

$$\tilde{p} = \frac{-(L_r - h_r)\tilde{\epsilon}_A - A_i\tilde{\epsilon}_L}{(H/P^*)[A_W(L_r - h_r) + A_i]} \tag{4.6}$$

$$\tilde{H} = H_r\tilde{r} \tag{4.7}$$

In this model open market policy is the only instrument, so that controllability of r and p simultaneously by the central bank is impossible. Of course, the availability of another instrument, such as government debt (a deficit policy) or government expenditures that affect the excess demand for commodities, permits, in a world of certainty, complete control of prices and interest rates. However, it is assumed in this model that only interest rates, and not the current aggregate price level, is contemporaneously known. This assumption precludes complete control of prices notwithstanding the number of instruments. Observation of interest rates alone is insufficient to reveal the complete state of the shocks to the system. As equation 4.5 indicates, only a linear combination of shocks is known from the observation of interest rates.

The central bank can devise a high-powered money policy, h_r, based on a known interest rate, which may influence both prices and interest rates. To demonstrate how such a policy might affect the variability of the endogenous variables and high-powered money, the variances of disturbances to these variables can be calculated from equations 4.5, 4.6, and 4.7 as

$$\sigma^2_{\tilde{r}} = \frac{\sigma^2_A - 2A_W\sigma_{AL} + A^2_W\sigma^2_L}{[A_W(L_r - h_r) + A_i]^2} \tag{4.8}$$

$$\sigma^2_{\tilde{p}} = \frac{(L_r - h_r)^2\sigma^2_A + 2(L_r - h_r)A_i\sigma_{AL} + A^2_i\sigma^2_L}{(H/P^*)^2[A_W(L_r - h_r) + A_i]^2} \tag{4.9}$$

$$\sigma^2_{\tilde{H}} = H^2_r\sigma^2_{\tilde{r}} = (P^*)^2h^2_r\sigma^2_{\tilde{r}} \tag{4.10}$$

where σ^2_A, σ^2_L, and σ_{AL} make up the variance–covariance matrix of $\tilde{\epsilon}_A$, $\tilde{\epsilon}_L$.

Minimizing equation 4.8 with respect to h_r yields the solution h_r (and hence H_r) $= \infty$, at which point $\sigma^2_{\tilde{r}} = 0$. This is easily understood in the context of the model. Since the interest rate is in fact controllable by the central bank, a policy of increasing high-powered money every time the interest rate rises will dampen the rise. An infinite response is equivalent to a "pegging" policy, where r is constant at its equilibrium value.

Under conditions of a constant interest rate policy,

$$\tilde{H} = P^*\left(\frac{-\tilde{\epsilon}_A}{A_W} + \tilde{\epsilon}_L\right) \tag{4.11}$$

$$\sigma^2_{\tilde{H}} = P^{*2}\left(\frac{\sigma^2_A}{A^2_W} - \frac{2\sigma_{AL}}{A_W} + \sigma^2_L\right) \tag{4.12}$$

$$\sigma^2_{\tilde{p}} = \frac{\sigma^2_A}{(H/P^*)^2 A^2_W} \tag{4.13}$$

It is easily seen that as A_W becomes small, which is another way of indicating a low wealth effect of government debt, the variability of high-powered money and prices becomes large. In the limit, where government bonds are not net wealth, the interest rate is independent of monetary policy and any attempt to control it will result in an infinite variability of money and prices.[5]

Minimizing $\sigma^2_{\tilde{p}}$ requires taking the derivative of equation 4.9 with respect to h_r, setting it equal to zero, and solving. The solution h^*_r is

$$L_r - h^*_r = \frac{A_i(A_W\sigma^2_L - \sigma_{AL})}{\sigma^2_A - A_W\sigma_{AL}} \tag{4.14}$$

The minimized price variability at h^*_r is

$$(\sigma^*_{\tilde{p}})^2 = \frac{\sigma^2_A\sigma^2_L(1 - \rho^2)}{(H/P^*)(\sigma^2_A - 2A_W\sigma_{AL} + A^2_W\sigma^2_L)} \tag{4.15}$$

where $\rho = \sigma_{AL}/\sigma_A\sigma_L$. From equation 4.14 it is apparent that if all the variability is in the demand for money, so that $\sigma^2_A = 0$, then $h^*_r = \infty$ and the interest rate should be stabilized, which will also result in complete stabilization of prices. On the other hand, if all the variability is in aggregate demand, then h^*_r should be set at L_r, which will also eliminate shocks to prices. In this case the optimal policy of the central bank is to "destabilize" the interest rate, that is, to lower the level of high-powered money in the response to interest rate fluctuations, so as to decrease to zero the interest rate responsiveness of the *excess* demand for money.[6]

Figure 4–1 plots the variance of the price level, interest rate, and high-powered money (as well as nominal broad money analyzed in the next

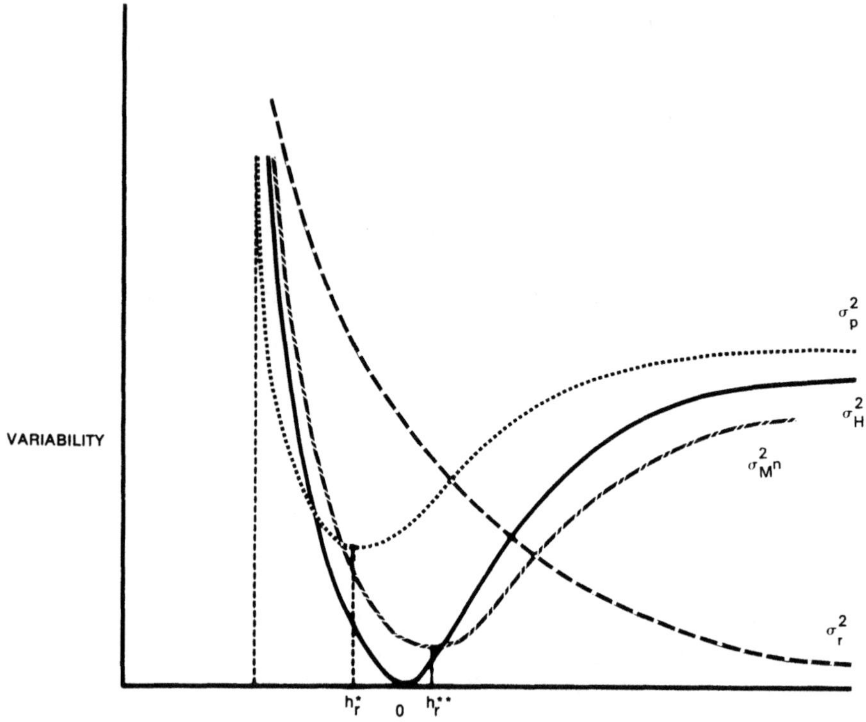

Figure 4–1 Effect of Various Linking Policies on the Variability of Interest Rates, Prices, Nominal High-Powered Money, and Nominal Money Supply

section) for various linking policies h_r. Interest rate variability is a steadily declining function of h_r, reaching zero when $h_r = \infty$. Nominal high-powered money is, of course, completely stabilized by a no-response policy of $h_r = 0$, but even when interest rates are completely stabilized, the variance of money is finite, reaching the asymptote derived in equation 4.13. The variability of the price level behaves somewhat like that of nominal high-powered money, except that zero variability cannot be achieved (except when either ϵ_A or ϵ_L is zero or there is a linear dependency between them). Price level variability increases, but at a decreasing rate, as interest rate stability is achieved. All variables become infinitely unstable as h_r approaches $L_r + (A_i/A_W)$ since the denominator of equations 4.8 and 4.9 becomes zero. This means that the government cannot strongly destabilize the interest rate, for setting h_r at this value will cause infinite fluctuations in prices and interest rates no matter where the source of disturbances to the system originate.

By inspecting equation 4.14, it is impossible to determine with certainty whether the minimized variability of prices occurs at a point where h_r^* is positive or negative, that is, whether the central bank should supply money when interest rates rise, dampening the rise, or restrict money, therefore "leaning against the wind," and amplifying the fluctuations of interest rates. If most of the disturbances to the economy occur in the real sector, then it is likely that h_r^* is negative, and the central bank should (to stabilize prices) exacerbate the fluctuation in interest rates compared to a constant money stock policy. If disturbances to liquidity demand predominate, then h_r^* will be positive and the Fed should attempt to dampen interest rate fluctuations.

The exact pegging policy derived in equation 4.14 requires the central bank to know the interest and wealth elasticities of aggregate demand, the interest elasticity of money demand, as well as the variance–covariance matrix of disturbances. Because of this, Poole himself advocated following one of the pure policies [i.e., money stock control ($h_r = 0$), or interest rate control ($h_r = \infty$)], since estimation of equation 4.14 is subject to too much error. There is, however, a very simple criterion for determining whether h_r^* is positive or negative. By analyzing equations 4.5 and 4.6, it can be shown that

$$h_r^* \gtreqless 0 \qquad \text{if and only if } \sigma_{\tilde{p}r} \lesseqgtr 0 \tag{4.16}$$

when $h_r = 0$ — or, the Fed should dampen interest rate fluctuation if and only if the correlation between interest rate and price level disturbances is negative under the conditions of a constant money stock policy. For example, if unanticipated changes in interest rates are associated with unanticipated changes in prices in the same direction, then equation 4.16 indicates that disturbances to aggregate demand must predominate and the Fed should restrict the money supply whenever interest rates rise unexpectedly.[7]

Targeting Broader Monetary Aggregates

Despite the allure of operating on an aggregate as simple as high-powered money or the monetary base, broader monetary aggregates are easily incorporated into the model. The demand for high-powered money is the sum of the demand for currency and reserves backing deposits, the latter subject to a reserve ratio k set by the central bank. Let us assume that the real demands for currency and deposits can be described by

$$C = C(r) + \epsilon_C \tag{4.17}$$

$$D = D(r) + \epsilon_D \tag{4.18}$$

so the real demand for high-powered money is $L = C + kD$ and $\epsilon_L = \epsilon_C + k\epsilon_D$. The disturbances to currency and deposit demand, like those to aggregate demand, are not revealed until the next period.

The disturbances to the nominal money supply, $\tilde{M}^n = \tilde{P}(\tilde{C} + \tilde{D})$ are, by expansion

$$\begin{aligned}\tilde{M}^n = \big[(k - 1)[(HD_rA_W + DA_i)\tilde{\epsilon}_C - (CA_i + HA_WC_r)\tilde{\epsilon}_D \\ + (C_rD - CD_r)\tilde{\epsilon}_A + h_r((C + D)\tilde{\epsilon}_A \\ - HA_W(\tilde{\epsilon}_C + \tilde{\epsilon}_D))\big] \div \big[H[A_W(L_r - h_r) + A_i]\big]\end{aligned} \tag{4.19}$$

where C and D are the equilibrium values of currency and deposits. This rather unwieldly expression can be simplified if one assumes that the proportional shocks to currency and demand and deposit demand are equal, that is,

$$\frac{\tilde{\epsilon}_C}{C} = \frac{\tilde{\epsilon}_D}{D} \tag{4.20}$$

Then equation 4.19 reduces to

$$\tilde{M}^n = \frac{(-HA_W(\tilde{\epsilon}_C + \tilde{\epsilon}_D) + M\tilde{\epsilon}_A)\left[\dfrac{CD(1 - k)}{C + D}\left(\dfrac{D_r}{D} - \dfrac{C_r}{C}\right) + h_r\right]}{H[A_W(L_r - h_r) + A_i]} \tag{4.21}$$

The variance of the nominal money supply can be clearly minimized at zero by setting

$$h_r^{**} = -\frac{CD(1 - k)}{C + D}\left[\frac{D_r}{D} - \frac{C_r}{C}\right] \tag{4.22}$$

Since it is frequently assumed that the demand for deposits is relatively more sensitive to interest rates than currency demand, then h_r^{**} would have to be positive to stabilize the broad money supply. This result is quite intuitive. If, as interest rates rise, deposits are more interest sensitive than currency, then the currency ratio will rise and the money multiplier (ratio of broad money to high-powered money) will fall in response to an increase in rates. For a given quantity of high-powered money, the money supply would contract. The Fed can offset this contraction by supplying more reserves when this occurs, simultaneously dampening the interest rate movement and offsetting the adverse shift in the multiplier.

In fact, if condition 4.20 holds exactly, the Fed can control nominal money perfectly. This policy has *no* implications for the stability of the price level, however; for if h_r^* is negative, then stabilizing nominal money instead of the high-powered money will worsen price level fluctuations.

If proportional shocks to currency and deposits do not prevail, then complete control of the nominal money stock is impossible. By continuity of the demand function, the minimized variability for nominal money will occur at positive values for h_r if disturbances to currency and deposit demand are nearly proportional. This result is plotted in figure 4–1. However, the minimized variability for nominal money may occur at a negative h_r, which means the Fed should amplify endogenous interest rate movements to stabilize disturbances to broad money.

Of course, if the reserve ratio k on demand deposit were set at unity, then complete stabilization of nominal money is always achieved by setting $h_r = 0$, or stabilizing high-powered money. As in the case of pegging rules described above, stabilizing nominal money by manipulating reserve ratios has no necessarily favorable implications for stabilizing the price level.

Evaluation of Costs of Price and Interest Rate Variability

By calculating the variance of disturbances to prices and interest rates and determining the variance minimizing policy, it is implicitly assumed that the public has a welfare function defined over the variances of these endogenous variables. Furthermore, since the analysis is done in terms of unanticipated shocks, anticipated movements in interest rates and prices, even if caused by variables outside of government control, are assumed to have no impact on welfare.

Although these assumptions appear strong, they are not unreasonable. Anticipated shocks and known paths of exogenous variables can be offset by governmental policy instruments, under the plausible assumption that these instruments exceed the number of critical endogenous variables. Even if this is not the case, anticipated movements in prices certainly have a lower economic cost than unanticipated movements. For these reasons, it does not appear unreasonable, in a fully optimizing model, to confine the analysis to unanticipated variability. But what exactly is the welfare cost of even unanticipated movements in interest rates and prices?

Interest-bearing securities are traded in the most liquid and extensive markets in existence. Now there exists a myriad of interest rate future markets where traders can hedge almost any movement in rates. Even before the existence of these markets, the depth and liquidity of the government securities market allowed trades in different maturities that were equivalent to futures trading, although the transactions costs were higher. Therefore unanticipated interest rate changes may not have a great financial impact. However, greater uncertainty of rates may bring about a greater yield on long-term contracts if risk aversion is sufficiently high. If this is true, the yield curve will display a greater slope in equilibrium due to the greater interest rate variability. Individuals may wish to stay "short" and take the interest rate risk rather than pay the premium required by lenders for a long-term commitment. If borrowing becomes a problem for liquidity constrained individuals or firms, or liquidity crises temporarily disrupt the normal functioning of capital markets, then interest rate uncertainty entails some risks and welfare loss.

Price level uncertainty is quite different insofar as there are no tradeable assets or securities that represent the price level.[8] Since virtually all contracts are denominated in nominal terms, there is no easy hedge for the transfers of income between parties induced by price level variability. Unanticipated price movements are the key to variability in aggregate supply in the rational expectations macroeconomic models. Of course, contracts can be pegged to the price level, but only in an ex post way, since the price level is revealed only in subsequent periods. Hence indexing will, in general, solve the redistributional problem but not alter the supply disturbances caused by unexpected price movements. Despite this, why more contracts are not specified in this manner is a puzzle. Perhaps the imperfections of the price indices, contracting costs, or insufficient length of the contract to guarantee price compensated payments contribute to the explanation.[9]

Another prominent nonindexed contract is of course interest-bearing securities which, in this country, are exclusively traded in nominal terms. Contracting in nominal terms takes on price level risk insofar as the expected rate of inflation is uncertain. This uncertainty can be "priced out" in the market place, but so far there is no convincing explanation for the absence of indexed securities.[10] The pervasiveness of nominal contracting makes unanticipated price level variability important, and perhaps more so than interest rate variability, which can be hedged in the capital market.

Conclusion

Central bank open market policy, which links the supply of high-powered money to the market rate of interest, is able to influence the variability of interest rates and prices in the economy. The linkage rule that minimizes the variability of prices may involve either smoothing interest rate fluctuations by increasing high-powered money when interest rates rise or increasing such fluctuations by constricting base money. A simple criterion is developed that demonstrates that the choice of interest rate rule depends solely on whether unanticipated disturbances to prices and interest rates are positively or negatively correlated. Fluctuations of interest rates can always be eliminated, but at the cost of increasing the variability of the price level.

Monetary aggregates broader than high-powered money are not, except in very special circumstances, under complete control of the central bank. Stabilizing such broader aggregates usually involves a decision rule of positive linkage of base money to the interest rate. Although a positive linkage rule will dampen interest rate fluctuations, the effect on the variability of the price level is uncertain, depending, as described above, on the correlation of the disturbances to prices and interest rates.

Finally, since there is no single rule that can minimize fluctuations of all the variables, some evaluation of the trade-offs must be made. Because markets to hedge interest rate fluctuations are widespread, it is probable that the central bank should give more weight to price level variability in choosing its decision rule.

Notes

1. This is now widely agreed upon by those who have studied the monetary mechanism. For details see Balbach (1981).

2. Each economic agent demands money dependent on the current prices he knows. The sum of these demands equals aggregate real demand even though the aggregate price level is unknown.

3. For a more detailed description, see Siegel (1982).

4. For simplicity in analysis, it is assumed $B^s = 0$ in equilibrium.

5. This result differs from that of Sargent and Wallace (1975), where such a pegging rule always leads to instability. The reason it does not here is that total government liabilities are nominally fixed (when government debt is undiscounted) no matter what the pegging rule is.

6. Equation 4.9 is the unconditional variability of prices, i.e., a measure of the unanticipated disturbances to the price level due to the shocks to the system in the current period. This measure is greater than the variance of the price level *given* the rate of interest, or the conditional variability of the nature of the disturbances (Siegel (1979)) that this conditional variance is identical to equation 4.15, the minimized unconditional variability.

These results are therefore in complete agreement with rational expectations theory which states that policy rules based on known variables (such as the interest rate) do not affect the degree of "uncertainty" in the economy, that is, the variability of endogenous variables based on all current information.

7. This procedure is operational since, for any money stock policy, if the correlation of

disturbances is positive, the Fed must be less accommodative to interest rate fluctuations and vice versa. Hence the Fed can zero in on the optimal interest rate rule.

8. Traded commodities are very imperfect hedges since these often differ markedly from the general price level.

9. Of course, it might be stated that if these reasons are sufficient to explain in the absence of price level indexing, then the cost of these redistributional effects cannot be that great since all the above obstructions can in general be substantially mitigated at small cost.

10. Some nominal securities will be desired to hedge against the holdings of high-powered money, but this total is small.

References

Balbach, Anatol B. "How Controllable is Money Growth?" Federal Reserve of St. Louis *Review* (April 1981), 3–12.

Barro, R.J. "Are Government Bonds New Wealth?" *Journal of Political Economy* (November/December 1974), 1095–1117.

Barro, R.J. "Rational Expectations and the Role of Monetary Policy." *Journal of Monetary Economics* (January 1976), 1–32.

Brainard, William. "Uncertainty and the Effectiveness of Policy." *American Economic Review* (May 1967), 411–433.

Friedman, Milton. "The Effects of a Full Employment Policy on Economic Stability: A Formal Analysis." In *Essays in Positive Economics*, Univ. of Chicago Press, 1953.

Poole, W. "Optimal Choice of Monetary Policy Instruments in a Simple Stochastic Macro Model." *Quarterly Journal of Economics* (May 1970), 197–216.

Sargent, T., and Wallace, N. "Rational Expectations, the Optimal Monetary Instrument, and the Optimal Money Supply Rule." *Journal of Political Economy* (April 1975), 241–254.

Siegel, J. "The Effectiveness of Monetary Reform Under Rational Expectations." *Economics Letters* (April 1979), 341–45.

Siegel, J. "Criteria for Achieving Optimal Interest Rate Rules in a Rational Expectations Macroeconomic Model." Mimeo, U. of Pennsylvania, 1982.

Woglom, Geoffrey. "Rational Expectations and Monetary Policy in a Simple Macroeconomic Model." *Quarterly Journal of Economics* (February 1979), 91–106.

DISCUSSION

Phillip Cagan

In the conduct of monetary policy we classify the sources of instability in the economy into those affecting the demand for money balances and those affecting the demand for goods. Increases in the demand to hold money raise interest rates and the velocity of money. This in turn reduces the aggregate demand for goods and services, which policy can offset by supplying more money. Increases in the demand for goods are viewed as not affecting the demand schedule for money but as reflecting shifts in the saving or investment schedules; these shifts raise interest rates, which policy can offset by reducing the money supply relative to its trend growth.

The problem of course is that we are largely in the dark about the source of these disturbances as they are occurring, and only identify them by their consequences some time after they occur. If policy operates by reacting to changes in the GNP or prices when they are finally observed, it will be operating late and, given the lags in monetary effects, will fail to offset disturbances until some time after they have occurred.

An opening for the justification of a stabilization policy is provided by the observation that its financial effects on interest rates occur quickly. There has quite naturally arisen a tradition in central banking to pay special attention to interest rates. But the problem of identifying disturbances is not avoided: a rise in interest rates could reflect an increase in the demand for money balances or an increase in credit and investment demand, while the appropriate monetary policy response is opposite in these two cases. A policy of preventing movements in interest rates is destabilizing if they are due to shifts in investment and would only be stabilizing if they were due to shifts in money demand. Moreover, stabilizing interest rates means that we lose the benefit of their market-determined movements as indicators of credit demand, while accompanying changes in the money supply do not distinguish between the two kinds of disturbances.

So the question arises whether there is any guidance that can be given to policy. In two extreme cases the guidance is clear. If disturbances occur only in money demand, then of course the correct policy is to stabilize interest rates, which prevents these shifts in money demand from affecting saving and investment. If disturbances occur only in investment, interest rates should be varied so as to keep saving and investment equal after they have shifted and also to counteract the effect of any change in interest rates on velocity by an equivalent opposite change in the money supply. These needed changes in interest rates will have to be estimated, but if the right amount of change is accomplished, aggregate demand can be maintained on its desired growth path. The policy-determined changes in the money supply will reinforce the market-induced changes in interest rates and make their fluctuations larger.

If a combination of both disturbances occurs, neither of the above special cases apply, and the proper policy actions would require unavailable knowledge of the nature of disturbances as they begin to occur. Nevertheless, traditional central bank behavior can be interpreted as proceeding on the assumption that money demand disturbances are mainly a serious problem at high frequencies, that is, are large only in the short run from day-to-day or week-to-week, and so can be offset by stabilizing interest rates over short periods. On the assumption that aggregate demand disturbances are longer run, mainly of a business cycle nature, policy should watch to see that monetary growth stays within bounds over the longer run at the same time that interest rates are moderated in the short run. This is the justification for the famous method of "leaning against the wind," that is, moderating high-frequency movements in interest rates and, in principle, though not followed, reinforcing low-frequency cyclical movements.

Siegel's model helps to formulate these issues. I have some technical reservations about the model, so far as it touches on the preceding issues, which I offer as suggestions to improve it where and when they are feasible. The time unit in which disturbances occur is left open. The model should allow far larger money demand disturbances in the short run rather than in the long run, relative to disturbances in the *A* function (pertaining to saving and investment). It also does not allow for lags (except for the time needed to observe disturbances), particularly lags in the effects on the price level. This is mitigated to some extent if *P* in the model represents aggregate demand, since the model would then avoid the very long lags we expect in the effect of money on prices. But then it would have little to say about fluctuations in prices, which would be a major shortcoming. Actually, the model assumes prices are perfectly flexible and that prices clear markets immediately, which is not realistic. (If that in fact were the case, we would have no problem in subduing inflation.) The model also focuses on the price level whereas policy is currently wrestling with the rate of change of prices.

Assuming we somehow fix up these shortcomings, I find such a formulation to be very useful pedagogically. I have used Poole's version of the model in class and, if my students were smart enough, I would use Siegel's version too. While accepting the model for pedagogical purposes, however, I do not see that such formulations carry us beyond the description of the problem, to provide usable answers. It is not only that we do not know the relative magnitude of the disturbances variances or of the slopes of the functions, which are needed for empirical application, but no allowance is made for uncertainty over the values of the slopes or over the general specification of the model. These are the important uncertainties that plague policy — not only the additive shifts in the two schedules of the model.

U.S. monetary policy abandoned its close operating tie to interest rates in October 1979, not because this analysis showed interest rates to be inappropriate, but because the inflationary environment made it impossible to track the *real* rate of interest, which is relevant to policy effects on the economy (as in Siegel's *A* function). The real rate cannot be satisfactorily estimated by subtracting the rate of inflation from the nominal rate of interest, because the adjustment of nominal rates to inflation has been incomplete, in part because of taxes (though in the past year and a half this adjustment appears to be complete for the current rate of inflation). Siegel's second model does take the real rate as being the nominal rate minus the rate of price change, but that assumes an adjustment in the nominal rate of inflation that is unrealistically instantaneous. Moreover, if economic adjustments to changes in anticipated interest rates and the anticipated rate of price change do not occur quickly, then it is not the variance from anticipated values that is relevant, as in Siegel's model;

the relevant variation is that of interest rates and the price level, or perhaps the rate of price change, around their equilibrium values. Siegel assumes equality between anticipated and equilibrium values, an assumption that has come to be widely made. But there is good reason to doubt that adjustments in expenditures and portfolios to changes in the anticipated rate of price change or in interest rates are rapid. Such adjustments require time for modifications not only in individual behavior but also in institutional and legal practices. Therefore, I would hesitate to be confident in Siegel's major result that policy regimes can be chosen on the basis of whether the correlation between price level and interest rates is positive or negative.

In recent years policy has also discovered that the stabilization of interest rates in practice tends to be overdone. The policy of moderating short-run interest rate movements tends to prevent the longer run movements that should occur, which is aggravated by an inflationary environment when large movements in nominal rates are needed to keep real rates at the proper level. In the face of these difficulties of interest rate stabilization under inflation, policy has placed more emphasis on monetary targeting.

The inflationary environment has also accelerated financial innovations that raise doubts about which money aggregate is appropriate for targeting. The present practical solution of using *M1B* and *M2* may or may not be satisfactory. This is a serious problem, even though I do not think anyone knows how serious it actually is in practice. In terms of Siegel's model it means that money demand can drift, and the disturbance term for this function is a random walk, which allows for such drift. However, the financial developments are fostering new transactions balances that raise the velocity of *M1B*; and, if these developments proceed in the same direction, the disturbances will be serially correlated. We can represent this drift by a random walk only if we add an unknown and changing trend to velocity, which complicates the error structure.

Siegel's model appears to avoid the problem of unknown trend in velocity because the equilibrium interest rate and price level are assumed to be known at the beginning of each period. We do of course know actual values, but we cannot know equilibrium values clearly unless there are no lags. In fact, lags in the real world mean that we do not know clearly what the consequences of past and current disturbances and policy on the equilibrium interest rate and price level are going to be. It is appropriate to treat the equilibrium interest rate and price level as known only if the period of analysis is very long, but long periods would destroy the purpose of this analysis.

Let me add a general comment on the present problems of policy. The uncertainty over the proper definition of monetary aggregates for targeting has raised criticisms of such targeting. Some critics (not Siegel) argue that monetary targeting cannot now succeed and should be abandoned. The force of that argument depends on the alternatives. What these are, other than looking at everything and acting with discretion, is unclear, though the main alternative would be to operate on the basis of current market conditions, that is, interest rates. The problems with money aggregates would have to be very serious indeed in this inflationary environment to justify returning to the use of interest rates. Today (October 1981) no one is sure why real rates of interest are so high, much less what real rate is appropriate under present conditions for the goal of gradually reducing inflation. I do not see how in this climate we can return to interest rate targets even in a partial way.

5 ON THE REAL EFFECTS OF IMPRECISE MONETARY CONTROL

Laurence H. Meyer
and Charles Webster, Jr.

This paper develops a model in which imprecise monetary control has important real effects. We identify two basic real consequences of short-run variability or erratic movements in the money supply: short-run variability in the variables affected by monetary policy and slow convergence of expectations of monetary change to the target set by the Federal Reserve System. The first of these effects has been explored in some detail previously. Our focus is on modeling the relation between the credibility of the policy authority and the policy authority's precision in meeting its announced targets, and on developing an estimate of the relation of policy credibility to the cost of reducing inflation. In this introduction, we develop each of these effects and outline our approach to analyzing the determinants and implications of policy credibility. In our analysis, we view the money supply as the intermediate target of monetary policy through which the effects of variation in the policy instruments are transmitted to the nominal and real variables policy affects.

Short-run variability in the money supply leads to short-run variability in inflation, output, etc. Assuming that stable levels of these variables are preferred, a cost is thereby imposed. Indirect effects arising from increased variability of inflation and output may be, for example, changes in desired portfolio composition in favor of real assets and away from financial assets, and toward shorter- as opposed to longer-lived investment projects. The Fischer and Modigliani (1978) and Fischer (1981) surveys of the real effects of inflation include a discussion of the real effects of inflation uncertainty, and a number of empirical studies have found that inflation uncertainty (more specifically, volatility in the inflation rate) affects the demand for money,[1] investment,[2] the term structure of interest rates,[3] and unemployment.[4] Friedman's (1977) Nobel lecture develops the view that inflation uncertainty undermines the efficiency of the resource allocation process and thereby results in output losses, and a number of empirical studies have confirmed this relationship.[5]

There have been several empirical studies specifically on the effects of short-run variability in the money supply[6] and they have generally concluded that the broad economic aggregates such as real and nominal income, employment, and inflation are relatively insensitive to short-run fluctuations in money due to the existence of lags between monetary change and the effects on these variables. The longer and more stable these lags are, the greater the dampening effect on short-run fluctuations in money. In particular, variations in money that wash out within a six-month interval were found to have minimal effects on key macro aggregates. On the other hand, more sizeable effects do occur when monetary change deviates from its target path for three or four consecutive quarters.

Our analysis focuses on a second real effect of imprecise monetary control, although there is no reason why both effects cannot be operative simultaneously. Our emphasis will be on the implications of short-run variability of money for the speed of convergence of expectations to the rate of monetary growth targeted by the Fed following a change in that rate. This speed of convergence will be shown to be directly related to the Fed's effectiveness in meeting its monetary growth targets. And the cost of slow convergence of expectations will in turn be a larger and longer temporary *real* effect of monetary change on unemployment and output.

Our point of departure is the analysis presented by Meltzer (1980) at this conference two years ago and developed in more detail in Brunner, Cukierman, and Meltzer (1980). Other recent discussions of the role of credibility can be found in a series of papers by Fellner (1979, 1980) and in Stein (1980). Meltzer describes the "basic inference problem" confronting the public as the attempt to infer the future course of monetary growth from reports of current growth rates. The problem is to separate the *transitory* from the *permanent* changes in growth rates. The optimal forecast, according to Meltzer, is, in this case, a distributed lag of past observed growth rates. Economic agents use repetitive observations of monetary growth to determine if a permanent change has occurred. If permanent changes are frequent and transitory changes are infrequent, economic agents are likely to view observed changes in monetary growth as permanent. In this case, the distributed lag on past monetary growth rates used to form expectations will be quite short and expectations will rapidly converge to the new monetary growth rate. On the other hand, if permanent changes are infrequent and transitory changes are frequent, economic agents will find it optimal to observe a relatively long series of monetary growth rates before concluding that a permanent change has occurred. In this case the distributed lag on past monetary change will be long, and expectations will converge quite slowly to the new monetary growth rate.

Meltzer goes on to note that the real costs of reducing inflation are lower the faster the adjustment of expectations of monetary growth to reductions in monetary growth. The purpose of our paper is to develop this insight of Meltzer more fully and to provide some empirical results on the magnitude of costs associated with short-run variability in money using a model that emphasizes the importance of the distinction between anticipated and unanticipated monetary growth. Our approach to modeling expectations is similar in spirit but different in technique from that suggested by Meltzer (1980) and Brunner, Cukierman and Meltzer (1980).

In the next section we develop a simple model of expectations formation relevant to situations in which the policy authority announces a change in policy. Our analysis focuses on the measurement and implications of the credibility the public places in the policy authority meeting its new announced objective. We develop a procedure for combining information about the policy authority's past behavior and the announced new behavior to form expectations about policy. We suggest that the public's expectations of the policy variable will be a weighted average of the value of the policy variable expected on the basis of past behavior and the value expected on the basis of the new policy. The initial weights reflect the initial degree of credibility the public places in the policy authority — the higher the credibility of the policy authority, the higher the weight attached to the announced new policy and the smaller the weight on past performance. These weights are allowed to evolve over time in response to the predictive performance that would be associated with using past performance to estimate current policy relative to the predictive performance that would be associated with assuming the policy authority would hit its new target.

In the third section, we introduce the empirical model we will employ to develop an empirical estimate of the real cost of imprecise monetary control, the Barro empirical rational expectations model[7] in which only unanticipated money affects real variables. The experiment we consider is the response to a change in monetary policy to a rule implying a lower rate of monetary growth and hence inflation. The faster the convergence of expectations of monetary growth to the rate set according to the new rule, the smaller the unanticipated monetary deceleration and the smaller the rise in unemployment during the transition to the lower rate of inflation. In the fourth section, we use simulations of the response of output, unemployment, and inflation to a change in the monetary policy rule under varying assumptions about the initial degree of credibility and the imprecision of monetary control.

In the fifth section, we develop the implications of these results for the question of whether a gradual or drastic monetary deceleration is preferred. While our results are not unambiguous on this issue, they suggest that the role of credibility may provide a case for a more drastic response, a finding in contrast with Meltzer's conclusion in the paper that motivated our study. We summarize our findings in the final section and suggest a number of important qualifications.

The Simple Analytics of the Relation Between Credibility and Monetary Control

In this section we set out the methodology we will employ to relate the evolution of the credibility of the Fed to the precision with which it controls the money supply. As a point of departure, we assume that the target rate of money growth has been constant for some period of time and that the monetary authority announces a change in the money growth rate. In forecasting the growth rate of the money supply, the public must implicitly evaluate whether the monetary authority has the will, ability, and political power to achieve and stick to the new money growth rate; that is, the public must make some judgment about the credibility of the monetary authority. The importance of the monetary authority's credibility can be seen by examining the polar cases of complete and zero credibility. If the monetary authority has complete credibility, then the public sets its expectation of money growth at the level announced by the monetary authority. The public's expectation is the same as the monetary authority's goal, and changes in the rate of money growth can be accomplished with no unexpected money growth; there is no unexpected inflation and the cost of reducing the rate of inflation is small. If the monetary authority has no credibility whatsoever, the public believes that monetary policy is carried out as before and the expected rate of money growth does not change or changes only very slowly as new data are used in estimating the expected money growth rate. With no credibility, the unexpected part of the money growth rate can be large and the resulting output loss huge.

To illustrate this we present a simple example. Denote the money growth rate as DM_t, the money growth rate target by μ, assume that money has been growing (on average) at the targeted rate μ_1 and that the monetary authority announces a change in the growth rate target to μ_2. Further assume that the actual money growth rates are normally distributed about the target rates:

$$DM_{it} \approx N[\mu_i, \sigma^2] \qquad i = 1,2 \tag{5.1}$$

The public, in forecasting the rate of money growth, must implicitly decide whether or not the rate of money growth has changed or assign some probability to the possibility of change. Let P_t be the probability that the policy has not changed in period t, based on information available through $t - 1$. Letting DM_t be the actual money growth rate, we can then write the public's expected money growth rate as

$$\begin{aligned} E(DM_t) &= E(DM_t | \mu = \mu_1)P(\mu = \mu_1) + E(DM_t | \mu = \mu_2)P(\mu = \mu_2) \\ &= P_t\mu_1 + (1 - P_t)\mu_2 \end{aligned} \tag{5.2}$$

If the growth rate in fact remains at μ_1, the unexpected money growth rate is

$$\mu_1 - E(DM_t) = (1 - P_t)(\mu_2 - \mu_1) \tag{5.3}$$

If, however, the growth rate has changed to μ_2, the unexpected money growth rate is

$$\mu_2 - E(DM_t) = P_t(\mu_2 - \mu_1) \tag{5.4}$$

From equations 5.2 through 5.4 we can see the crucial role that credibility plays in the determination of unexpected money growth. If the announced change in policy occurs but is not widely believed (P_t large), from 5.4 we can see that the unexpected portion of money growth will be large. Alternatively, a change in policy that is widely believed (P_t small) but fails to be realized also results in large unexpected money growth — as can be seen from equation 5.3.

From the above discussion we can clearly see the crucial role played by the P_t term and the importance of specifying how the P_t values are generated. In modeling this situation we place ourselves in the situation of the public when a new money growth rate is announced for the next time period. For the first time period, the value of P_t, P_1, must be determined subjectively — based presumably on the monetary authority's past record in achieving its announced goals. For the second time period we assume that the public has observed the rate of money growth in the first period and can use that observation as well as its prior subjective judgment to determine P_2. Unfortunately, since the actual money growth rate is randomly distributed around the target, the public only sees DM_t, never μ, and must determine P_2 in the presence of random variability around the monetary target. For time period 3, the public has observed money growth for two time periods and can determine P_3 from DM_1, DM_2, and its prior subjective probability. P_t is determined using the prior subjective probability and observations on $DM_1, DM_2, \ldots, DM_{T-1}$, where the role of the prior judgment should fall as the number of observations since the announced policy change, T, increases.

To formally model changes in P_T we first note that

$$P_T = P(\mu = \mu_1 | DM_1, DM_2, \ldots, DM_{T-1}) \tag{5.5}$$

Using Bayes theorem we can write

$$P(\mu = \mu_i | DM_1, \ldots, DM_{T-1}) = \frac{P(\mu_i)}{f(DM_1, \ldots, DM_{T-1})} f(DM_1, \ldots, DM_{T-1} | \mu = \mu_i) \tag{5.6}$$

where a discrete density function is denoted by $P(\ldots)$ and a continuous density by $f(\ldots)$. We can use equation 5.6 to solve for P_T:

$$\begin{aligned} \frac{P_T}{1 - P_T} &= \frac{P(\mu = \mu_1 | DM_1, \ldots, DM_{T-1})}{P(\mu = \mu_2 | DM_1, \ldots, DM_{T-1})} \\ &= \frac{P(\mu_1)}{P(\mu_2)} \times \frac{f(DM_1, \ldots, DM_{T-1} | \mu = \mu_1)}{f(DM_1, \ldots, DM_{T-1} | \mu = \mu_2)} \end{aligned} \tag{5.7}$$

Using the assumption of normally distributed DM_t, we can write 5.7 as

$$\frac{P_T}{1 - P_T} = \frac{P(\mu_1)}{P(\mu_2)} \left(\frac{2\pi\sigma_1^2}{2\pi\sigma_2^2} \right)^{(T-1)/2} \frac{\exp\left[\frac{-1}{2\sigma_1^2} \sum_{t=1}^{T-1} (DM_t - \mu_1)^2 \right]}{\exp\left[\frac{-1}{2\sigma_2^2} \sum_{t=1}^{T-1} (DM_t - \mu_2)^2 \right]} \tag{5.7a}$$

To use equation 5.7a, we must make two additional assumptions. First, we assume that $\sigma_1^2 = \sigma_2^2$; that is, the precision with which the monetary authority hits its target is unchanged as the target changes. The second assumption is to assign to $P(\mu_1)$ the value P_1, which is the public's subjective probability that the monetary authority has in fact changed policy. This assumption introduces a subjective element into the analysis, but it cannot be avoided — how does the public evaluate an announced policy change in the absence of any evidence?

Making these assumptions and simplifying, 5.7a can be written as

$$\frac{P_T}{1 - P_T} = \left(\frac{P_1}{1 - P_1}\right) \exp\left\{\left(\frac{-1}{2\sigma^2}\right)\left[\sum_{t=1}^{T-1} (DM_t - \mu_1)^2 - \sum_{t=1}^{T-1} (DM_t - \mu_2)^2\right]\right\} \tag{5.7b}$$

Manipulation of the exponent term in equation 5.7b allows us to write

$$\frac{P_T}{1 - P_T} = \left(\frac{P_1}{1 - P_1}\right) \exp\left\{-\left[\sum_{t=1}^{T-1} \frac{(\mu_2 - \mu_1)^2}{2\sigma^2} + \frac{(\mu_2 - \mu_1)}{\sigma^2} \sum_{t=1}^{T-1} (DM_t - \mu_2)\right]\right\} \tag{5.8}$$

From equation 5.8 we wish to examine the impact upon P_T of P_1, T, and σ^2.

From 5.8 we can see that for $0 < P_1 < 1$, the value of P_1 has no long-run impact but could have a very important short-run effect. For small T the exponent in equation 5.8 is likely to be small and the P_1 term will predominate in the determination of P_T. This is intuitively quite appealing, saying that in the absence of much data subjective judgment plays an important role.

If the money growth rate is changed from μ_1 to μ_2 the second term in the exponent of equation 5.8 will be, on average, zero; and it can be seen that P_T will change with the term

$$\left(\frac{T - 1}{2}\right)\left(\frac{\mu_1 - \mu_2}{\sigma}\right)^2 \tag{5.8a}$$

From 5.8a we can see that if $\mu_2 - \mu_1 \neq 0$ and if $0 < P_1 < 1$, as more observations become available 5.8a gets larger and P_T goes to zero, regardless of the specific values of P_1, μ_1, and σ^2. This means that ultimately prior judgment has no effect; in the long run enough evidence will swamp any initial lack of credibility of the monetary authority.

From 5.8a we can also see the importance of the term $[(\mu_2 - \mu_1)/\sigma]^2$. This term controls the speed with which P_T converges to zero: the smaller this term, the slower P_T converges. The term $[(\mu_2 - \mu_1/\sigma)]^2$ can be interpreted as the *signal-to-noise ratio*. It is a measure of how large the change in the target is relative to the size of randomly occurring changes: that is, it is a measure of the relation between the permanent and transitory changes emphasized by Meltzer. This term measures how difficult it is to separate a policy-induced change in the money growth rate from the normal variability of the growth rate. This ratio becomes smaller as σ^2 increases: it follows that a larger σ^2 leads to slower convergence of P_T to zero and therefore to a larger portion of unexpected money and larger output losses.

The impact of the $[(\mu_2 - \mu_1)/\sigma]^2$ term suggests that this analysis of policy credibility has an important implication for the question of whether a gradual or drastic deceleration of money growth would be preferable. While a gradual policy would have only small effects on unexpected money each period, the possibility exists that a gradual policy would involve a change in growth rates so small that it would be difficult to separate this change from the normal fluctuation in the money growth rate. Thus a drastic policy, because it leads to a large signal-to-noise ratio, may be preferable. This will be investigated in detail below.

A Simple Empirical Rational Expectations Model Incorporating Bayesian Learning

In order to develop the implications of policy credibility for the response of output, employment, and inflation to a change in the policy, we need a model in which credibility matters, that is, a model in which the effect of policy actions depends on whether the policy is anticipated or unanticipated. A natural model to employ for this purpose is Barro's simple empirical rational expectations model in which *only unanticipated monetary change affects real variables*. The equations we use are a slightly modified and reestimated version of those presented by Barro (1976, 1978) and Barro and Rush (1980). The equations are all estimated with annual data with the sample period extending through 1980. The starting points for each equation are the same as in Barro and Rush (1980): 1941 for the expected money growth equation, 1946 for the output equation, 1948 for the price level equation, and 1949 for the unemployment equation.

Modified Barro Model

$$UN_t = \underset{(-79.62)}{-2.69} - \underset{(-3.30)}{5.1}\, DMR_t - \underset{(-6.61)}{10.2}\, DMR_{t-1} - \underset{(-2.96)}{4.6}\, DMR_{t-2} - \underset{(-10.64)}{5.5}\, MIL_t \qquad R^2 = 0.877 \qquad (5.9)$$

$$\log(Y_t) = \underset{(456.)}{5.85} + \underset{(4.29)}{0.994}\, DMR_t + \underset{(4.03)}{0.924}\, DMR_{t-1} + \underset{(2.12)}{0.494}\, DMR_{t-2} + \underset{(93.91)}{0.036}\, t + \underset{(6.28)}{0.584}\, MIL_t \qquad R^2 = 0.998 \qquad (5.10)$$

$$DM_t = \underset{(3.88)}{0.094} + \underset{(2.16)}{0.285}\, DM_{t-1} + \underset{(2.80)}{0.324}\, DM_{t-2} + \underset{(5.94)}{0.079}\, FEDV_t + \underset{(3.54)}{0.030}\, UN_{t-1} \qquad R^2 = 0.89 \qquad (5.11)$$

$$\log(p_t) = \underset{(29.42)}{1.06} \log(M_t) - \underset{(-6.40)}{0.99} - \underset{(-4.23)}{0.98}\, DMR_t - \underset{(-3.43)}{0.84}\, DMR_{t-1} - \underset{(-4.40)}{1.07}\, DMR_{t-2} - \underset{(-3.87)}{0.93}\, DMR_{t-3} - \underset{(-3.00)}{0.66}\, DMR_{t-4} - \underset{(-1.84)}{0.32}\, DMR_{t-5} - \underset{(-3.66)}{0.005}t \qquad R^2 = 0.998 \qquad (5.12)$$

where

UN	= $\log U/(1 - U)$
U	= the unemployment rate (based on total labor force including military personnel)
MIL	= ratio of military personnel to male population aged 15–44 years in which a selective military draft was in effect
DM	= $\log M_t - \log M_{t-1}$
M	= money supply ($M1B$)
DMR	= unanticipated monetary change = $\hat{DM} - DM$
$\hat{DM}$	= the predicted value of DM from equation 5.11
$FEDV$	= $\log(FED) - [\log(FED)]^*$
FED	= real expenditures of the federal government
$[\log FED]^*$	= an exponentially declining distributed lag of log FED, a measure of the normal value of FED
Y	= real GNP
p	= the implicit GNP price deflator
t	= time trend

The Barro model consists of four equations determining the unemployment rate, expected monetary growth, the price level, and real output. These are listed above as equations 5.9 through 5.12. The unemployment and real output equations, 5.9 and 5.10, include current and past unanticipated monetary growth as arguments. Anticipated monetary change is neutral even in the short run in this model; that is, anticipated monetary change affects the price level but not real variables. The unemployment equation also includes a military draft variable (*MIL*), the ratio of military personnel to male population aged 15–44 in years in which a selective draft was in effect; the output equation also includes a time trend along with the military draft variable.

Barro determines anticipated and unanticipated monetary growth by estimating a policy reaction function for the Fed, equation 5.11. Anticipated monetary change is defined as the predicted value of monetary change from the reaction equation; unanticipated money is defined as the residuals from that equation. The reaction function specifies expected monetary change as a function of past monetary growth, lagged unemployment, and a variable defined as the difference between federal government expenditures and normal federal government expenditures where the latter is an exponentially declining distributed lag of past federal government expenditures.

The price level, given by equation 5.12, depends on the actual money supply, current and lagged unexpected monetary growth, and a time trend. This equation differs slightly from Barro's but retains the spirit of the Barro model.[8]

Barro's model incorporates a particular specification of the way in which the public employs new information to form expectations about future policy. This approach to incorporating new data into expectations formation has been labeled "least squares learning" and has been studied by B. Friedman (1979) and Taylor (1975). If the policy authority alters its behavior, economic agents gradually learn of this by reestimating the reaction function with updated data. We have shown elsewhere that ultimately the estimates of the reaction function in Barro's model may converge to those of the altered rule, but this learning occurs slowly, leaving a long period of unanticipated monetary change following any change in the policy rule.[9] We believe the Bayesian learning procedure developed in the second section is more sensible in cases where the public has reason to believe that policy may have been changed; for example, in cases where the Fed announces a policy change.

Using the Barro model, we estimate the response of output, inflation and unemployment to an announced change in monetary policy. The old policy is given by the policy reaction function estimated over the sample period and updated as under least squares learning. The new rule is either a gradual or immediate move to a rate of monetary growth much lower than that implied by the old policy; in particular, 2% per year (DM_t = .02). We assume the public believes with probability P_t that the old rule ($D\hat{M}_{1t}$) remains relevant and with probability $1 - P_t$ that the new rule ($D\hat{M}_{2t}$) is relevant. The public's expectation of monetary growth is then a weighted average of the old and new rules, with the weights being the probabilities the public assigns to each:

$$D\hat{M}_t = P_t D\hat{M}_{1t} + (1 - P_t) D\hat{M}_{2t} \qquad (5.13)$$

Neither rule will precisely predict the behavior of monetary growth, assuming the Fed imprecisely controls monetary growth. The procedure used to assign values of P_t initially and to allow P_t to evolve over time in response to the actual pattern of monetary growth is as described in the second section. In the following section we develop how the response to the policy change depends on the precision of monetary control and how the lack of credibility affects the cost of reducing inflation.

Policy Credibility and the Cost of Eradicating Inflation

In the previous sections we have set up a model to examine the impact of policy credibility on the cost of eradicating inflation. In this section, we perform a number of simulation experiments to determine how policy credibility is affected by the precision with which the policy authority meets its objectives and how policy credibility affects the costs associated with a change in the monetary policy rule to one implying a lower rate of inflation.

The Experiment

The specific experiment we examine is a change in the money growth rule from a reaction function in which the money growth rate depends upon other economic variables to a fixed money growth rate. We assume that through time period $t = 0$ the Fed determines money growth using the reaction function given by equation 5.11 above. Actual money growth is

$$DM_t = D\hat{M}_{1t} + \epsilon_t \qquad (5.14a)$$

where $D\hat{M}_{1t}$ is the predicted values of monetary growth from the reaction function, equation 5.11, and where ϵ_t is a random factor generated from the information in the residuals of equation 5.11 over the sample period, 1941–1979. For $t > 0$ money growth is determined by the money growth rule

$$DM_t = \mu_t + \epsilon_t$$
$$\epsilon_t \approx N(0, \sigma^2) \tag{5.14b}$$

where μ_t is the Fed's targeted (and announced) rate of growth of the money supply. For our experiments we assume the same variance for both the reaction function prior to the policy change and the money growth rule after the policy change; that is, we assume that the Fed can hit its reaction function target just as accurately as it can hit its monetary growth rule target. To determine the expected rate of growth of the money supply we use the method discussed in the previous sections. In particular, the public's expectation of monetary growth is given by equation 5.13, which is a weighted average of equations 5.14a and 5.14b, where DM_{2t} is simply μ_t.

To find the impact of unexpected money growth we assume that Barro's model, equations 5.9, 5.10, and 5.12, adequately captures the "laws of motion" of the economy. Since the deviation of the unemployment rate from full employment and output from potential output is determined by the unexpected money growth, the Barro model gives us a convenient way to evaluate the cost of an unexpected monetary deceleration.

For each simulation, we use historical values of Y_t, DM_t, p_t, $FEDV_t$, MIL_t, and UN_t from 1941 through 1979. We then generate data for 30 time periods after 1979 (1980–2009), setting $MIL_t = 0$, $FEDV_t = .16$ (roughly its average value in the 1970s) and generate values for $\hat{DM}_t$ using equation 5.13. ϵ_t is generated from a random number generator and μ_t is the Fed's announced policy. We examine two different Fed policies: the first, which we refer to as a "drastic" policy, involves an immediate reduction of money growth to 2% per year. The second, which we refer to as a "gradual" policy, involves a reduction in money growth to 6% in the first year, 5% in the second, 4% in the third, 3% in the fourth, and a 2% money growth rate in the fifth and later years. The long-run money growth rate implied by the reaction function is about 6% and this yields an implied long-run inflation rate of about 6% under the "old" policy.

The Results

For our simulations, we vary both the variance around the money growth rule and the degree of credibility that the public initially has in the Fed.

We run each simulation 100 times and present the average results in table 5–1. For each trial we present the unemployment rate for the period with the largest average unemployment rate (*UMAX*) and the cumulative output loss for the period with the largest average cumulative output loss. Results are presented for both gradual (*G*) and drastic (*D*) policies. For example, for trial 1, $\sigma = .01$, the public believes with probability .4 that the Fed has not changed policies, and an immediate reduction is imposed on money growth to 2% growth per year. In this situation the maximum unemployment rate is 7.4% (the natural rate is 6.5%) and there is a cumulative output loss of $38 billion. Had the policy been gradual instead of drastic, the maximum unemployment rate and cumulative output loss would have been 7.0% and $29 billion respectively, as shown in table 5–1 for trial 2.

It is evident from the results of Table 5–1 that an increase in the variance of the money supply around its target unambiguously results in a higher unemployment rate and in a greater output loss. The increase in output loss as the standard error associated with money supply control is doubled varies from virtually none in trials 1 and 9 (with $P_1 = .4$) to an increase by roughly a factor of three in trials 6 and 14 (with $P_1 = .99$), but in all cases (except in trial 1) the increase in the maximum cumulative output loss and in the maximum unemployment rate is substantial. The difference between trial 1 and the other trials is that the credibility of the

Table 5–1. Mean Results when the Policy Regime Changes

Trial	σ	P_1	*D/G*	*UMAX*	*CLMAX*
1	.01	.4	D	7.4	38
2	.01	.4	G	7.0	29
3	.01	.8	D	9.0	117
4	.01	.8	G	7.8	110
5	.01	.99	D	10.0	159
6	.01	.99	G	8.6	224
7	.01	1.0	D	13.5	1649
8	.01	1.0	G	11.5	1685
9	.02	.4	D	7.5	40
10	.02	.4	G	7.3	75
11	.02	.8	D	9.6	175
12	.02	.8	G	8.5	235
13	.02	.99	D	11.8	381
14	.02	.99	G	9.7	703
15	.02	1.0	D	14.7	1818
16	.02	1.0	G	11.8	1862

Fed is strong in trial 1 *and* the change in the money growth rate target is large enough not to get lost in the noise.

The effect of the Fed's initial credibility is also evident from the results reported in table 5–1. If $P_1 = 0$, corresponding to a situation in which the public completely believes and acts as if the Fed will do exactly what it says it will do, monetary deceleration can be accomplished with no cost. If, on the other hand, $P_1 = 1.0$, and the Fed is not believed, the public totally ignores the Fed's announcements and predicts money growth by adding the data since the alleged policy change to the data set from which the reaction function is estimated. If the data set from before the policy change contains a large number of observations, the length of time that it takes for the expected money growth from the reaction function to converge to an expected money growth rate close to μ_t can be quite long,[10] resulting in a large unexpected money growth rate.

For example, for the case of the drastic policy, when the standard deviation of the money growth rule is .01, *UMAX* increases from 7.4 to 13.5 as P_1 increases from .4 to 1.0, the *CLMAX* increases from $38 billion to $1649 billion. For the gradual policy change, the unemployment rate increases from 7.0 to 11.5 and the cumulative output loss increases $29 billion to $1685 billion. This indicates the enormous importance of the Fed's credibility; if the public has little faith in the Fed's ability and/or desire to reduce the rate of growth of the money supply, the cost of a monetary deceleration can be enormous — in this case, roughly one year's GNP.

The Implications for the Choice Between Gradual and Drastic Policies

The results in Table 5–1 show mixed results for the effects of a gradual versus a drastic policy change. In all cases, the maximum unemployment rate is larger for the drastic policy than for the gradual policy. This is to be expected, as the drastic policy imposes large costs immediately while the gradual policy imposes its costs over a longer period of time. The reverse side of this is that the rate of inflation falls faster for the drastic policies. With respect to the cumulative output loss, however, the results are not so clear.

For smaller values of P_1, where the public has relatively more confidence in the monetary authority, and for the lower money supply variance, the gradual policy is better. However, where there is little faith in the monetary authority or where the variance of the money supply growth rate is high, the drastic policy is superior. The reason for this can be seen by examination of equations 5.4 and 5.8a. From equation 5.4 we know that the higher the belief of the public that the Fed is in fact carrying out its announced policy, the lower is the unexpected money growth and the lower is the cost of reducing inflation. However, from 5.8a we see that the speed with which the public changes its belief that the Fed has, in fact, changed its policy is dependent upon the ratio of the size of the money growth rate change to the variance of money growth. The higher the initial degree of belief in the Fed, the less the degree of belief has to change, the less the unexpected money growth, and the lower the cost of reducing inflation. The higher the variance, the less apparent it is, purely from examining the data, that policy has changed; that is, the more difficult it is to determine whether a change in the money growth rate reflects policy change or is mere random noise. With the high variance, a (continuing) small change in the money growth (gradualism) could go relatively undetected for a number of time periods.[11] In this case, for a policy change to be noticed it must produce a large enough change in the money growth rate to swamp the purely random noise.

Our analysis of drastic versus gradual policy actions concerns only the costs resulting from the inability to separate random and nonrandom changes in the rate of monetary growth. It should be pointed out, however, that there are a number of additional considerations that are relevant to the choice between gradual and drastic policies. In particular, the existence of *distribution effects* associated with unanticipated policy; of *nonlinearities,* which make the total cost of adjustment an increasing function of the speed of adjustment; and of *uncertainty* about the economy's response to policy actions provide a case for gradualism that must be weighed against the possible case for more drastic action based on the analysis of the signal-to-noise ratio.

The existence of long-term nominal contracts that embody expectations about future inflation is the source of the distribution effects arising from unanticipated policy actions. Both Stein (1980) and Meltzer (1980) note the possibility of such distributional effects in their discussions of the case for gradualism.

Adjustment costs that vary with the speed of adjustment may arise from simple nonlinearities in the economic structure. In Perry's (1978) Phillips curve, for example, inflation depends on the *inverse* of the unemployment rate. Each increment in the unemployment rate yields a smaller reduction in inflation in this case. As a result, a drastic policy will yield a much larger cumulative output loss than will a more gradual policy.[12]

Brainard (1967) has shown that in the presence of uncertainty about the economy's response to policy actions, it is desirable to act cautiously. Given the limited confidence with which we can predict how much disruption would be associated with drastic policy, Brainard's analysis further reinforces the case for gradualism.

We make no attempt here to weigh the case for gradualism based on the existence of distribution effects, nonlinearities, and multiplier uncertainty against the case for more drastic action suggested by our analysis of the signal-to-noise ratio. However, the considerations mentioned above suggest there may be an optimal rate of policy change, large enough to permit the public to pick up quickly evidence of the policy change in observations of monetary growth but not so large as to result in, for example, large distribution effects.

Conclusion

In this paper we have developed an analysis of the relation of the precision with which a policy authority meets its announced objectives to the credibility of the policy authority and of the implications of policy credibility for the cost of adjusting to changes in policy. We focus on the transitional costs in the form of higher unemployment during the adjustment to a lower rate of monetary growth and inflation. Our analysis suggests that imprecise monetary control raises the cost of reducing inflation and our empirical results demonstrate that the effects of policy credibility on the cost of reducing inflation can be extremely large. Improvements in operating procedures of the Federal Reserve System, and the demonstration that the Federal Reserve has the will — as well as the technical ability — to stick with its announced targets, are investments in improved credibility. Such investments may have dramatic payoffs for the economy.

Our analysis required a model in which the effect of policy actions depends on whether they are anticipated or unanticipated. We have used Barro's empirical rational expectations model in our analysis, despite our reservations about that model. Because unemployment is affected only by unanticipated policy in Barro's model, it provides a framework that maximizes the effects of policy credibility. It would be valuable to develop empirical evidence on the implications of policy credibility in more eclectic models where, for example, long-term contracts result in inertia in the inflation process so that both anticipated and unanticipated policy may affect unemployment and output. But as long as the effects of a policy change vary depending on whether or not the change was anticipated, policy credibility will matter.

Notes

1. Smirlock (1981) found that increased inflation uncertainty reduces the real demand for money. This is consistent with the proposition that wealth owners substitute out of financial assets and into real assets in response to increased inflation uncertainty.

2. Able (1979) found that increased inflation uncertainty reduced investment in plant and equipment.

3. McElhattan (1973) found that increased inflation uncertainty raises the premium in the long rate compared to the short rate.

4. Levi and Makin (1980) introduced an inflation uncertainty variable into a Phillips curve and found that increased inflation uncertainty reduces the level of employment below what would be associated with a given amount of unexpected inflation.

5. Friedman's proposition that increased inflation uncertainty might reduce output and employment has been confirmed empirically by Blejer and Liederman (1980) as well as by Levi and Makin (1980).

6. Corrigan (1973) and Pierce and Thomson (1973).

7. For a discussion of this model see Barro (1976 and 1978) and Barro and Rush (1980).

8. We deleted two explanatory variables from Barro's price equation: the interest rate and the ratio of government expenditures to income. We eliminated the interest rate because Barro's model did not include an equation to determine the interest rate, and we could not simulate the model without adding such an equation, treating the interest rate as exogenous, or reestimating the price equation excluding the interest rate. We chose the latter solution, and it leaves us with a price equation that can be rationalized as a reduced-form in the same spirit as the unemployment and output equations.

9. See Meyer and Webster (1981).

10. In experiments we ran with 30 observations before the policy change, it took over 30 observations *after* the policy change for the expectations from the reaction function to be close to μ_t.

11. We should emphasize that the procedure used determines the degree of credibility in the gradual policy, as a whole. The P_t term refers to the belief in the *entire* policy, not just the policy up until time t.

12. See Meyer and Rasche (1980) for a comparison of the cumulative output loss associated with Perry's Phillips curve under gradual and drastic policies.

References

Able, S. "Uncertainty, risk aversion, and the neoclassical investment model: An empirical study." Ph.D. Dissertation, Indiana University, 1979.

Barro, R.J. "Unanticipated money growth and unemployment in the United States." *American Economic Review* (March 1976), 101–115.

Barro, R.J. "Unanticipated money output, and the price level in the United States." *Journal of Political Economy* (August 1978), 549–580.

Barro, R.J., and Rush, M. "Unanticipated money and economic activity." In S. Fischer, ed., *Rational Expectations and Economic Policy,* Chicago: University of Chicago Press, 1980.

Blejer, M., and Leiderman, L. "On the real effects of inflation and relative-price variability: Some empirical evidence." *Review of Economics and Statistics* (August 1980), 539–544.

Brainard, W. "Uncertainty and the effectiveness of policy." *American Economic Review* (May 1967), 411–424.

Brunner, K., Cukierman, A., and Meltzer, A. H. "Stagflation, persistent unemployment, and the permanence of economic shocks." *Journal of Monetary Economics* (October 1980), 467–492.

Corrigan, E.G. "Income stabilization and short-run variability in money." Federal Reserve Bank of New York *Monthly Review* (April 1973), 87–98.

Fischer, S., and Modigliani, F. "Towards an understanding of the real effects and costs of inflation." *Welwirtschaftlisches Archiv* (1978), 810–833.

Fischer, S. "Towards an understanding of the costs of inflation II." In K. Brunner and A. Meltzer, eds., *The Costs and Consequences of Inflation,* North-Holland: Carnegie-Rochester Conference Series on Public Policy, November 1981.

Fellner, W. *Towards a Reconstruction of Macroeconomics: Problems of Theory and Policy*. Washington, D.C.: American Enterprise Institute for Public Policy Research, 1976.

Fellner, W. "The credibility effect and rational expectations: The implications of the Gramlich study." *Brookings Papers on Economic Activity* 1 (1979), 167–178.

Fellner, W. "The valid core of the rationality hypothesis in the theory of expectations." *Journal of Money, Credit, and Banking* (November 1980), 763–787.

Friedman, B.M. "Optimal expectations and the extreme information assumptions of rational expectations' macro models." *Journal of Monetary Economics* (January 1979), 23–41.

Friedman, M. "Inflation and unemployment." *Journal of Political Economy* (1977).

Levi, M., and Makin, J. "Inflation uncertainty and the Phillips curve." *American Economic Review* (December 1980), 1022–1027.

McElhattan, Rose. "The term structure of interest rates and inflation uncertainty." Federal Reserve Bank of San Francisco *Review* (December 1973), 27–35.

Meltzer, A. "The Case for gradualism in policies to reduce inflation." In *Stabilization Policies: Lessons from the '70s and Implications for the '80s*. Proceedings of a Conference Sponsored by the Center for the Study of American Business and the Federal Reserve Bank of St. Louis, 1980.

Meyer, L.H., and Rasche, R.H. "On the costs and benefits of anti-inflation policies." Federal Reserve Bank of St. Louis *Review* (February 1980), 3–14.

Meyer, L.H., and Webster, C. "Monetary policy and rational expectations: A comparison of least squares and Bayesian learning." Paper presented at the Carnegie-Rochester Conference on Public Policy, November 1981.

Mullineaux, D.J. "Unemployment, industrial production, and inflation uncertainty in the United States." *Review of Economics and Statistics* (May 1980), 163–168.

Perry, G. "Slowing the wage spiral: The macroeconomic view." *Brookings Papers on Economic Activity* (1978:2), 259–291.

Pierce, J.L., and Thomson, T.O. "Some issues in controlling the stock of money." In *Controlling Monetary Aggregates II: The Implementation,* Federal Reserve Bank of Boston, 1973.

Sargent, T.J., and Wallace, N. "Rational expectations and the theory of economic policy." *Journal of Monetary Economics* (April 1976), 193–228.

Smirlock, M. "Inflation uncertainty and the demand for money." In *Empirical Studies of the Demand for Money,* Proceedings of a Conference sponsored by the Center for the Study of American Business, 1981.

Stein, H. "Achieving credibility." In W. Fellner, ed., *Contemporary Economic Problems, 1980.* Washington, D.C.: American Enterprise Institute, 1980, 39–76.

Taylor, J.B. "Monetary policy during a transition to rational expectations." *Journal of Political Economy* (October 1975), 1009–1021.

Taylor, J.B. "Staggered wage setting in a macro model." *American Economic Review,* Papers and Proceedings (May 1979), 108–113.

DISCUSSION

Robert H. Rasche

Meyer and Webster's announced intention in this study, to develop "an estimate of the relation of policy credibility [of the Fed] to the cost of reducing inflation" is both an important and difficult objective. Given the latter, it is hardly surprising and quite excusable that their output sheds little light on this problem. My remarks are divided into two parts: first I shall enumerate the things that I see as the deficiencies in the Meyer-Webster framework and analysis. Following this I shall list some of the empirical problems with which, in my judgment, a constructive analysis of the credibility problem must cope. At this point I will admit unabashedly that I do not have a well-developed analytical framework that can cope with these problems, although I have several suggestions on how a productive analysis of such a topic might be pursued.

Many of the deficiencies of the Meyer-Webster analysis derive from their assertions about initial conditions. They start their analysis with the proposition that in the beginning "the target rate of money growth has been constant for some period of time and that the monetary authority announces a change in the money growth rate." This is certainly not an appropriate statement of the initial condition for the U.S. economy, nor to my knowledge, any other economy in which announced monetary growth rates are currently disseminated. A more appropriate statement of initial conditions might be obtained by paraphrasing a famous source:

> In the beginning the monetary target was without form and void, and confusion was upon the face of the markets.

There appear to be at least two reasonable alternatives for the state of the world when a monetary target is initially announced: (1) complete credibility for the monetary authority or (2) a diffuse prior with respect to the precision with which the monetary authority can achieve its announced intentions. This latter is not really a lack of credibility of the monetary authority, but rather the complete absence of an information base from which private economic units can make judgments on the future performance relative to the announced targets.

Neither of these initial states of the world can be accommodated within the Meyer-Webster framework. The first problem we encounter is how to get the Meyer-Webster Bayesian learning process started. In their equation 5.8, we now have an announced target for the future, μ_2, but there is no well-defined notion of the target for the past, since no such announcements had ever been made. This may not be a fatal shortcoming of the framework, if there has been a transition phase, such as we experienced in the U.S., from a regime with no targets through a regime of unannounced targets. Then if one were willing to ignore the first two subsamples and argue that the analysis is appropriate only to the final regime, one could argue for a μ_1 equal to the last unannounced target, which presumably is known ex post.

Even if this problem is overcome, starting the learning process is not well defined. Consider the case of complete credibility (perfect naivete) on the part of private economic units. This would be represented in the Meyer-Webster framework by a degenerate prior distribution on μ, that is, $P_1 = 0.0$. Under these conditions, from equation 5.8, $P_t = 0.0$, all t, and nothing the monetary authorities can do will lose them credibility. This implication strikes me as clearly counterfactual, at least with respect to the U.S. experience.

It should be noted that the same problem holds in the Meyer-Webster framework for the other polar case of $P_1 = 1.0$, or perfect incredibility. If we take the reciprocal of equation 5.8,

$$\left(\frac{1-P_t}{P_t}\right) = \left(\frac{1-P_1}{P_1}\right) \exp\left\{\sum_{t=1}^{T} \frac{\mu_2 - \mu_1}{2\sigma^2} + \frac{(\mu_2 - \mu_1)}{\sigma^2} \sum_{t=1}^{T} (DM_t - \mu_2)\right\}$$

Let $P_1 = 1.0$. Then regardless of μ_2, μ_1, $\sigma^2 > 0$, or the observed history of DM_t,

$$\left(\frac{1 - P_t}{P_t}\right) = 0 \qquad \text{(all } t\text{)} \qquad \text{hence} \qquad P_t = 1.0 \qquad \text{(all } t\text{)}$$

In short, if we allow private economic units to start with complete incredibility with respect to the intentions of the monetary authority, nothing that the authorities do would ever improve their credibility.

Now it could be argued that the analysis of equation 5.8 presented above is deficient and/or erroneous, in that perfect credibility or incredibility should be represented by a degenerate prior in which $P_1 = 1.0$ (or 0.0) and $\sigma^2 = 0.0$. At best this presents the problem of defining the product of zero and ± infinity. More realistically, it exposes the second deficiency of the Meyer-Webster framework: namely, they assume some given precision of the monetary control process that is known with certainty to private economic units, and which is stationary over time. There does not appear to be any justification for either of these assumptions.

First, it would seem appropriate to interpret σ not as the technical precision with which the monetary authority hits its target, but with the public's perception of how well the authority hits its target. As such, it is probably more appropriate to regard the public as possessing some estimate of σ, say s, that changes as more information is made available. In short, private decision makers are faced with the problem of updating their priors in a world where both mean and variance are unknown; not just a world of unknown means as assumed by Meyer and Webster. This complicates the analysis, but is a situation that has been investigated in the literature on statistical decision theory (see Raiffa and Schlaifer, 1961, pp. 298–309). Moreover, once we admit that the precision of the process is something to be determined and/or refined from the data, then the framework is capable of analyzing the impact of events like the October 6, 1979 announcement. Presumably this should be treated as an intervention (to borrow a term from time series analysis) with respect to the prior on the precision of the monetary control process. It seems reasonable within such a Bayesian learning framework that such an announcement could have permanent beneficial effects if the change in operating procedures in fact increases the observed precision with which targets are hit. Conversely the beneficial impact of the increased signal to noise ratio can be depreciated rapidly if experience fails to confirm the presumed increase in precision.

The second part of my criticism of the Meyer-Webster analysis is directed to their adopted empirical framework, equations 5.9 through 5.12. The primary problem is stated quite precisely by Meyer and Webster: "Barro's model incorporates a particular specification of the way in which the public employs new information to form expectations about future policy." The significant point for the present analysis is that the particular specification *is not* the Meyer-Webster specification. From the Meyer-Webster perspective, equation 5.11, and the additional definition of unanticipated monetary change as the residuals of that regression, is a specification error. Since 5.11 is misspecified under the Meyer-Webster hypothesis, equations 5.9, 5.10, and 5.12 are all subject to undetermined biases through measurement error present in DMR_t. This is acknowledged by Meyer and Webster, who state "We believe the Bayesian learning procedure developed in the second section is more sensible in cases where the public has reason to believe that policy may have been changed; for example, in cases where the Fed announces a policy change."

In spite of this, Meyer and Webster proceed to construct simulation exercises as if the parameter estimates in equations 5.9, 5.10, and 5.12 are unbiased under their hypothesis. Clearly the appropriate way to proceed is to respecify an equation for the expected monetary growth rate that incorporates a Bayesian learning procedure, jointly estimate this relationship and the remaining equations of the model (Barro's equations or some alternative set), and then simulate the correctly specified system of equations. Until this is done, truth in advertising requires the labeling of the simulation results, "Caution: The use of these results may be hazardous to your understanding of current policy problems."

A final remark: The entire Meyer-Webster analysis presumes that there is an important difference in the impact of anticipated and unanticipated monetary growth rates on economic activity. There is a growing literature alleging support of that hypothesis, represented here by the citations to Barro's work. Many such results have been shown to be extremely sensitive to the choice of specification and/or sample period. Most important, the message of the Meyer-Webster analysis should be that the hypothesis of differential impact of anticipated versus unanticipated money growth and the expectations formation mechanism are joint; one cannot be ordered prior to the other, nor is it appropriate to draw conclusions about one apart from the other.

Reference

Raiffa, H., and Schlaifer, R. *Applied Statistical Decision Theory,* Boston: Division of Research, Graduate School of Business Administration, Harvard, 1961.

IV LUNCHEON SPEECH

6 TRANSMUTING PROFITS INTO INTEREST
or How to Free Financial Markets and Bankrupt Business

Albert M. Wojnilower

It is an unusual privilege to address this audience of businessmen and scholars, two groups rarely to be found voluntarily in the same location. For the businessmen it is probably relevant that I have a record of over seventeen years of rather successful interest rate forecasts (with the only major error, according to my own biased scoring system — the failure to anticipate the 1971 wage and price controls). This record, however, is of little interest to academics because the predictions were not derived from any explicit forecasting model.[1]

What may, however, hold some passing interest or irritation for the scholars here is that a respectable academic journal, the *Brookings Papers on Economic Activity*, recently published an article of mine entitled "The Central Role of Credit Crunches in Recent Financial History."[2] What some may find irritating in that paper is not any particular formal challenge — when it comes to formal economics, we can all agree that I am not in the same league with the scholars at this conference — but rather the implicit methodological challenge posed by the article's historical and institutional approach.

People act differently in crowds, casinos, mobs, and societies than they do as individuals. Group behavior is the essence of financial markets.

Current financial theorizing, which postulates narrowly individual and narrowly pecuniary motives, omits a key part of the story.

In contrast to individuals, groups and societies can alter the prevailing rules of conduct and contract when they are dissatisfied with the outcomes. These days they are particularly trigger happy about doing so. The system observes, questions, and modifies itself. In particular, virtually every business cycle of at least the last 30 years has prompted major innovations in financial rules and practice. This means that, if forecasting techniques are to keep pace, they must adapt from cycle to cycle —which is a serious and perhaps mortal challenge to econometric techniques that depend heavily on assumptions that the underlying financial structure is stable when in fact it is not.

In an attempt to oblige both audiences present here, my plan is to review the major themes of the Brookings article as they appear in the light of subsequent developments and as they may illuminate the outlook for the future.

Credit Availability Is What Counts, Not the Cost

The chief thesis propounded in the Brookings article is that essentially all recessions of the last 30 years were triggered by credit crunches — sudden and generally unexpected disruptions in the supply of credit quite analogous in nature and impact to the sudden gasoline shortages of 1974 and 1979. By contrast, high interest rates alone, even rates "incredibly" beyond the experience of market participants, have merely slowed the economy without prompting recessions. In short, "no recession without a credit crunch."

Some credit crunches were brought on by collisions with the regulatory structure. In 1959 or 1966, for example, yields on marketable instruments rose above deposit-interest rates and threatened the life of major depositary institutions through disintermediation. In 1980, consumer and some business credit was abruptly cut off when the Federal Reserve, under pressure from the White House, invoked a panoply of credit controls. Other more serious crunches resulted from credit panics, as in 1970 when Penn Central defaulted on its commercial paper, or in 1974 when the Franklin National and Herstatt Bank failures shook the certificate of deposit and foreign exchange markets.

One of my heresies is the belief that the credit crunches brought on by financial regulation were wholesome. They brought a much quicker halt to surges in inflation and interest rates than would otherwise have occurred, and thereby prevented the cyclical peak in inflation and interest rates from lasting long enough to become embedded in experience and expectations. The recessions these credit crunches triggered were relatively brief and mild, partly because the booms they followed had not much time to get out of hand and partly because as soon as the collision between the economy and the regulatory constraints were relieved — a matter of months or even weeks — activity promptly began a rapid return to normal. But most importantly, induced credit crunches were and remain valuable because they are the mutually exclusive alternative to credit panics, which if not "bailed out" instantly and decisively bring on the serious recessions and depressions.

How does this view look in October 1981 as compared with August 1980 when the Brookings article was drafted? At that juncture, when the Federal funds rate was only 9% and the Treasury bond yield 11%, the economy was widely regarded as still mired in recession with little early prospect of significant improvement. My view, vindicated by events, was that a vigorous recovery was beginning, and I fully anticipated the rise in long-term interest rates to the levels that now prevail. I never expected, however, with industrial production failing to regain its early 1979 peak and with inflation slowing, that the prime bank loan rate would shortly exceed bond yields and actually hang at 18% or higher for a whole year. Indeed so high a level of the predominant interest rate clouds the distinction between the availability of and the demand for credit. Even when rates are low, lenders refuse many loan applicants because they don't believe the borrower will be able to meet the payments. This problem of loan qualifications is clearly much more serious at high rates. Are individuals and firms still desirous of borrowing almost as much or even more at rates of 20%, but unable to do so because lenders no longer regard them as creditworthy; or would the lenders be willing, but is it the borrowers who are fearful? Both tendencies are at work; the problem is how to tell which tendency is the stronger.

Despite the extraordinary rise in interest rates, the economy roared ahead into the spring of 1981 and crept ahead until July. To that point, the credit availability hypothesis clearly survived an exceptionally strenuous test. After July 1981, however, economic activity turned down. But this recent weakening does not necessarily mean that a recession is being born without benefit of credit crunch. Credit crunches, like lightning, do not come as bolts from the blue. They strike from economic storm clouds that are already overhead. We have had economic slowdowns during which no credit crunch occurred, but from which the economy rallied without falling into a full-fledged recession, and we have had slowdowns from which the economy appeared to be recovering until it was plunged into a more pronounced decline by a late bolt of credit lightning. These experiences, as well as, probably, our present circumstances, are analogous to what happens to the broken-field runner on the football field. The runner stumbles as he is hit, but he will gain a lot more yardage and perhaps even recover his momentum unless tackled again while off balance. If our economy were now thrust by a credit panic into a deep and long-lasting recession, its statistical beginning would be marked as August 1981, but this would not be much more meaningful than crediting the first and only the first tackler for bringing down the ball carrier. On the other hand, should no such panic develop, the economy may well start stumbling forward again.

The repeated easing of the Federal Reserve's money market stance since midyear and the consequent counterseasonal drop in short-term interest rates, the tax cuts now taking effect, and various industry-specific factors do indeed suggest that the economy may soon regain slightly better footing. The counterweight is, however, that soon some or all of the monetary aggregate measures by which, for better or — more probably — for worse, we set our monetary course will grow more rapidly. Then the prevailing rulebook will call for the Federal funds rate, which has now dropped to 15% or less, to embark on a roundtrip back up to the 20% of July 1981. Just when the business community manages the beginnings of a collective sigh of relief that interest rates may be ebbing just a bit, they will shoot up again. In that event it is odds-on that a serious credit crunch and wave of industrial bankruptcy would be precipitated, engulfing prudent and imprudent with little distinction.

Will such a disaster come to pass? Probably not — because the administration is likely to modify or set aside the monetary rulebook if it calls for higher interest rates any time soon. At least such good sense is what I both urge and predict. I refer to "the administration" rather than the Federal Reserve because, at least for the time being, Federal Reserve policy is ipso facto dictated by the administration, whether the parties themselves realize it or not. But not even the British, despite Mrs. Thatcher's doctrinaire views and the de jure subjugation of the Bank of England to the government, have come close to holding their monetary expansion within the official targets. This fall from grace has not prevented the British from achieving substantial disinflation, but of course also 12% unemployment; the annihilation of businesses and their profits; the weakening of the pound sterling; and long-term government bond yields of 16%, not seen since the wild inflation of the earlier 1970s — long before the present regime came to power.

High Interest Rates Cause Inflation, Maybe More Than the Other Way Around

The probability that monetary policy may soon bend a little brings me to my next theme, which is that high interest rates cause inflation, quite possibly more than the other way around. Interest rates high enough to cause serious economic trouble provoke inflationary political responses. Particularly in an unregulated financial environment, it is much easier to assuage the pain of high rates through tax reduction and more inflation, than to find a dependable way to bring the rates down. Eventually, of course, regulation is reinstituted; so far as I know, all societies that have left historical records have regulated interest rates and/or credit. When most mortgage rates in the U.S. have become floating rates, every change in the Federal Reserve discount rate will become a political issue and the discount rate will change much less frequently than before.

It is no news, only a bit impolite, to remind both the audiences here of the long-recognized link between inflation and entrepreneurial activity. Profit depends on an improvement in revenues relative to costs. Revenues depend on unit sales and prices. In a mature economy, large gains in physical sales are hard to come by; price increases of 5% or 10% usually seem easier to accomplish than comparable increases in unit sales. In any event, widespread sales and price gains depend upon an expanding economy. Cost reductions depend mainly on productivity gains which, so long as business plans for growth, also can be realized only as the economy grows. The time when the economy expands beyond previous sales peaks happens to be, however, the time when wage and other input prices are apt to be moving up. Thus entrepreneurial business benefits from, indeed requires for its survival, intermittent puffs of inflationary stimulus.

As long as we kept interest rates below free market levels, this provided business with a subsidy that to some important extent substituted for inflationary stimulus of a monetary character. To be sure, the interest rate ceilings deprived the small savers of a fair return. However, because the employers for whom they worked were then more prosperous, the small savers had better job and advancement prospects. Because many borrowing opportunities were more restricted and it was harder to accumulate a retirement nest egg, they saved more of their income. And when they or their children wanted an affordable mortgage it was no problem. Tears shed for the small saver are crocodile tears.

In the classical economic model on which monetarist prescriptions are based, there is precious little room for entrepreneurship or profits. Equity owners and their managers are supposed to get by on the minimum return needed to keep them or the creditors from liquidating the business. In such a world, as you readily can verify from recent statistics or perhaps your own income statements, there is much interest but little profit. For many years and as recently as 1979, corporate profits before tax were some 75% larger than net interest paid by business. For the last several years, including this year [1981] to date, total property income (profits plus interest) has been rising rapidly. But by now, profits and interest are about equal. About the only good thing that can be said for supply siders — the cultist nonsense of their prescriptions was exposed at these meetings last year — is that they do at least recognize the importance of the entrepreneurial dimension and the inevitability of its destruction under sustained monetary restraint.

To recapitulate, the deregulation of interest rates has been inflationary in that it (1) withdrew an anti-inflationary subsidy benefiting mainly the business sector; (2) made it virtually impossible to contain and reverse inflation and interest rate upswings quickly, with the result that such upswings have come to be regarded as typical rather than transitory; and (3) led to political responses (as well as market adaptations to be discussed below) that are inflationary.

Those of you not acquainted with my earlier work may think of me as an inflationist. Emphatically the opposite is true. But, equally emphatically, it is necessary to recognize that our current inflation is not the disease, but only the fever. It is only a symptom of the fundamental trouble — which is, primarily, our international weakening. Fixation on symptoms at the expense of treating the underlying malady can kill the patient. In January 1979, I wrote an essay that summed up the whole problem in the title, which was "The Financial Equivalent of War."[3]

Overburdening the Lender of Last Resort

Each time the financial system has been chastened by the interaction of monetary policy and regulatory constraints, it has evolved, as do bacteria in response to antibiotics, new forms able to resist such discipline. Banks learned, among other things, to sidestep branching restrictions through the invention of certificate of deposit and Eurodollar borrowing; to escape the need for and risks of long-term asset ownership through short-term liability management; to offset the impact of potential quantitative credit controls through the proliferation of legally binding future lending commitments; and to shoulder off interest rate risks to borrowers through floating rates.[4] Floating rates are particularly pernicious because they remove any competitive pressure to postpone longer-range projects due to high interest rates: all borrowers wind up paying essentially the same rates, regardless of when they choose to borrow. Banks were supported in these efforts to avoid constraints by a durable bipartisan commitment, developed and sustained through a series of Democratic and Republican national administrations, to free the financial system from essentially all regulation.

Economists know — although we often find it difficult to persuade our clients — that no amount of deregulation and innovation can enable a financial system to escape the bearhug of a determinedly anti-inflationary monetary policy. But if key participants in the economy believe that as a result of their ingenuity they, as individuals, can escape, they make it much harder for a restrictive monetary policy to succeed. They become willing to take greater risks and to bid up asset prices and interest rates even higher in the effort to outlast less courageous or more reckless competition. Meanwhile, every rise in interest rates makes it politically more difficult for the government to press home its restrictive policy, and the greater the exposure taken by the private sector, the more the Fed's hand may be stayed for fear of touching off an uncontrollable wave of bankruptcies.

The saving of a drowning person must be a harrowing experience for the rescuer as well as the rescued. To serve as lifeguard, to be the lender of last resort, is the central bank's ultimate *raison d'être* but also its most soul-searching ordeal. Yet in connection with each of the last four business downturns, crises erupted — the disintermediation crunch of 1966, the Penn Central commercial paper default of 1970; the Franklin National and Herstatt bank failures of 1974; and perhaps — the facts have not been made public — the collapse of the silver bubble in 1980, which impelled the Federal Reserve to intervene as emergency lender of last resort. Each occasion reinforced the Federal Reserve's determination to forestall the need for repeating so traumatic an encounter in the future. But of course each occasion also confirmed the bathers in their view that they could cavort with impunity because rescue will always come in time so long as the party in apparent jeopardy is important enough. From this point of view, deregulation is like removing the ropes, the depth markers and buoys, and putting all the responsibility for safety on the lifeguard. It is a game of chicken with the financial survival of our economy.

The push to deregulate commercial banking continues apace. Banks are to be allowed, through holding companies, to expand into still other lines of business, including the securities business. Although in principle only banks and not their holding companies are eligible for deposit insurance and Federal Reserve accommodation, in practice, major bank holding companies reason quite correctly that, if an affiliate came under a shadow dark enough to cloud the name of the bank, the Federal Reserve lifeguard will have no choice but to plunge in for the rescue lest a larger and more hazardous panic develop.

In other respects, however, the thrust toward deregulation is losing steam. Public policy toward thrift institutions, for example, has changed dramatically. For over a decade, the financial authorities strove relentlessly to exterminate the industry, on grounds that special purpose institutions protected by regulation deserved no place in a free financial system. The home building industry, foolishly, allowed itself to be persuaded that it had a future separate from the thrifts. Now, however, the all-saver legislation and related regulatory changes signal a shift of priorities toward averting the toppling of these particular dominoes. It is noteworthy, too, that in prescribing that 75% of the net proceeds from all-saver inflows be invested in mortgage or farm credit instruments, the new tax law includes probably the first affirmative credit control we have ever enacted. As other business mendicants show up on the government's doorstep, we should expect more such ad hoc responses, which will frame out the new regulatory system that free marketeers of a generation hence can attempt to pull down.

On the interest rate front, what with NOW accounts and checkable money market funds, the deregulation of deposit interest has been substantially accomplished. All the same, it is rather interesting that recent legislative moves to supersede state usury ceilings for consumer loans (as was done last year for mortgages) have not attracted strong support; that announced increases in the interest rate ceilings for passbook saving were rescinded; and that the campaign to abolish the prohibition of interest on demand deposits seems to have died away. Of course, the damage has been done. Just as the price of gasoline is forced up when the crude oil price increases materially (and the price of crude when demand pushes up the price of gas), so the deregulation of deposit and loan interest rate ceilings has unleashed much higher levels of interest rates than prevailed under controls. When rents are decontrolled, we get the benefit of more housing construction. But when interest rates are freed, additional increases in money and credit do not necessarily follow and are no blessing if they do. Over the last 20 years, in my judgment, financial innovation and deregulation (and its interaction with the tax system) and not inflation has prompted most of the rise in nominal interest rates.

Now the emphasis is shifting toward getting rates down. One approach, illustrated by the all savers certificates, the liberalized IRA limits, and other aspects of the new tax law, is to accomplish this through tax exemption for interest income and limitation of interest deductions. This would be a much more sensible direction in which to go, except for that accident of history that has linked the maintenance of our infrastructure of streets, sanitation, schools, hospitals, etc., and possibly the very survival of our federal system and its division of powers between the national and state governments to the subsidy that tax exemption has conferred on municipal borrowing. As interest and other property income become increasingly tax free, tax exempt securities offer less and less advantage to issuer and investor. The financial system has its own peculiar ecological balance. As with nature, what appear to be perfectly sensible interventions may have highly undesirable fallout. We may be virtually sure that, current plans notwithstanding, Federal subsidies to states and localities will soon be larger rather than smaller.

Financial Investment and Gambling: The Diminishing Difference

In this world, the states of the future for which borrowers and lenders choose to make provision are highly complex and interdependent. To think of the public as having a straightforward set of expectations shaped by a small number of variables is a factual error and predictably produces poor policies and forecasts. The market remains full of paradoxes, which seem to multiply daily with the new paradoxes in public policy and the further removal of the few anchors and benchmarks still left from an earlier time when, in finance as in society, the range of the permissible was narrower. Market horizons are short: for most professional investors, whether of their own or others' money, only about three months or even less and probably no more than a year for borrowers and issuers. Most sizable institutional funds receive report cards from their clients every three months — and their professionals want to gain accounts, commissions, and promotions now, not in the hereafter. Optimism, the willingness to fight the odds, is a biological necessity for survival. Not surprisingly, one usually finds in the financial markets, as among gamblers, a group bias toward optimism and a widespread willingness to overpay and overstay for the lure of a big killing. Such attitudes, especially now that they have also been adopted into the bosom of government economic policy, make for spastic markets. Nothing in this regard has changed for the better since a year ago.

A year ago [1980], the yield curves in the corporate, government, and the municipal bond markets differed dramatically from one another, suggesting the absurd notion that participants in these closely related markets held radically different interest rate expectations. To a somewhat lesser extent, the same discrepancies persist. A year ago, the historical record showed cyclical turns in long-term rates that were lagging behind both short rates and the cycle. This occurred despite the fact that speculators are always lying in wait to scalp bond prices around times of turning points; and so they would, one might think, learn to read the short rate signals. Nothing has happened to contradict this pattern. As of a year ago, the record showed that corporations had managed the timing of their short- and long-term borrowings so as to — exaggerating somewhat — pay the highest possible interest rates over both the short and long run. Since then, their continued reluctance to borrow at long term except after clearly defined cyclical rate peaks has produced new records for unnecessary interest payments. Within companies, as before although to a lesser degree, the production and sales side continues to extrapolate the same or greater inflation, especially for wages and product prices, while the financial side accepts the revenue forecast but predicts lower interest rates. This is often true even if the economist plays a prominent role in or actually makes both forecasts. Along the same lines, the household public continues to prefer investment in tangibles and high-yielding short-term liquid assets, which are essentially inflation hedges, while the institutional managers who run the public's trust and pension funds continue to invest predominantly, although perhaps less ardently, in stocks and bonds.

How is one to summarize the state of expectations of such a marketplace? One negative conclusion is that so-called "inflationary expectations" are nothing but a phlogiston or ether that analysts invent and form to desired shape to explain what they don't know how to explain. Why should interest rates be so much higher now than in 1974–1975, when inflation was as rapid then as in 1979–1980, and when, more importantly but too easily forgotten, sophisticated financiers and businessmen believed that commodity shortages and runaway prices would not merely typify the future but also make it fun? I have never used inflation as an input to my interest rate forecasts except insofar as it affects the growth of nominal GNP and credit flows or might enter the government's policy function. Subject to the same exceptions — this will please the academics in this audience more but the businessmen less — neither have I paid any attention to Federal budget deficits.

The dominant factors in the market's interest rate expectations have been and remain, I believe, the cyclical outlook for (real) business and for short-term interest rates. These often used to be nearly synonymous, but the Federal Reserve's gradual shift to a mechanical day-to-day operating rule governed by monetary aggregates and the reserve base has loosened or broken the tie. It used to be assumed that the market and the Federal Reserve would recognize a business downturn and react to lower short rates at about the same time; if the Fed lagged, the drop in rates would be delayed. Business upturns also would be spotted simultaneously, but the Fed might hold short rates down until it was satisfied the upturn had really taken root. Nowadays, by contrast, short-term rates are hostage to large fluctuations in the diverse monetary aggregates whose timing is highly erratic with respect to one another and the general business situation.

One regularity does stand out, however: the correction of any significant departure of the monetary aggregates from their targets in either direction has been associated with a movement of at least five full percentage points (and sometimes more than twice that) in the Federal funds rate. Since October 1979, there have been six such movements each compressed into a few months. No wonder the market scrutinizes the weekly figures so anxiously, since the crossing of a critical threshold portends such enormous changes in rates. When rates have already risen substantially, the danger to the trader on the bandwagon is that monetary growth will subside and rates decline; when Federal funds rates have already fallen from about 20% to 15% or less as is currently the case, the threat is that monetary growth may accelerate and short-term rates rise as rapidly as they fell. No decision maker I have ever known in the financial market or in any nonfinancial company reacts to monetary data other than for what those data may imply for credit access or nominal interest rates.

This "new" monetary rulebook leaves only a residual role to the business outlook in influencing interest rate fluctuations. Any relevant change in the business situation would have to be rather major not to be swamped by the enormous but commonplace "technical" swings in short rates. So far, moreover, the no-growth monetary policy, in place essentially since the dollar crisis of fall 1978, has shown itself to be a pretty effective antirecession policy also. As a result, market participants pay little heed to any possibility of deep or prolonged economic contraction. The paradoxical outcome is liable to be that another garden-variety recession may not bring down long-term rates at all.

At present, I would judge, the largest body of market participants is reasoning in terms of a brief recession seen as already underway. From their point of view, bonds are a hazardous holding because they are apt to be dumped as soon as, in the not-too-distant future, the market scents the coming of a business recovery. To put it more directly, the only way to get bond yields down a lot may be to persuade the market that we are launched into a business recession from which early recovery is impossible. If I am right about the stickiness of bond yields, that would be another reason, in addition to bankruptcy risk, why any recession planted now could well sprout into something rather frightful.

The Brookings paper deplored the way in which our financial system was being restructured, in the name of free markets, to increase the rewards to myopia and gambling at the expense of business enterprise. The epidemic acceleration of market trading volume, documented in my paper, has persisted. Average GNP per working day is on the order of $12 billion. For the rather incomplete sample of security dealers and markets that reports trading volume, securities turnover (including futures and options) has been exceeding $70 billion daily. Treasury bill and bond options trading, with huge potential for enlarging all types of Treasury securities turnover, is set to start shortly. The combined volume of commodities and foreign exchange trading probably approximates that in the securities market. In all important categories, volume has increased at least on the order of threefold over the last five years; in some cases, much more. Price volatility has also intensified to a bizarre pitch. In the Treasury bill market, for example, the average day-to-day yield change (not including intraday fluctuation) in the two years prior to October 1979 was 7 basis points; since then it has been 26 basis points. On 30-year Treasury bonds, the prices of which are supposedly governed by rather inflexible 30-year expectations, the average day-to-day price change had been a quarter of a point; in the last two years, it has been nearly a full point.

Many small businessmen sadly complain that their attention is increasingly taken up by commodity or foreign exchange (and soon interest rate?) hedging, as price fluctuations reach magnitudes that overwhelm any conceivable managerial expertise in production or marketing. Meanwhile, the high interest rates have hardly dented the demand for credit to finance mergers. Top executives of large companies have no choice but to preoccupy themselves with buying out others or avoiding being swallowed up themselves. And, even more than in the summer of 1980, the disquieting trend persists for

> the most talented business school graduates [to] vie for employment in investment banking and related fields, correctly assessing the potential for early and large rewards; while it is left to lesser mortals to organize, for smaller rewards, the production and distribution of the goods and services that give underlying value to the claims and securities that the financial market shuffle about.[5]

Can this be good? The boundaries among investment, speculation, and gambling are very thin. The excitement that pulses over the dice tables, commodity pits, and securities exchanges is the same. By common consent, gambling is regulated because we recognize the addiction it exercises over the many who are susceptible: but for the grace of God, there go I. The actions of individuals — I know them personally — in taking hundreds of millions of dollars in open positions in financial futures, or of committees in switching around pension fund managers in search of above-average performance, are no different from gambling; and the dangers to innocent bystanders and posterity are greater. Freeing the financial markets has been tantamount to allowing them to be consumed by the betting fever. As a result, the financial community has largely lost its ability to maintain the imperatives of "order, continuity, and triviality" that human institutions must satisfy in order to survive. Thus it is certain that, as I have been intimating, new boundaries to financial behavior will eventually be written into law to restore a "semblance of social *and* psychic safety."[6] Most likely this will not be done soberly and parsimoniously, but haphazardly in response to a real or imagined crisis.

Where Is the Model?

Long before now, if this were a purely academic gathering, I would have been challenged to present my mathematical model, my fistful of equations that purport to encapsulate the world. I have no such model. The models I have seen, with their distributed lags and dummy variables, bear no more relationship to the financial world that I know than do antiseptic model electric trains to the noise, smell, sweat, surprises and boredom, intelligence and stupidity, goodwill and malice, and sheer danger of a real railroad.

There is worthwhile knowledge to be gained from models, but only by those who recognize how pitifully brief is their useful life, especially once they become well understood, and how rich are the many aspects of human motivation, especially of social and collective behavior, that models fail to reach.

If this be treason, make the most of it.

Notes

1. Rational expectations theorists might note, however, that no man need have been an "island" during these years since these forecasts (and the similar ones by my friend, Henry Kaufman) were widely available at the price of a newspaper. The subject of "islands," on which people are ignorant of what is happening on other "islands," because it is too expensive to find out, is a current item of debate on the academic island of rational expectations.

2. *Brookings Papers on Economic Activity*, 1980:2, pp. 277–326.

3. The Brookings article outlines the case as follows: "The fundamental causes of the inflation are noneconomic. . . . They involve the changes in the internal and external relations of the United States after World War II as it gained and then lost world hegemony. Now an introverted economy heavily oriented toward providing domestic amenities is compelled by its loss of geopolitical dominance to give up a significant margin of its standard of living. This is the cost of building military preparedness, producing the additional exports to pay the higher price of oil imports, developing expensive energy substitutes, subsidizing or replacing mass production industries doomed by foreign competition, and maintaining the relatively restrictive macroeconomic policies necessary to protect the international value of the dollar, whose stability is vital to our external political influence and to keeping down the oil price. Inflation is a standard historical response for societies forced to reduce their economic aspirations — and is useful up to a point in averting divisive internal strife about how the new burdens are to be distributed" (pp. 325–326).

4. Donald Hester explored these and other innovations more fully in a subsequent Brookings paper: "Innovations and Monetary Control," *Brookings Papers on Economic Activity*, 198:1, pp. 141–189.

5. Peter L. Berger, *Facing up to Modernity: Excursions in Society, Politics, and Religion*, Basic Books, 1977, p. 315.

6. Ibid., pp. xiv–xv.

List of Contributors

William A. Allen, Assistant Advisor on Monetary Policy, Bank of England.

Phillip Cagan, Professor of Economics, Columbia University.

R. Alton Gilbert, Senior Economist at the Federal Reserve Bank of St. Louis.

W. Lee Hoskins, Senior Vice-President and Chief Economist at the Pittsburgh National Bank.

David E. Lindsey, Assistant Director, Division of Research and Statistics, Board of Governors of the Federal Reserve System.

Laurence H. Meyer, Professor of Economics, Washington University.

Michael Parkin, Professor of Economics, University of Western Ontario.

William Poole, Professor of Economics, Brown University.

Robert H. Rasche, Professor of Economics, Michigan State University.

Kurt Schiltknecht, Director, Economic Division, Swiss National Bank.

Jeremy J. Siegel, Associate Professor of Finance, Wharton School, University of Pennsylvania.

Charles Webster, Jr., Assistant Professor of Economics, Washington University.

John Wenninger, Manager. Monetary Research Department, Federal Reserve Bank of New York.

Albert Wojnilower, Managing Director for the First Boston Corporation.

List of Conference Participants

William Allen, Bank of England
Leonall Andersen, Gustav Adolphus College
Anatol B. Balbach, Federal Reserve Bank of St. Louis
Rachel Balbach, Centerre Bank
James Barth, George Washington University
Ramachandra Bhagavatula, Citibank, N.A.
John Biggs, Washington University
Norm Bowsher, Federal Reserve Bank of St. Louis
Dan Brennan, Federal Reserve Bank of St. Louis
Albert E. Burger, Jr., Federal Reserve Bank of St. Louis
Phillip Cagan, Columbia University
Kenneth Chilton, Center for the Study of American Business
Norman Coats, Ralston Purina Company
Donald Cox, Washington University
Lesley Daniels, Washington University
Larry Davidson, Indiana University
Thomas Davis, Federal Reserve Bank of Kansas City
Arthur Denzau, Washington University
William Dewald, Ohio State University
Ben Eisner, Seven Up Company
Bernard Feigenbaum, Washington University
Nicholas Filippelo, Monsanto Company

Charles Freedman, Bank of Canada, Ottowa
Christopher Garbacz, University of Missouri at Rolla
David Garino, Dow Jones & Company
William Gavin, Federal Reserve Bank of Cleveland
R. Alton Gilbert, Federal Reserve Bank of St. Louis
Kevin Grier, Washington University
Rick Hafer, Federal Reserve Bank of St. Louis
Bruce Halliday, Fontbonne College
Clifford Hardin, Center for the Study of American Business
Scott Hein, Federal Reserve Bank of St. Louis
Robert Holland, Illinois State University
Jerome J. Hollenhorst, Southern Illinois University-Edwardsville
Donald Hooks, University of Alabama
W. Lee Hoskins, Pittsburgh National Bank
Homer Jones, Federal Reserve Bank of St. Louis, Retired
Jim Kamphoeffner, Federal Reserve Bank of St. Louis
Denis Karnosky, Office of Under Secretary for Monetary Affairs
Robert Kelleher, Federal Reserve Bank of Atlanta
Donald Kemp, Monsanto Company
William Kester, St. Louis Post-Dispatch
Richard Lang, Federal Reserve Bank of Philadelphia
David E. Lindsey, Board of Governors of the Federal Reserve System
James Little, Washington University
J.A. Livingston, Philadelphia Inquirer
Clifton Luttrell, Federal Reserve Bank of St. Louis
Kevin Maloney, Washington University
Joseph McKenna, University of Missouri-St. Louis
Paul Merz, St. Louis University
Ann-Marie Meulendyke, Federal Reserve Bank of New York
Laurence H. Meyer, Washington University
Hyman P. Minsky, Washington University
Greg Neihaus, Washington University
Eric Newhouse, Associated Press

Mack Ott, Pennsylvania State University
Michael Parkin, The University of Western Ontario
James Parthemos, Federal Reserve Bank of Richmond
Seymour Patterson, Northeast Missouri State University
Douglas Pearce, University of Missouri-Columbia
James Pearce, Federal Reserve Bank of Dallas
William Poole, Brown University
Lawrence Radecki, Federal Reserve Bank of New York
Fred Raines, Washington University
David Ramsey, Illinois State University
Robert H. Rasche, Michigan State University
David Resler, First National Bank of Chicago
Fred Ribe, Congressional Budget Office
Lawrence K. Roos, Federal Reserve Bank of St. Louis
Peter Schaal, University of Alabama
Ted Schafers, St. Louis Globe-Democrat
Zalman Shiffer, Bank of Israel
Kurt Schiltknecht, Schweizerische National Bank
Jeremy J. Siegel, Wharton School of the University of Pennsylvania
David Small, Washington University
Michael Smirlock, Washington University
Paul Smith, University of Missouri-Columbia
Jerome L. Stein, Brown University
Frank Steindl, Oklahoma State University
Neil Stevens, Federal Reserve Bank of St. Louis
Courtenay C. Stone, Federal Reserve Bank of St. Louis
Werner Sublette, Northeast Missouri State University
Casey J. Sylla, Northwestern Mutual Life Insurance Company
John Tatom, Federal Reserve Bank of St. Louis
Dan Thornton, Federal Reserve Bank of St. Louis
Ronald Tracy, Southern Illinois University-Carbondale
Michael Trebing, Federal Reserve Bank of St. Louis
Marcia B. Wallace, Center for the Study of American Business

Charles Webster, Jr., Washington University
John E. Wenninger, Federal Reserve Bank of New York
Harvey Wilmeth, Northwestern Mutual Life Insurance Company
Albert J. Wojnilower, First Boston Corporation
John Woolley, Washington University
Gene C. Wunder, Northeast Missouri State University
Jai-Hoon Yang, Morgan Guaranty Trust Company

GPSR Compliance

The European Union's (EU) General Product Safety Regulation (GPSR) is a set of rules that requires consumer products to be safe and our obligations to ensure this.

If you have any concerns about our products, you can contact us on ProductSafety@springernature.com

In case Publisher is established outside the EU, the EU authorized representative is:

Springer Nature Customer Service Center GmbH
Europaplatz 3
69115 Heidelberg, Germany

Batch number: 10830937

Printed by Printforce, the Netherlands